More Praise for *Bringing Out the Best in Yourself at Work*

"This well-written, practical, and clear book moves the Enneagram teachings significantly forward into the world of business applications. Dr. Lapid-Bogda provides both rich examples and meaningful insights in bringing the Enneagram into any organization. This is a vital read for anyone interfacing the Enneagram with organizations."

> —*David N. Daniels, M.D., clinical professor, Department of Psychiatry and Behavioral Sciences, Stanford Medical School, and coauthor of the bestselling book* The Essential Enneagram

"Entertaining, knowledgeable, readable, and insightful, *Bringing Out the Best in Yourself at Work* is replete with stories, examples, and applications of how the nine Enneagram types operate in the workplace. Ginger Lapid-Bogda has observed carefully how people of each type think, feel, and behave, and she encourages her readers similarly to observe themselves for self-improvement. Her style is fresh, light, and bright. This book's positive outlook, clarity, and attention to detail will place it at the top of many a reading list."

> —*Kathy Hurley and Theodorre Donson, coauthors of the bestselling* What's My Type? *and creators of The Enneagram of Transformation® Certification and Training Program*

"A fine book about bringing the Enneagram to business, filled with many useful real-world examples. Anyone who works with people should read this book!"

> —*Michael J. Goldberg, J.D., organizational consultant and author of* The 9 Ways of Working

"I've known Ginger as a lively and savvy presenter; now I know her as a clear, persuasive writer. She's done a fine job of taking critical consulting areas such as communicating effectively, managing conflict, creating high-performance teams, and developing leadership, and running them through the filter of the nine Enneagram personality styles, showing how these general concepts appear at work in nine different epiphanies. Her book will make an oft-consulted, very useful contribution to both the business and Enneagram communities."

—*Jerome P. Wagner, Ph.D., internationally known Enneagram teacher and author of* The Enneagram Spectrum of Personality Styles

"A winner! This book is both a solid and accessible introduction to the Enneagram and a fine overview of the system's applications at work. It is useful at every turn, offering many practical suggestions to successfully enhance communication and resolve conflicts. Full of real-world examples, *Bringing Out the Best in Yourself at Work* also offers detailed advice on how to apply the Enneagram to team building and effective leadership. Use it to change old patterns and succeed at new challenges."

—*Thomas Condon, Enneagram teacher and author of* The Enneagram Movie and Video Guide

"In this remarkable book, Ginger Lapid-Bogda clearly communicates the essence of the Enneagram and its practical applications for effective leadership in organizations. As a colleague in a range of projects with her, I have long admired her competence and grace as a teacher, trainer, and consultant. I'm delighted to see this material become widely available for people who seek a deeper understanding of the dynamics of interpersonal and team behavior. The illustrative stories, short activities, and crisp, accessible explanations make this a resource book readers will return to again and again—and recommend to their friends!"

—*Saul Eisen, Ph.D., professor of psychology and founder, Graduate Program in Organization Development, Sonoma State University*

BRINGING OUT THE BEST IN YOURSELF AT WORK

BRINGING OUT THE BEST IN YOURSELF AT WORK

How to Use the
Enneagram
System for Success

GINGER LAPID-BOGDA, Ph.D.
With a Foreword by Helen Palmer

McGraw·Hill

New York   Chicago   San Francisco   Lisbon   London   Madrid   Mexico City
Milan   New Delhi   San Juan   Seoul   Singapore   Sydney   Toronto

The **McGraw·Hill** Companies

Library of Congress Cataloging-in-Publication Data

Lapid-Bogda, Ginger.
    Bringing out the best in yourself at work : how to use the Enneagram system for success /
Ginger Lapid-Bogda.—1st ed.
        p.   cm.
    Includes bibliographical references and index.
    ISBN 0-07-143960-9
    1. Enneagram.   2. Quality of work life.   3. Self-actualization (Psychology).   I. Title.

BF698.35.E54L37   2004
155.2'6—dc22   2004009318

7 8 9 10 11 12   DOC/DOC   0 9 8

ISBN 0-07-143960-9

Interior design by Think Design Group

McGraw-Hill books are available at special quantity discounts to use as premiums and sales
promotions, or for use in corporate training programs. For more information, please write to the
Director of Special Sales, Professional Publishing, McGraw-Hill, Two Penn Plaza, New York, NY
10121-2298. Or contact your local bookstore.

This book is printed on acid-free paper.

This book is dedicated to my son, Tres,
who has been using the Enneagram since he was seven years old
to know himself better,
to have compassion for his parents,
and to work effectively with his friends and teachers.

Contents

Foreword

*T*he Enneagram is arguably the oldest human development system on the planet, and like all authentic maps of consciousness, it finds new life in the conceptual worldview of each succeeding generation. Because of its enduring value, the Enneagram map has moved through time like seed that blossoms in the cracks of human history when it is needed. Then it goes dormant again, lying unnoticed in plain sight, often for protracted periods of time, as public attention turns elsewhere.

I'm especially delighted that Dr. Lapid-Bogda's book positions the Enneagram in the language and framework of contemporary organizations. In doing so, she creates a context in which terms like "professional development," "conflict management," and "high-performance teamwork" seem comfortably at home within a map of human evolution.

Drawing from an impressive background of organization development and consultancy experience, she writes for those of us who work in today's pressure cooker of rapid change and quick decisions weighted with lasting consequences. Her skill lies in quietly directing attention to the inner patterns that impede our working well with each other. And rather than focus on outer behaviors, she skillfully shows the reader how each type is inwardly organized to participate in key areas of business activity.

Most of us wouldn't think of going to work every day as a professional development program, yet our patterns are constantly triggered by the job and the people around us. You'll find that knowing your type will help you to recognize when automatic patterns start to engage. Sixes, for instance, can tell when their thinking becomes doubtful, and Sevens will recognize a flood of interesting plans. Nines may find themselves suddenly waking up to discover their attention has wandered off, and so on for all nine profiles.

All of this is encouraging, because you can recognize your two selves: the self that acts on automatic, and a secondary aspect of yourself that can watch the mechanics of your own mind. In our time, there is practically no education for the observing self, yet you will be using witnessing consciousness (self-observation) to discover your type, and later on to recognize and relax the patterns that do not bring out your best in the key areas of work described in this book.

The Enneagram originally came about as a map to assist self-observation. Its power still lies in "educating" the observing self, which is already free of automatic conditioning. At a time when corporate survival depends on working cooperatively with each other, history's oldest professional development tool is being renewed because we need to understand one another's point of view.

One commonly asked question about the system is "Which type is most suitable for a specific job?" or "How can we build an ideal team?" And the answer is "Find mature human beings." People aren't hired for their type. They are hired for their skills, their creativity, their past experience, and whether they act like grown-ups. This book is an excellent guide for understanding how different types of people can learn to communicate effectively, perform well on teams, manage conflict, and lead with compassion. The way to use the Enneagram system for success in these key areas is by way of knowing yourself and others as they actually are, which, as the title suggests, brings out the best in ourselves at work.

—Helen Palmer, author of the internationally bestselling books The Enneagram in Love and Work *and* The Enneagram: Understanding Yourself and the Others in Your Life; *cofounder of the Trifold School for Enneagram Studies*

Acknowledgments

This book would not have been possible without the support of many individuals and organizations. First, Mary Nadler did an amazing job of editing the initial manuscript, but more important, she saw the real potential of the information and encouraged me to aim high. David Balding of the Enneagram Consortium provided advice and encouragement from the very beginning. A special acknowledgment goes to Wolfgang Fenchel for translating my ideas into the visual images used in the book.

My knowledge and experience with organization development and the behavioral sciences would not be what it is without the pioneering work of National Training Laboratories (NTL) and my many years of involvement with the Organization Development Network (ODN). I am especially indebted to several organization development colleagues who are also close personal friends—in particular, Saul Eisen, Phil Hanson, Beverly Kaye, Susan Nero, Dick Mayer, and my best friend for over twenty years, Michael Collins. A special thanks to Warner Burke for his support over the years and his intellectual contributions to the field of OD. Two additional OD colleagues are no longer alive, yet they still inspire me—Alice Sargeant and Uma Umapathy.

My indebtedness to the Enneagram community is wide. Helen Palmer and David Daniels, from whom I first learned the Enneagram and with whom I later certified as an Enneagram teacher, gave me an excellent foundation that I draw on every day. Others who have influenced me both intellectually and personally include Don Riso and Russ Hudson, Kathy Hurley and Theodorre Donson, Tom Condon, Peter O'Hanrahan, Jerry Wagner, Michael Goldberg, and Claudio Naranjo, without whom the Enneagram system would not be as evolved as we currently know it.

In addition, a number of colleagues from the IEA (International Ennea-gram Association) have provided me with invaluable feedback and support of various kinds. My special thanks to Judith Searle, Arnaldo Pangrazzi, Anne Muree, Uranio Paes, Andrea Isaacs, Barry Keesan, Bart Wendell, Brian Grod-ner, Tom Flautt, Laurie O'Brien, Lenka Jordanov, Bea Chestnut, Francoise Chesaux, Antonio Barbato, Oscar Ayala, Jack Labanauskas, and Sandy Perry.

Several other individuals have also supported this effort in a variety of ways: David Coleman, Pat Hunt, Russ Bogda, Lucy Weiger, Charles Miller, Nancy Stetson, Nancy Golen, Clarence Thomson, Maurice Monnette, and Marianne Triplette. This work has also been inspired by many of my clients, with par-ticular acknowledgment to Marie Campbell, Catherine Lee, Dev Vrat, Angel Cruzado, Chris Samsel, and Richard Wyatt.

Those closest to me have given more than moral support—my nephews Jon Platt, Ben Platt, and Marshall Platt; my brother, Martin Snapp; and espe-cially my thirteen-year-old son, Tres Bogda. Tres not only gave me ideas for the book, he also gave me the time and encouragement to write. My assistant, Natalie Toy, was involved in each step of the book's progress.

Finally, thank you to my literary agents, Muriel Nellis and Jane Roberts, at Literary and Creative Artists, for their efforts to find the best publisher for this book, and to Donya Dickerson, Mary Glenn, Ellen Vinz, Eileen Lamadore, and Irina Lumelsky from McGraw-Hill, all of whom saw the value of this book and the benefit of making it available to a wide audience.

Introduction

*B*ringing out the best in yourself at work is something everyone can do. All it requires is your ability to pay attention to your most precious asset—*you*. If you are already able to do this, then you should be able to answer yes to all of these questions:

- Are you able to communicate effectively at work so that others truly understand what you mean to say? Do you objectively hear what others say to you?
- Can you give constructive feedback to the people with whom you work in such a way that they do not feel defensive and that you actually help them to improve their performance?
- Can you manage conflict at work, including taking responsibility for your contribution to a situation, de-escalating a conflict, and approaching others in a respectful and productive way?
- Do you know how to develop both your own behavior and that of other team members in order to increase team performance?
- Do you understand your own leadership strengths and weaknesses, as well as those of the leaders for whom you work? Do you know how to capitalize on your leadership strengths and how to work on your development areas? Do you understand your boss so that you can work more effectively with him or her?
- Do you know practical and powerful developmental activities, customized to your own needs, that can help you to know yourself better and to work successfully with others?

Did you answer a resounding *Yes!* to all of the above questions? Few people can. However, all of these skills for bringing out the best in yourself at work can be learned when you use the Enneagram as a means to increase your social intelligence. Since the 1920s, social science and management research have shown that social intelligence is critical to a person's overall success in the workplace. However, it has not been apparent how a person can go about developing social intelligence. Social intelligence is actually two different yet interconnected factors: *intra*personal intelligence, which is the ability to know oneself accurately and to use that knowledge to operate successfully in life, and *inter*personal intelligence, which is the ability to understand and work well with others. An individual's "emotional intelligence" (EQ), as social intelligence is frequently called, is a greater predictor of success in almost every field of work than either prior work experience or standard IQ score. *The Enneagram is the single most powerful tool available to help you develop your "emotional intelligence."* This book will show you exactly how to develop your social intelligence, guiding you in learning how to apply your new awareness and skills in both the most common and the most critical work situations.

There are nine different Enneagram styles, representing nine distinct habits of thinking, feeling, and taking action, connected to nine unique personal and spiritual developmental paths. Because this book integrates the Enneagram with time-tested theories and skills from the behavioral sciences, you will learn not only what approach you should take, but also why that approach will work for you. This level of understanding will enable you to draw on your new-found skills in any situation you encounter.

Rather than simply telling you that you can use the Enneagram for self-awareness, self-mastery, and improved interpersonal interactions, this book *shows* you how to apply the Enneagram in a business context. Strategic approaches are offered, using real-life vignettes and anecdotes as the foundation for descriptions of different Enneagram styles in action. In-depth analyses of Enneagram style behavior are provided, along with concrete suggestions for improving your skills. The readable, anecdotal approach will help you to internalize the information presented so that you can more easily learn to do the following:

- Identify your Enneagram style
- Communicate more effectively
- Provide better feedback to others
- Prevent conflict or, once it has occurred, resolve differences successfully
- Create and participate in highly productive teams

- Understand how your greatest leadership strength can become your greatest weakness, and know what to do about this
- Develop a customized method for transforming yourself

This book has evolved from my thirty years of experience as an organization development and change consultant for Fortune 500 companies, service organizations, law firms, and nonprofit agencies. Every one of my consulting projects has required me to help individuals within an organization to know themselves better, to change their behavior, and to work more effectively with others. This has been the case regardless of the area of work, whether it was strategic planning, executive retreats, problem solving and change, organizational redesign, diversity, team development, conflict resolution, or executive coaching. It has also been the case for all of my clients, regardless of organizational level (whether CEOs, managers, or individual contributors) or specific circumstances—for example, whether the person is high performing, under great professional duress, in charge of an important project, and/or a member of a team.

Although I trained as a gestalt therapist in the early 1970s and was well versed in the psychological literature, it was not until I encountered the Enneagram in the early 1990s that I realized a tool existed that could help people to understand themselves and others with accuracy. As I shared the Enneagram and its insights with clients, colleagues, friends, and family, I began to understand its remarkable power. *The Enneagram is the single most useful, profound, insightful, and practical tool available to help us grasp the depth and complexity of the human personality.*

In recent years, clients and colleagues began to ask me when I would write a book that integrated the insights of the Enneagram with the practical applications of behavioral science and management theory. This book represents that integration. I hope you will find the information as valuable as my clients and I have found it to be.

What Is the Enneagram?

No one knows the precise origins of the Enneagram, though its roots appear to lie in Asia and the Middle East and date from several thousand years ago. The word *enneagram* derives from the Greek words *ennea* ("nine") and *gram* ("something written or drawn") and refers to the nine points on the Enneagram model. The Enneagram system offers profound insights into the nine very different ways in which people feel, think, and behave.

Various parts of the Enneagram have been articulated by Gurdjieff, who was prominent in Europe beginning in the 1930s; by Oscar Ischazo, from Bolivia, who has been working since the 1950s to refine the system; and by Chilean-born Claudio Naranjo, M.D., whose Enneagram work became well known beginning in the 1970s, when he began teaching the system in Northern California. From the foundational work of these three teachers, others have made major contributions to our understanding of the Enneagram system, among them Helen Palmer and David Daniels, Don Richard Riso and Russ Hudson, Kathy Hurley and Theodorre Donson, Tom Condon, and Jerry Wagner.

Shown below is the Enneagram model, which is explained in Chapter 1.

While the Enneagram system contains multiple levels of complexity, it can be easily grasped and readily used. You may be surprised to find that even a first exposure to the Enneagram will promote your self-awareness and provide you with avenues for self-development. As you become more familiar with the system, you will be able to understand the Enneagram more deeply and can then easily apply this knowledge to multiple interpersonal situations. People often express amazement at how well the Enneagram describes them. The Enneagram is an insightful system, acting as a multiple mirror that reflects the various facets of an individual's internal character structure.

Far more than just a psychological framework, the Enneagram is a key that can open the door to a deep understanding of the self and the connections among personality, psychological development, and spiritual transformation. Although the Enneagram is not a religion, it has a spiritual as well as a psychological foundation. It parallels many aspects of Christian mysticism, the Kabbalah, and Sufism and attracts people of all religions. Most other personality systems, by contrast, have only a psychological basis. While the Enneagram may be used solely as a psychological tool, many prefer to use the system with the psychological and spiritual elements intertwined.

In this book, no distinction is made between the psychological and spiritual dimensions of the Enneagram, as the psychological and spiritual issues for a particular Enneagram style are in essence the same. On an initial reading, the descriptions of Enneagram applications throughout may appear more psychologically than spiritually oriented. However, once you have gained the self-insight that comes from understanding your style and are engaging in the actions suggested throughout the book, you will find that you are growing in both the psychological and spiritual arenas. While your psychological growth will enable you to function more effectively on a day-to-day basis, your spiritual development may emerge in a variety of ways, depending on your own inclination and receptivity—for example, increased knowledge and acceptance of who you are and greater compassion for others.

Because the Enneagram is both very powerful and easy to use, it is becoming increasingly popular internationally. The Enneagram describes people of every culture accurately. While there may be cultural nuances to the actions of individuals who come from different countries but have the same Enneagram style, the underlying personality dynamics and motivations remain the same across cultures. The same is true for gender: men and women of the same Enneagram style may display some gender-influenced differences, but the pattern and dynamics of the style remain unchanged.

Applications of the Enneagram Throughout Business

The Enneagram is currently being used in many fields and disciplines, among them business, education, psychotherapy, entertainment, medicine, sales, and law. In business, for example, an increasing number of organizations are using the Enneagram in both training programs and organizational change initiatives, since the Enneagram system provides a thorough foundation for understanding why people behave in the ways that they do. Among the organizations making use of the Enneagram are the Walt Disney Company, Silicon Graphics, Kaiser Permanente Research Center, the Federal Reserve Bank, the CIA, and Rational Software. These and other companies and institutions use the

Enneagram in the areas of communication skills, conflict resolution, coaching, leadership development, team effectiveness, strategic planning, and organizational culture change.

Many additional applications exist in different industries. In the legal field, the Enneagram is used in situations that include jury selection, case presentation, the development of legal arguments, the development of teams to represent particular clients, mediation, leadership in law firms, and relationships between lawyers. In sales, the Enneagram helps salespeople to improve presentations and customer interactions. Health-care professionals use the Enneagram to improve both interactions with patients and working relationships with other health professionals.

Because the Enneagram reveals enduring truths about the human character, the system is timeless in its usefulness. Human beings will always need and seek ways to improve their interpersonal effectiveness, and this is as true within the work environment as it is in other areas of life—perhaps even more so, given the importance of interpersonal contact to the capacity of an individual or an enterprise to succeed.

Prior to 1940, most organizations viewed employees almost as machines or widgets, with time-and-motion studies used to increase individual performance. Since that time, however, management theory and practice have grown to support the perception of workers as human beings, and great attention is now paid to the areas of employee motivation, personal and professional development, and interpersonal effectiveness. The Enneagram provides a great step forward in helping people to develop their humanity at work.

Who Should Read This Book

Everyone who interacts with others in a business environment should read this book. Employees and managers of all levels and from all industries, human resource personnel, organizational consultants, trainers, and coaches can all achieve profound improvements in their interpersonal effectiveness by working through the chapters in this book.

How This Book Is Organized

While most books about psychological styles are organized according to personality type, this book is organized according to application areas—particular skills that can be used to solve recurring business issues. You can thus use this book as a continuing resource, consulting it as needed when you encounter particular challenges at work.

Each of the seven chapters has a specific focus. The chapters build on one another, moving from the identification of one's Enneagram style to the application of the Enneagram in increasingly complex business situations. Individuals unfamiliar with the Enneagram should first read Chapter 1, "Discovering Your Enneagram Style." Those who already have a firm understanding of their Enneagram style can begin with the chapter that best suits their needs; while designed to follow a logical progression, Chapters 2 through 7 can be read in any sequence desired. Finally, the Resources section offers books, websites, and other reference material for further study.

My intention in writing this book has been to integrate the Enneagram with the behavioral sciences, as these are the two most useful fields of knowledge and practice available to help people work most effectively in organizations. The uncanny wisdom of the Enneagram represents centuries of accumulated knowledge and insight and is unparalleled in its accuracy, its ability to both explain and predict behavior, and its capacity to show people how to change if they wish to do so. The behavioral science theories and practices used in this book have been field-tested for decades, and they work. Together, the Enneagram and the behavioral sciences provide a powerhouse approach to assist people who want to improve how they function in an organizational setting.

The ideas in this book stand on the foundational work of many organizations and individuals, all of whom have contributed to illuminating how people work together and how that process can be improved. It is my greatest hope that this book follows in that tradition.

BRINGING OUT THE BEST IN YOURSELF
AT WORK

Chapter 1

Discovering Your Enneagram Style

ccording to the Consortium for Research on Emotional Intelligence in Organizations, a person with emotional intelligence (EQ) possesses both personal competence and social competence. Social competence—that is, social awareness and skills—depends on an individual's personal competence. Personal competence begins with *self-awareness*—emotional awareness, accurate self-assessment, and self-confidence—and then expands to include self-regulation and self-motivation. The most accurate and useful system available to help develop both personal and social competence is the Enneagram, which is why companies all over the world—Hewlett Packard, Sony, and Disney—are embracing it, and the CIA uses it to predict the behavior of foreign leaders. To use the Enneagram, a person must first accurately identify his or her own Enneagram style from among the nine unique personality styles identified by numbers One through Nine.

Each of us has only one place on the Enneagram. *While your Enneagram style remains the same throughout your lifetime, your characteristics may soften or become more pronounced as you grow and develop.* As you read this chapter, you will find information and exercises to help you identify your Enneagram style. As you do the activities, you may find that two, or even three, Enneagram styles seem to match you. This is not unusual. While you have one core pattern, there are four other Enneagram styles linked to your own; these related styles add to the Enneagram's richness and are explained later in this chapter. It is easier to learn about these connecting styles after you have identified your own basic style.

To determine your Enneagram style, you will need to take stock of yourself, making an honest assessment of your strengths and weaknesses. The following exercises, checklists, and concepts are your guides in this process, so please take your time and do them all in sequence. Accurately identifying your own Enneagram style is crucial to understanding and using the ideas in the entire book.

Begin by going through the following two warm-up exercises. They will help you get started in thinking about yourself, and the answers will be useful to you as you proceed through the rest of the chapter's activities.

Warm-Up Exercise 1: Identify Your Strengths and Weaknesses

Please write down your answers to the question that follows. Identify two to three people, preferably from a work context, who have known you well over a period of time. What would they think are your three greatest strengths and your three greatest weaknesses? If you limit your thinking to one person's perceptions, you will likely write down characteristics that would be only that person's point of view. If you use your perceived perspectives of several people, the information is likely to be more accurate and useful.

Three Strengths	Three Weaknesses
1.	1.
2.	2.
3.	3.

This exercise may look simple, but it is actually revealing something about your Enneagram style. Try to remember your responses here as you go through the remaining activities in the chapter; you will probably see some of the exact words you picked as you read about and determine your own Enneagram style.

Warm-Up Exercise 2: Chart Your Emotional Index

Because we are human beings, we all have emotions. However, we do not all have an identical range of emotions, nor do we all feel with the same degree of intensity. Feelings actually fall into four main groupings: *Mad, Sad, Glad,* and *Afraid*. All human emotions are variations on these basic categories.

Feelings vary in strength and can be sorted into low, medium, or high intensities. Please read the emotions checklist on the next two pages and place a check next to every feeling you *frequently* experience. Think about this as a checklist of your emotional repertoire—not just feelings you may have experienced in the last week or month, but emotions you have tended to feel fairly regularly over your life.

MAD

High Intensity	Medium Intensity	Low Intensity
☐ Embittered	☐ Agitated	☐ Bothered
☐ Enraged	☐ Aggressive	☐ Cynical
☐ Furious	☐ Belligerent	☐ Displeased
☐ Hostile	☐ Disgusted	☐ Dissatisfied
☐ Incensed	☐ Frustrated	☐ Irked
☐ Infuriated	☐ Indignant	☐ Provoked
☐ Outraged	☐ Irritated	☐ Peeved
☐ Seething	☐ Resentful	☐ Tense
☐ Vengeful	☐ Revolted	☐ Upset

SAD

High Intensity	Medium Intensity	Low Intensity
☐ Anguished	☐ Abandoned	☐ Bored
☐ Defeated	☐ Apathetic	☐ Disappointed
☐ Depressed	☐ Discouraged	☐ Disillusioned
☐ Desperate	☐ Distressed	☐ Helpless
☐ Devastated	☐ Hopeless	☐ Lonely
☐ Humiliated	☐ Melancholic	☐ Pained
☐ Powerless	☐ Pessimistic	☐ Somber
☐ Purposeless	☐ Sorrowful	☐ Unhappy
☐ Worthless	☐ Weak	☐ Vulnerable

GLAD

High Intensity	Medium Intensity	Low Intensity
☐ Blissful	☐ Animated	☐ Alive
☐ Delighted	☐ Cheerful	☐ Calm
☐ Ecstatic	☐ Excited	☐ Carefree
☐ Enthusiastic	☐ Grateful	☐ Content
☐ Euphoric	☐ Optimistic	☐ Lighthearted
☐ Joyful	☐ Passionate	☐ Peaceful
☐ Thriving	☐ Proud	☐ Pleased
☐ Vibrant	☐ Satisfied	☐ Relaxed
☐ Vigorous	☐ Thankful	☐ Secure

AFRAID

High Intensity	Medium Intensity	Low Intensity
☐ Alarmed	☐ Anxious	☐ Cautious
☐ Defenseless	☐ Apprehensive	☐ Concerned
☐ Distressed	☐ Disoriented	☐ Confused
☐ Fearful	☐ Disturbed	☐ Doubtful
☐ Frightened	☐ Insecure	☐ Guarded
☐ Intimidated	☐ Startled	☐ Hesitant
☐ Panicked	☐ Stressed	☐ Reluctant
☐ Petrified	☐ Troubled	☐ Suspicious
☐ Traumatized	☐ Worried	☐ Wary

The pattern of your checks is important. To analyze what you see, look over your marks. It helps to start with larger patterns first and then move to a more detailed assessment.

Larger Patterns
- Overall, do you have many checks (over 50 percent) or very few (under 25 percent)?
- Which of the four feeling categories have the most checks, and which have the least?
- Do your checks show that you generally favor a particular intensity level?

More Detailed Patterns
- Within each of the four feeling categories, do you notice any patterns regarding your intensity level?
- Comparing the checks within one category to those in another, do you notice any particular differences or similarities?

Your responses and analysis may give you very helpful information, because your emotional patterns are strongly related to your Enneagram style. This connection is most easily explained by the concept of Centers of Intelligence.

Each Enneagram style is rooted in one of three Centers—the Head Center, the Heart Center, or the Body Center. Our emotional repertoire often reflects our main Center. The notion of a primary Center, which stems from a long Eastern philosophical tradition, refers to the way in which we typically react, often internally, to events in our lives.

While we all have heads, hearts, and bodies, each of us tends to favor one of these three modalities. The following explanation of the Emotional Index response patterns may help you to both clarify your primary Center and identify your Enneagram style, as each Center contains three of the nine Enneagram styles. The Emotional Index patterns described here are tendencies only; they reflect trends that occur roughly 75 percent of the time.

HEAD CENTER EMOTIONAL PATTERNS If you had many checks in the Afraid category, particularly marks next to medium- and high-intensity words, your Enneagram style may be in the Head Center (also called the Mental Center). The Head Center contains Enneagram styles Five, Six, and Seven. These three mental styles share the tendency to engage first in elaborate analysis as a reaction to their common emotion, fear.

Fives respond to fear by withdrawing, retreating into their minds in order to understand. If your Emotional Index marks were also predominantly low-intensity in the other three feeling categories, you may be a Five. When Fives withdraw, they tend to detach emotionally, hence their lower-intensity scores.

Sixes react to their worry and fear by anticipating negative scenarios and planning alternatives to circumvent what could go wrong. As a result, the Six Emotional Index scores will often show a high number of checks in all three Afraid intensity levels.

Sevens take a different route in dealing with fear, moving from worry very quickly into pleasurable possibilities. Although Sevens do not appear fearful on the surface, they are actually running from fear and pain—an avoidance reaction. Their Emotional Index scores will often show not only many checks in the Afraid list but a similar high number of marks on the Glad list.

HEART CENTER EMOTIONAL PATTERNS If you had numerous checks in all four Emotional Index categories, your Enneagram style may be in the Heart Center—styles Two, Three, and Four. Individuals with these Heart (Emotional) Center styles work hard to project a particular image, and they use their emotions to perceive how others are responding to them.

Twos try to create an image of being likable, and they look to others for affirmation of their self-worth. Because they tend to be warm, optimistic, and enthusiastic, the Two Emotional Index usually contains a high number of checks in the Glad category.

If you have checks in all four categories but fewer Sad marks, you may be a Three. Threes work to project an image of success, and they seek the respect and admiration of others for what they accomplish. Allowing oneself feelings of sadness does not correspond with the "can-do" orientation of most Threes.

Fours, on the other hand, are very familiar with feelings of sadness and melancholy, so the Sad category is the one in which they often have the highest number of marks. As the most inwardly focused of the three Heart Center styles, Fours try to create an image of being unique or special, and they use their emotional sensitivity to defend against rejection.

BODY CENTER EMOTIONAL PATTERNS If your Emotional Index marks were highest in the Mad category, your Enneagram style may be in the Body Center, also called the Gut Center or Instinctual Center—styles One, Eight, and Nine. Anger lies in the emotional substructure of these three styles.

Medium intensity checks in the Mad category combined with a range of Sad marks may indicate that you are a One. The One's anger, while deep, often manifests as frequent irritations followed by flares of resentment. Tending toward self-criticism, Ones can also become discouraged and depressed, hence their familiarity with the range of Sad emotions.

If you had a large number of checks—particularly high-intensity marks—in the Mad category, you may be an Eight. Eights tend to express their anger frequently and directly. Their anger, which begins in the gut and moves rapidly up and outward, is stimulated by various events, such as an injustice done to someone, weakness in others, someone taking ineffective control of a situation, and someone's lying.

The Nine's anger, sometimes called "anger that went to sleep," lies deep below the surface. The anger gets activated when Nines feel either ignored or forced to do something. However, the Nine Emotional Index may or may not show high Mad marks; Nines tend to avoid anger and conflict, preferring a feeling of rapport and comfort with others. Therefore, it is just as common for Nines to have an Emotional Index that has primarily low- or medium-intensity marks in all four categories.

The purpose of these two warm-up activities has been to get you started in thinking about yourself and your Enneagram style. As you move through the next pages, keep your responses to both activities in mind. The information gained will be useful as you proceed to learn about the Enneagram system and discover your Enneagram style.

Exercise 3: Discover Your Enneagram Style

For each Enneagram style, you will find a descriptive paragraph, followed by four words and a question to ask yourself. The four words include two positive and two negative words or phrases associated with that style. Next to the style description is an illustration with a single word below it. The picture and word together symbolize a main characteristic of the style and give you additional information to consider as you identify your Enneagram style.

Begin by reading through all of the Enneagram descriptions on the following pages. In reviewing the paragraphs, ask yourself: *Which of these descriptions most accurately describes my inner workings, **not** what is necessarily visible to others?* If you are over forty years old, also think about how you were in your thirties, twenties, and even your teenage years. If more than one paragraph description seems accurate, please reread those particular paragraphs to determine which one fits you the best.

Keep in mind that the Enneagram descriptions used here may not be in the exact words you would choose to describe yourself, but they may be similar. These descriptions work best when you take the entire paragraph into consideration rather than focusing on only one sentence or even one word. For example, when you read the Enneagram Six paragraph, you will see a statement concerning the Six's "supporting underdog causes." Fighting for social justice is common to several Enneagram styles, so this comment needs to be read in the context of the whole style description.

The question at the bottom of each paragraph is particularly helpful in clarifying whether that style matches your own behavior. These questions focus on an Enneagram style characteristic that is habitual and often unconscious. For example, the One question *Do I have a voice or message in my head, like a tape recorder, that continually criticizes me for what I do wrong?* may describe each of us, as we can all be self-critical. However, self-recrimination is unending for Ones. Ones describe this internal judge as a voice that is perpetually on 75 percent of the time or more. Some Ones even describe being awakened from a deep sleep by their self-critic. It is therefore very important that you look at these questions closely.

Ones

With high internal expectations for behavior, I hold myself and others accountable to meet these important standards. It is easy for me to see what is wrong or incorrect in a situation, as well as to see how things can be improved. I may come across as overly demanding or critical, but it is simply hard for me not to have things done the right way. I take great satisfaction in assuming responsibility, and I enjoy a refined, aesthetic sense of perfection. When I say I will do something, I make sure it is done properly. When others act unfairly or irresponsibly, I get resentful, although I try not to show it.

Enneagram Style (1)
DILIGENCE

| ↑ Hardworking | ↓ Judging |
| Disciplined | Inflexible |

Do I have a voice or message in my head, like a tape recorder, that continually criticizes me for what I do wrong?

Twos

Enneagram Style
GIVING

My greatest strength is being sensitive to other people's needs—sometimes with people I do not even know. It is as if I have an invisible antenna that can read other people's needs, often before they do. I like to think of myself as a warmhearted, friendly, and generous person. Good relationships are important to me; I work hard at developing them. Sometimes it is hard for me to resist helping others, even though I may be overwhelmed or in need of help myself. I may then feel taken for granted or unappreciated for my efforts and can become emotional or insistent.

| ↑ Caring | ↓ Indirect |
| Tuned into others' feelings | Overly accommodating |

Do I intuitively know what someone else needs but have a hard time articulating my own needs, even to myself?

Threes

Enneagram Style
PERFORM

I am most motivated by a need for success, achievement, and being the best. Generally, I have done well with whatever I have set as a goal. I strongly identify with work, and I believe that a person's value is largely based on what he or she accomplishes. Because I am so busy, I often set aside feelings or self-reflection so I can get everything done. I can get frustrated with people who do not use my time well or who do not step up to the task. Although I am a competitor, I can also be a good team player (although I often head up the team!).

| ↑ Confident | ↓ Competitive |
| Results-oriented | Workaholic |

Do I do all the things I do so that others will value and respect me?

Fours

I am a sensitive person who finds richness and meaning in authentic relationships with others. Because I enjoy symbolic aesthetic expression, I may be drawn to the arts in various forms. My artistic sense is for the sophisticated and unique. I often feel that other people do not understand me; I can react strongly to this with anger or sadness. I am happiest when I feel special and deeply connected. I am also willing to experience the sadder parts of life; in fact, melancholy has a wistful quality for me. Often, I find the ordinary boring and the distant or unavailable appealing.

Enneagram Style   4
MOOD

↑ Creative   ↓ Intense
   Expressive   Self-conscious

When I feel something very strongly, do I hold onto my emotions intensely for long periods of time, often replaying my thoughts, feelings, and sensations?

Fives

I see myself as an analytical person who thrives on time alone to recharge my energy. I enjoy observing situations rather than being in the middle of them, and I do not like too many demands being placed on me. I like to reflect on my experiences when I am by myself so I can enjoy, understand, and sometimes relive them. Because I have such an active mental life, I am never bored when I am alone. I would like to live a simple, uncomplicated life and be as self-sufficient as possible.

Enneagram Style   5
KNOWLEDGE

↑ Analytical   ↓ Detached
   Objective   Unassertive

When a situation gets emotional or intense, am I able to easily disconnect from my feelings of the moment and then reconnect later at a time and place of my choice?

Sixes

One of my greatest strengths is my sharp, incisive mind, which goes into high gear when I imagine something is threatening my security or safety. My inquisitive mind also allows me access to keen insights or intuition. Trusting others is a central issue for me, and I often scan my environment to determine whether a danger may be forthcoming. Suspicious of authority, I am also committed and loyal to organizations to which I belong. I may either avoid danger or approach it head-on, and I am usually active in supporting underdog causes.

↑ Loyal
  Responsible

↓ Worrying
  Hypervigilant

Do I constantly worry, thinking about what could go wrong and trying to plan so these negative possibilities will not occur?

Sevens

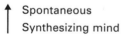

I am an optimistic person who enjoys coming up with new and interesting things to do. I have a very active mind that quickly moves back and forth between different ideas. I like to get a global picture of how all these ideas fit together, and I get excited when I can connect concepts that initially do not appear to be related. I like to work on things that interest me, and I have a lot of energy to devote to them. I have a hard time sticking with unrewarding or repetitive tasks. If something gets me down, I prefer to shift my attention to more pleasant things. Having multiple options is important for me; otherwise, I feel boxed in.

↑ Spontaneous
  Synthesizing mind

↓ Unfocused
  Rebellious

Do I continuously seek new and stimulating people, ideas, or events to keep life exciting and moving forward?

Eights

I place a high value on being strong, honest, and dependable, and I approach issues of importance in a straightforward way. I like strength and directness in others, and I can usually tell when someone is not telling me the truth or is being devious. I will protect innocent people, especially when an injustice has been done, yet I have trouble tolerating weakness in others. If I do not agree with those in authority or if no one is taking charge, I will step in and take control. It is hard not to display my feelings when I'm angry, and I am usually ready to stick up for friends and family.

Enneagram Style
CHALLENGE
8

 Direct
Assertive

 Controlling
Excessive

Do I have a strong exterior, one that is sometimes intimidating to others (intentionally or unintentionally), that hides a less visible but vulnerable interior?

Nines

Because I can usually see and appreciate all points of view, I am good at helping people resolve their differences. This ability to grasp the advantages of all sides makes me nonjudgmental but may make me appear indecisive. I do not like conflict, and it takes a lot for me to show my anger directly. I enjoy engaging in a number of activities, and I sometimes get so completely involved in an activity that I may forget about something else I am supposed to be doing. Easygoing and likable, I seek a comfortable, harmonious, and accepting life.

Enneagram Style
HARMONY
9

 Affable
Accepting

Puts things off
Avoids conflict

Do I automatically blend with other people's positive energy, but get quite distressed when I am around negativity, anger, and conflict?

Now that you have read the nine Enneagram descriptions, take a piece of paper and rank the style numbers in order, from most like you to least like you. Most people ultimately find that their Enneagram style is one of the top four choices in this ranking exercise.

Follow the next steps in order; they will help you gain more certainty regarding your first-choice Enneagram paragraph description.

- Reread your top four paragraph descriptions. *Do one or two of them seem more accurate than the others?* If yes, keep these in mind as you proceed. If not, keep the initial four choices.
- Next, review your list of strengths and weaknesses from Warm-Up Exercise 1. *How do your lists compare with your top-choice paragraphs?* If you find a good match between your strengths and weaknesses list and one of your top paragraphs, this is likely to be your Enneagram style.
- Finally, *does the pattern of your responses to the Emotional Index in Warm-Up Exercise 2 seem to match one of your top-choice paragraph descriptions?* A yes answer here suggests that you have found your Enneagram style.

If you are now reasonably sure of your Enneagram style, the following information will give you more details about your selection. If you are not yet certain of your Enneagram style, that is fine; the information here will help you to further clarify the differences among the nine different styles.

The Enneagram Model

The big picture of the Enneagram system can be helpful to you. As you review the Enneagram model, shown four different ways, you can use the information to confirm or disconfirm what you initially thought was your style, and to learn the Enneagram system as well.

Descriptive Labels
Sometimes people are able to identify their Enneagram style when they read the names commonly applied as Enneagram style labels. The label names come from a variety of Enneagram teachers and books. While no single label is standard throughout the Enneagram literature, the numbers (One through Nine) and general style descriptions are consistent with each other.

As you review the Enneagram model in Figure 1.1, please read the Enneagram labels and think about which set or sets of words best describe you.

Personality Characteristics
Figure 1.2 displays the most prominent characteristics of the nine Enneagram styles. Determine which set of characteristics most accurately describes you.

FIGURE 1.1 Descriptive Labels

Do any of these word combinations sound like something you may have thought about yourself or have had others say about you?

Several words on the chart below are italicized to indicate that a definition of the word appears in the sidebar on the following pages. These italicized words, whose meanings may be unclear at first glance, are included here because they frequently appear in the Enneagram literature.

FIGURE 1.2 Personality Characteristics

The italicized words from Figure 1.2 that may need explanation are as follows:

Twos

Manipulative refers to the interactive dynamic between Twos and others (often unconscious to the Two) in which Twos give to others as if not expecting anything in return. However, what a Two really wants is to be liked, needed, and treated as worthy. A forty-year-old software engineer in management describes this behavior to his colleagues: "At family functions, I offer each person a foot rub. If the person refuses, I get quite upset and wonder why they don't like me!"

Threes

Changes image describes the way Threes intuitively adjust their persona or image to the situation they are in. Striving to gain the respect of others, they know how to read their context and then dress and behave accordingly. A Three priest, for example, was taking a management course with business leaders. He dressed in casual business attire, and for six months no one knew that he was actually a member of the clergy. Neither his physical appearance nor his statements revealed this information. When questioned about his attire and behavior, he commented, "I thought people might discount what I had to say if they knew my profession."

Fives

Fives *compartmentalize*, a process in which a person puts information, experiences, and even personal behavior into mental categories or "boxes," each separated from the other. As a Five explains, "I have boxes for my boxes!"

Sevens

Mentally reframes describes the way Sevens tend to respond when faced with unpleasant situations, such as pain, conflict, or criticism. Sevens will reframe something to give it a positive rather than negative meaning. For example, after having missed a strategic business meeting, a Seven project manager said, "Yes, but I was with an important client, getting more work for our group!"

The *synthesizing mind* associated with Sevens describes the process of jumping from idea to idea, thing to thing, and experience to experience, yet connecting all these events into a larger whole. This is sometimes called the *monkey mind* in Eastern spiritual tradition—the Seven's mind works like a monkey, grabbing branch after branch in rapid succession. A highly successful lawyer talks about his inner process: "While I'm listening to the conversation at the meeting I'm leading, I start thinking about a strategy for my biggest client, what I'm going to write in a brief, when to pick up my kids, and where I'm going to go for dinner, all the while still listening to the meeting." What he has neglected to say is that he also paced around the room the entire time and took three cell phone calls.

Nines

For the Nine, two of the descriptive words need clarification. *Merges* refers to the Nine tendency to connect and blend with other people's energy, enthusiasm, and personality. For this reason, many Nines initially think they have all nine Enneagram patterns. In a way, they do, because Nines at some time connect in this merged way with people from all places on the Enneagram.

The word *narcotizes* is a term from the Enneagram literature that means a tendency for a person to move away from the priority in front of him or her and engage in repetitive, secondary activities instead. Each Nine has a preferred way of doing this. For example, a prominent businessman describes himself this way: "I bring a briefcase full of work home. After dinner, I enjoy washing all the dishes, and my wife likes that. After that, she says that I disappear. I start to work but then go outside to garden for a few minutes, and that turns into hours. If it's too cold or too dark to garden, I do my work in front of the television. I start switching channels, and the time gets away from me. I end up bringing the same work home night after night."

Focus of Attention

Tom Peters, author of the bestselling *In Search of Excellence*, noticed that the issues to which managers give the most attention are the ones that become priorities in their organizations; this is what is meant by *focus of attention*. So it is with the Enneagram. Depending on our Enneagram style, we pay greater attention to certain data, while we allow other information to recede into the background. Figure 1.3 shows the focus of attention for each Enneagram style. As you read this, ask yourself, *In most situations, where does my attention go, often subliminally, first and foremost?*

FIGURE 1.3 **Focus of Attention**

Worldview

The fourth model describes the *worldview* of the nine Enneagram styles. A person's worldview, sometimes called a mental model or paradigm, is a set of tacit assumptions about how the world works and one's role in it. As you can see, each Enneagram style operates from a very different set of implicit assumptions. *Which worldview in Figure 1.4 comes closest to your own?*

FIGURE 1.4 **Worldview**

The world is a place where I cannot assert myself;
instead, I will create harmony.

The world can be tough, and only the strong
survive. I will protect the innocent.

The world is imperfect, and I
work toward its improvement.

The world is full of exciting
opportunities so I look
to the future.

The world is full of people who
depend on my help; therefore,
I am needed.

The world is a threatening and
unsafe place. I must be loyal
and question authority.

The world values winners, so
I avoid failure at all costs.

The world is invasive, so I need privacy to
guard my resources and refuel my energy.

In the world, others have something
that I am missing. What is wrong?

Your Enneagram Style

At this point, you have completed three exercises to help identify your style:

- List of strengths and weaknesses
- Emotional Index
- Enneagram style descriptions

You also reviewed four different Enneagram charts in order to gain additional insights about the nine styles and compare this information with your top-choice paragraph descriptions. Now, ask yourself these questions:

- What do I think is my Enneagram style?
- Does it still seem that more than one style fits me?

Ultimately, you need to trust yourself when assessing your own Enneagram style. *You* know yourself best, after all. While feedback from others can be helpful, one person cannot necessarily determine another's Enneagram pattern based only on observable behavior. The Enneagram goes beyond external, observable traits, delving into inner motivations and internal processes. It is this depth that makes the Enneagram so powerful. Consequently, we should be careful not to assume we know someone else's place on the Enneagram, and we should also not assign ourselves an Enneagram style prematurely.

Delving Deeper into the Enneagram

The Enneagram system has two additional features: each Enneagram style has "wings" as well as stress and security points. These features add complexity and richness to the Enneagram. If you already know your Enneagram style, these additional features of the Enneagram system will give you more insight into yourself. If you have not yet placed yourself on the Enneagram, that is also fine. The information that follows may help you understand why, for example, you selected the top four choices that you did.

Wings
Wings are the Enneagram styles on each side of your actual Enneagram style. These are secondary styles of your core personality, which means that you may also display some of the characteristics of these Enneagram styles. Wings

do not fundamentally change your Enneagram style; they merely add additional qualities to your core personality. You may have one wing, two wings, or no wings at all. It is also common to have had one wing more active when you were younger or to have had another appear as you matured.

Here are two questions that may help you determine whether you have any wings to your basic Enneagram style:

1. Have you exhibited any characteristics of the styles on either side of your core Enneagram style at some time in your life?
2. Did your top four Enneagram paragraphs contain numbers directly next to each other?

If the answer to the second question is yes, one of those paragraphs may be your core style and others may indicate one, or possibly two, wings. People often select one of their wings among their top four paragraphs.

People of the same Enneagram style and identical wings may use their wing qualities differently. However, the general wing descriptions for all nine Enneagram styles (see Figure 1.5) may serve as guidelines to help you explore this aspect of the Enneagram and also help you to identify your wing or wings.

General Stress and Relaxation Reactions

In situations of stress, an individual's behavior typically becomes an accentuated version of the negative qualities of that person's Enneagram style. For example, Ones often become more critical; Twos tend to overextend their giving and then become angry; Threes tend to fixate even more on work; Fours often become hypersensitive; Fives may become more detached; Sixes may become immobilized by high anxiety; Sevens may become more frenzied; Eights might be more dominating; and Nines may get less accomplished.

When a person is feeling secure or relaxed, the strengths of his or her style often become more apparent. Ones may start to exhibit more excellence in what they do; Twos often become more freely giving and generous; Threes tend to become highly effective; Fours may become more joyful in their creativity; Fives often grasp how everything fits together; Sixes may share more pure insight; Sevens may implement more of their innovative ideas; Eights tend to make important things happen more often; and Nines often generate greater harmony in their lives.

Stress and Security Points

In addition to the stress and security reactions described above, the Enneagram system also shows the dynamic pattern of how each Enneagram style,

FIGURE 1.5 **Wing Descriptions for All Nine Enneagram Styles**

9 1 2
Wings for Ones

Ones with a Nine wing may be more relaxed, react less quickly, and enjoy nature's perfection.

Ones with a Two wing may be more generous and gregarious and may focus their work on helping people.

1 2 3
Wings for Twos

Twos with a One wing may be more serious, critical, and dedicated to work.

Twos with a Three wing may be more in the spotlight and focused on being successful.

2 3 4
Wings for Threes

Threes with a Two wing may be more empathic and pursue work and activities that help others.

Threes with a Four wing may be more emotional and have stronger aesthetic interests, such as writing, painting, or photography.

3 4 5
Wings for Fours

Fours with a Three wing may be more energetic and sophisticated and may pursue higher-profile work.

Fours with a Five wing may be more subdued, private, and analytical.

4 5 6
Wings for Fives

Fives with a Four wing may be more emotional and artistic.

Fives with a Six wing may be more skeptical and cautious.

5 6 7
Wings for Sixes

Sixes with a Five wing may be more internally focused and passionate about information gathering.

Sixes with a Seven wing may be more upbeat and risk-taking.

6 7 8
Wings for Sevens

Sevens with a Six wing may be more overtly fearful and deliberate.

Sevens with an Eight wing may be more assertive and direct.

7 8 9
Wings for Eights

Eights with a Seven wing may be more high-spirited, independent, and adventurous.

Eights with a Nine wing may be warmer, calmer, and more consensually oriented.

8 9 1
Wings for Nines

Nines with an Eight wing may exhibit more personal power and take more control of situations.

Nines with a One wing may be more punctual, discerning, and judgmental.

under conditions of stress or security, might move along the Enneagram. The *stress point* is the place on the Enneagram to which you move when you are feeling under pressure; the arrow points *away* from your core Enneagram style. The *security point* is the place on the Enneagram to which you move when you are feeling relaxed; the arrow points *toward* your core Enneagram style. *When feeling stressed or secure, individuals do not change their core Enneagram style; they simply start showing some characteristics of their stress or security points.*

Stress Points

Under stress, the Enneagram arrows flow counterclockwise. The Enneagram style toward which your arrow points is your *stress point*.

The Inner Triangle: Stress

If you look at the inner Enneagram triangle—styles Nine, Six, and Three—you will see the counterclockwise movement of the arrows. Under stress, Nine moves to Six, Six moves to Three, and Three moves to Nine (see Figure 1.6). *Stress* refers to any kind of pressure, ranging from mild demands, such as moderate deadlines, to circumstances of extreme duress, such as being passed over for a promotion.

Because Nines go to Six under stress, when pressured by issues such as severe time constraints or an impending conflict, Nines may begin to worry excessively like Sixes. Under moderate stress, Nines may also show more of their mental agility and insight. Sixes who are under pressure to take action

FIGURE 1.6 **The Inner Triangle: Stress**

may actually forgo some of their self-doubts and, like Threes, go for results. They sometimes also become more driven, even to the point of becoming workaholics.

Threes under stress move to Nine, and, like Nines, they may begin doing soothing sorts of activities, such as engaging in repetitive exercising or watching a great deal of television. Such pastimes provide comfort for those Threes experiencing anxiety related to situations of possible failure or interpersonal conflict.

The Hexad: Stress

Now look at the interior lines of the Enneagram, with the inner triangle removed (Figure 1.7). This configuration, called a *hexad*, shows the six other Enneagram styles and their interconnections under stress.

Ones move to Four under stress, which often occurs when their sense of responsibility becomes a burden or they are deeply disappointed. At these times, Ones can get depressed for long periods of time.

Fours under stress move to Two, most typically when they are feeling isolated or rejected. Fours in stressful situations may begin to give to others excessively but fail to take care of themselves. Fours under stress may also lose sight of who they are and, like Twos, try to become what they believe others want them to be.

Twos move to Eight when they are stressed, which commonly occurs when they overextend themselves but do not feel appreciated for their efforts, or when they are frustrated about their inability to keep another person from being abused. An angry Two often becomes powerful, like an Eight.

FIGURE 1.7 **The Hexad: Stress**

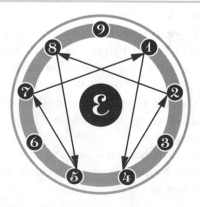

Eights under stress move to Five, often after they have fought too many battles, overworked themselves to excess, or just feel too vulnerable. Eights under stress often retreat into their own worlds, moving away from other people and from the demands those people might place on them. During this time, Eights typically engage in self-reflection and recharge their energy.

Fives under stress move to Seven and tend to become more extroverted and lively. For example, a Five having to give an important speech to a large group is, like anyone, under pressure. Giving a speech can be doubly stressful for Fives because they typically prefer private conversations and predictable interactions with others. On the podium, however, Fives often become upbeat, charming, and engaging—in other words, more like Sevens. And like Sevens, Fives under stress may also lose their focus.

Sevens move to One under stress, which often results when the workload piles up or when a Seven feels trapped. Under pressure, Sevens may focus somewhat obsessively on getting the work done and may become critical about the smallest work details.

There are wide variations in how people behave in relation to their stress points. Please note that stress may not be altogether negative for some people, who may, under pressure, demonstrate the positive characteristics of their stress point. For other people, stress is undesirable; these individuals will tend to exhibit more of their stress point's negative qualities.

Security Points

Under security or relaxation, the Enneagram styles flow clockwise toward the points where the arrows originate. The Enneagram style at which your arrow originates is your *security point*.

The Inner Triangle: Security

When secure, Nines move to Three and often become highly productive, efficient, and focused on results, like Threes. (See Figure 1.8. Note that the movement under security is in the *opposite* direction to the arrows shown in the figure.)

Relaxed Threes move to Six, where they can take the time to think through the challenges they face. At these times, their keen insights about people, work, and relationships often emerge.

Sixes move to Nine when they feel secure and relaxed; no longer filled with angst about what might happen, Sixes can let their minds relax, and they engage in enjoyable activities.

FIGURE 1.8 The Inner Triangle: Security

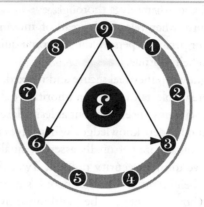

The Hexad: Security

Looking at the six Enneagram patterns in the hexad of the Enneagram diagram, shown in Figure 1.9, you can see that Ones move to Seven, Sevens move to Five, Fives move to Eight, and so forth (opposite to the directions the arrows point).

Ones move to Seven when secure. Typically, Ones tend to be responsible and reliable; they have difficulty relaxing and letting go at work and even at home, because there is always so much that needs to be done. However, when

FIGURE 1.9 The Hexad: Security

Ones are relaxed, typically when on a vacation, they take pleasure in every new experience and enjoy themselves thoroughly.

Sevens move to Five when relaxed. Instead of moving quickly from idea to idea, task to task, or person to person, they become quieter and more reflective, and they enjoy their solitude.

Fives move to Eight when they feel secure and relaxed. At these times, Fives begin to become more visible, taking more authoritative stances; they can exert authority under other circumstances, too, but at less relaxed times their authority tends to be based on expert knowledge. When Fives move to Eight, their authority often takes on a more personally assertive quality.

When Eights move to their security point at Two, they often relax with great pleasure, turn their attention to other people's needs, and become generous and giving. Although Eights can be highly intuitive when they are not relaxed, their more usual intuition comes from the gut, as if they *sense* or *know* something to be true. When Eights are relaxed, however, their intuition also comes from the heart, as if they *feel* something to be true.

Twos move to Four when they feel relaxed. This movement often draws out a Two's artistic and creative side, perhaps through drawing, painting, or writing. Although Twos can also take pleasure in the aesthetic under normal conditions, when they are relaxed, their aesthetic endeavors often emerge from a deeper place in their interior life.

Fours move to One when they feel secure, which often enables them to become more self-disciplined and more focused on external reality. Fours at their security point can begin to become more balanced, fluctuating less from the swings of interior moods and achieving more equilibrium among their thoughts, feelings, and actions.

Please note that there are also wide variations in how people behave in relation to their security points. Security may not be altogether positive for some people, who may, when relaxed, actually demonstrate the negative characteristics of the security point. For other people, security and relaxation are desirable; these individuals will tend to exhibit more of the security point's positive qualities. The most useful way to think about your stress and security points is to view them as two additional places on the Enneagram where you can gain insight into your thoughts, feelings, and behaviors.

Revisiting Your Enneagram Style

As you think back to the top four choices of Enneagram style you made earlier, it is possible that you selected your core Enneagram style and a stress or security point. For example, you may have selected Two, Eight, and Four. If so, Two may be your core style, and Eight and Four your stress and security points, respectively. Or, you may have selected Seven, One, and Five; if your core pattern is Seven, your stress and security points are One and Five.

It is most common for an individual's core Enneagram style to be among the top four choices made. In addition, people often find that they have chosen a wing, a stress point, or a security point among their top four. Occasionally, all of these appear in the top four paragraph choices. Now that you know more about the Enneagram system, go back and look at your four top selections again.

Conclusion

The next chapters will help you to understand how your Enneagram style gives you reasonably predictable behaviors at work in almost every type of situation. If you have already been able to identify your Enneagram style, the chapters that follow will show you how to gain self-insight and improve your interpersonal relationships. If you are still unsure about your Enneagram style, the upcoming chapters will also be of benefit by demonstrating further the likely behavior patterns for all nine Enneagram styles in common work situations, such as communication, feedback, conflict, teams, and leadership. So please don't become discouraged if you do not know your Enneagram style at this point. After you have read all of the remaining chapters, it will be clear to you that the behaviors, thoughts, and feelings of a certain style really describe you with a high degree of accuracy.

The following story will help demonstrate the value of the Enneagram in business applications:

Leon and Stan, both senior attorneys at a large firm, could not tolerate being in the same room together. Because Leon, a Three, and Stan, a Six, avoided all contact with each other, their hostile relationship was not actually a problem for them; it did, however, pose a huge dilemma for the firm. Leon, a rainmaker, provided one-third of the firm's revenue, while Stan's area of legal specialization made it necessary for him to be involved in 95 percent of the firm's cases.

At the urging of the firm's managing director, Leon and Stan consented to work on their relationship with a consultant. They planned to first meet separately with the consultant to clarify their individual concerns. They agreed to meet jointly later to resolve their differences. Well versed in the Enneagram, the consultant taught both attorneys the Enneagram system and helped them identify their particular styles. They met individually with the consultant for four months.

At the end of that time, Leon and Stan were able to work together comfortably on common projects. Through the individual sessions, both had realized that their issues with each other actually reflected more about themselves than about the other person. Neither felt the need for a joint meeting.

As a Three, Leon had dismissed Stan because he felt annoyed by Stan's perpetual worrying and pessimistic attitude. Leon began to realize that Stan's "can't-do," worst-case scenario thinking disturbed him because a focus on the negative raised the specter of failure and potentially impeded Leon's need to get quick results. Leon came to understand that these were his issues as a Three, and he began to appreciate Stan's insights and careful deliberations.

Stan, a Six, had perceived Leon as a showman, with more bravado than substance. Upon reflection, Stan gained the insight that he actually wished he could be more like Leon, who seemed to function without any perceptible self-doubt. Using the Enneagram, Stan came to appreciate that Leon also worried, but that he used his anxiety to move toward action.

While the two never became close friends, each went on to use the insights of the Enneagram for his own self-development and for improving both his work with clients and his relationships at home.

Chapter 2

Communicating Effectively

Communication is *the* single skill that every employee in every company must demonstrate continually in his or her work. The success of senior leaders, individual employees, managers, and support staff in every industry and profession can be made or broken on the effectiveness of their communication skills. We communicate in person at staff meetings, in one-to-one conversations, and in the halls; we also communicate through e-mail, telephone, letters, videoconferences, and presentations. Our intention is almost always to come across well, to be understood, and to influence others. However, the reality is that we do not always achieve these goals; in truth, even the most effective communicators can sometimes be misunderstood. Everyone can benefit from improving his or her communication skills.

Have you ever been misunderstood in any of the ways described below?

1. I feel hurt and angry when I am told that I criticize others, because I work so hard to control my responses.
2. I feel unappreciated and indignant when I hear that someone does not perceive me as the kind and generous person I believe myself to be.
3. I am upset and perplexed when someone tells me that I come across as cold, abrupt, or insincere.
4. I feel hurt and angry when my behavior is misinterpreted or when I am told that I am overly sensitive.
5. I am taken aback when someone says that I am aloof and act superior, and I can't understand how anyone could perceive me that way.
6. I react very strongly when people tell me I am pessimistic; after all, I keep most of my negativity to myself and try to be constructive.

7. I get distressed when I discover I am not taken seriously at work, because I have more ideas and know more about most topics than other people do.
8. I try hard to contain myself, so I feel distraught when I hear, yet again, that I overwhelm others.
9. I get confused and then quietly angry when others do not consider my polite requests and suggestions.

Have you ever been in a situation in which something you said was misperceived? Or, have you ever realized after listening to someone else that you did not truly hear what the other person was saying? In either of these cases, Enneagram-based communication distortions were at work. When we talk, we often distort what we say as a result of our Enneagram speaking style, body language, and blind spots; when we listen, we often filter what the other person is saying to us through Enneagram-based selective listening.

We cannot always know the Enneagram style of the person with whom we are communicating, but if we know our own Enneagram style, we can improve our side of any communication. Knowing *how* we communicate is the first step. We can then decide what we want to change. The sender-receiver model in Figure 2.1 shows the general types of communication distortions.[1]

After a brief review of both sending and receiving distortions, this chapter summarizes what people of each Enneagram style do that contributes to their being misunderstood as well as to their misunderstanding others.

FIGURE 2.1 Sender and Receiver Distortions

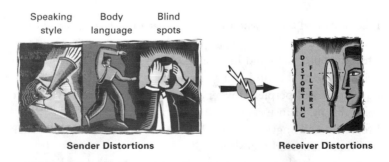

---

1. The "sender-receiver" model originally appeared in *Looking Out/Looking In* by R. Adler and N. Towne (1978).

Three kinds of distortions may be present when we send a communication to someone else: speaking style, body language, and blind spots. *Speaking style* refers to the overall pattern by which we talk as well as to what we actually talk about. Some of us speak slowly, while others get right to the point; some of us sound like honey and others like machine guns. Some tell stories, while others talk about tasks. Some people talk about feelings, and others talk about ideas or events. Some people hardly talk at all.

SENDER DISTORTIONS AT WORK

Speaking Style

Thomas, an attorney who is a Three on the Enneagram, has a concise, direct speaking style. His intention is to be truthful and straightforward, but his messages are often interpreted as abrupt and dismissive. From his own point of view, he is focused, clear, and honest when he talks to others. Some of Thomas's coworkers, however, perceive his speaking style to be rushed and rude; to them, it feels as though Thomas wants to finish the conversation quickly so he can get back to his primary goal, work. Who is correct—Thomas, or those who perceive him to be rude?

Body Language

Sam, a successful management consultant who is a Six on the Enneagram, was presenting the results of an organizational effectiveness survey to the senior staff of a manufacturing plant. The plant manager commented that the narrative survey report contained too many harsh criticisms of the plant. Sam became defensive, and a comment was made from the audience that he seemed angry. Sam pounded his fist on the table, furrowed his brow, and stated, "I am not angry!" Those in the audience tried to muffle their laughter as Sam's body language, rather than his words, showed his true feelings.

Blind Spots

Leadership roles seem to always find Eric, an Eight, even when he expresses the desire to remain an individual contributor. Because he is organized, smart, strategic, and an excellent developer of less experienced staff, Eric was asked to take a senior leadership position. Eric was panicked that he would fail at his new job because of his tendency to erupt angrily. For this reason, he

continued

requested the services of an executive coach. Through coaching, Eric discovered that it was not his anger that he needed to work on, but rather his blind spot—his deep vulnerability and subsequent strong reactivity. In working with Eric, the coach was able to elicit a strong reaction in him by saying one of two things: something untrue and defaming about Eric, or something negative about someone for whom he cared. Even with forewarning from his coach that one of these types of comments was forthcoming, Eric would erupt with anger, frustration, and sadness. For Eric, the exploration of this blind spot was the key to his growth and future success.

Our posture, facial expressions, hand gestures, body movements, energy levels, and hundreds of other nonverbal messages form the integrated impression known as *body language*. The combination of our speaking style and our body language accounts for approximately 80 percent or more of the meaning others hear in what we communicate; only 20 percent or less of a perceived message comes from the actual content of what we say.

As important as body language is to communication, most of us are unaware of our own body language because it is largely unconscious. Our body language is as automatic as breathing. We rarely pay attention to taking a breath, yet we do it all day long.

Blind spots contain information about ourselves that are not apparent to us, but are highly visible to other people. We unknowingly convey this information through an amalgam of our speaking style, body language, and other inferential data. Have you ever been told—and been surprised to hear—that you cleared your throat regularly, pulled at your hair, crossed your feet while standing, or said "um" ten times during a speech? This is the type of information contained in our blind spots. Each Enneagram style has specific blind spots through which unconscious and unintentional messages are sent to others.

The receivers of the messages we send also distort what they hear through their *distorting filters*. These are unconscious concerns or assumptions, often based on Enneagram style, that alter how we hear what others say. For example, if you focus on whether or not your listener likes you (as Twos often do), or if you pay attention to whether other people are demanding your time and energy (as Fives typically do), you will not be clearheaded enough to accurately hear what others are really saying to you. Most communication courses teach a technique called *active listening*. This technique involves listening to another person very closely and then paraphrasing what you have just heard the other person say to you. Even in this situation, one in which we are try-

RECEIVER DISTORTIONS AT WORK

Oscar, a One, was the newly appointed board president of a nonprofit organization. He was aghast at the chaos he found in the organization, and he was concerned that he did not have the support of the entire board of directors. At his first board meeting as president, Oscar was bombarded by criticism from a new board member, Faith, a Four on the Enneagram. As soon as Oscar said something, Faith would ask *why* questions—"Why isn't there this policy?" "Why can't we try that?" and "Why is this practice in place?" Furious, Oscar wondered why Faith was being relentlessly critical of both him and the organization.

For her part, Faith was ready to quit the board after the first meeting. She found all of her attempts to solicit information or propose suggestions met by hostility from the board president, Oscar. Other board members seemed to enjoy her energy and creativity, but Oscar clearly did not.

Oscar, a One, felt thrown into a work situation that seemed to him to be completely out of control. Consequently, he heard Faith's comments through his own filter, mistaking her questions of inquiry for criticisms.

Faith, a Four, was in both a new work and a new social situation, and she felt misunderstood and rejected by Oscar. These common Enneagram Four distortions—being misunderstood and feeling rejected—prevented Faith from understanding Oscar's genuine concerns and from seeing his constructive plans for the organization.

ing our best to listen accurately, most of us either miss some information or misinterpret what we have just heard. That is because all of us unconsciously engage in selective listening to at least some degree, simply because we are human.

As noted, each Enneagram style has specific communication distortions of speaking style, body language, blind spots, and distorting filters. The following examples, which illustrate instances of miscommunication that happened with some of my clients, show the communication distortions of each style.

The best way to avoid having others misperceive what we say is to alter the way in which we say things. We can only do this by becoming aware of our speaking distortions and then working to change our behavior. Similarly, the way to ensure that we hear others more accurately is to minimize our distorting filters. Again, this comes from first understanding the distorting filters of our own Enneagram style, and then working to minimize or remove them— one filter at a time.

How Ones Communicate

Enneagram Style
DILIGENCE

Oscar feels hurt and angry when he is told that he criticizes others, because he works so hard to control his responses.

Speaking Style

Precise, direct, exacting, concise, and detailed • Share task-related thoughts • Use words such as *should, ought, must, correct, excellent, good, wrong,* and *right* • React quickly to ideas • Defensive if criticized

"Diligence" best defines Oscar's speaking style, as he works very hard to find exactly the right words to express his thoughts. Such words as *good, should,* and *ought* are interwoven, directly or implicitly, in his speech. Oscar reacts quickly to ideas and becomes defensive if he feels criticized. His speaking style is demonstrated by the following example:

Oscar and a colleague, Cameron, were about to go to a professional meeting. The first thing Oscar said to Cameron was this: "You're not wearing a suit?"

Cameron, surprised by this unsolicited remark, replied, "What? Why are you saying that to me?"

Oscar's response was rapid and sincere: "What you're wearing is too casual for this meeting. You need to wear a suit. I'm just trying to help you!"

Oscar never used the words *correct* or *must,* but he was clearly correcting Cameron when he said, "You're not . . ." and "You need to . . ." Oscar's quick response and defensive explanation are also characteristic of the One's speaking style.

Body Language

Erect posture • Taut muscles • Eyes focused • Body language may reveal a negative reaction • Clothing well coordinated and pressed

During this interaction, Oscar's body language became increasingly tense; from his point of view, he was truly trying to assist his colleague, not criticize him. As the discussion continued, Oscar's jaw tightened, his eyes became intense, and he stood up straight and moved backward. The importance Oscar placed on his own appearance (being well groomed, having coordinating clothing and accessories, and wearing the correct attire) was something he wanted to share with his coworker, even though Cameron was not the least bit interested.

Blind Spots

Appear critical, impatient, or angry • Tenacious regarding their own opinions

The interaction also reveals one of Oscar's blind spots. Oscar was unaware that he was criticizing Cameron's choice of clothing, and he maintained his criticism even after Cameron's negative response. Ones can appear critical and impatient even when they are trying hard not to do so.

Distorting Filters

Being criticized by someone else • Preoccupation with their own ideas • Whether, in the One's view, other people are behaving correctly and responsibly

Because Ones work diligently to do the right thing themselves, they often filter and distort what others say for any suggestion of criticism directed toward them. Oscar felt criticized by Cameron's indignant response. Ones also continue to believe their own ideas so strongly that they may not accurately hear what the other person is actually saying. Oscar was so convinced that Cameron was dressed incorrectly (and annoyed that he had not taken the time to consider the appropriate attire) that he was not able to hear the hurt and anger Cameron expressed.

How Twos Communicate

Terry feels unappreciated and indignant when she hears that someone does not perceive her as the kind and generous person she believes herself to be.

Enneagram Style ②
GIVING

Speaking Style

Ask questions • Give compliments • Focus on the content of other person • Few references to self • Soft voice • Angry or complaining when they dislike what others say

"Giving" is a word Terry often uses in describing herself in her interactions with other people. In her speaking style, Terry typically asks questions of other people, gives compliments, and rarely focuses on herself. In fact, when she is asked questions about herself, she often deflects the conversation back to the other person. When Terry does not like what she hears, however, her soft and sympathetic voice can transform into something far less pleasant.

Talking on the phone to Michael, a colleague, Terry asked how he was doing. Michael responded that a close friend of his had recently died in a bizarre mountain climbing accident; the friend had been taking a personal development course that combined mountain climbing with personal growth training, and he had been attempting to overcome his fear of heights. At the top of a ninety-foot cliff, he had suffered a fatal heart attack. Michael said that the course instructor had shown little visible concern at the time and had ignored the incident in later discussions with the remaining students. Terry, a friend of the instructor's, became agitated on hearing this and accused Michael of planning to instigate trouble for the instructor.

Body Language

Smiling and comfortable • Relaxed facial expressions • Open, graceful body movement • When agitated, furrowed brow and facial tension

This example illustrates the transformation of the Two's speaking style, with a soft, lilting voice becoming one filled with complaining and anger. The body language also changes and is palpable even over the phone, as the Two's smiling and relaxed countenance changes so that the brow becomes furrowed and there is overall facial tension. In Terry's perception, her friend, the instructor, was potentially under siege.

Blind Spots

A secondary or hidden intention may lie beneath their generosity, helpfulness, and attention-giving • If uninterested in the other person, disengage precipitously

Shortly after this conversation, Terry called Michael back because she was worried that he was angry. Terry's first remark to Michael was, "I just want to make sure that you deal with your feelings." She then added, "And don't do anything that will hurt the instructor." This comment illustrates the first Two blind spot, that of a stated intention to be helpful that masks a deeper motivation—in this case, protecting the instructor. Terry perceived, incorrectly, that Michael was planning to take further action. In other cases, Twos may try to act in a helpful manner, but have other types of unexpressed intentions—for example, to be appreciated, to feel important, or to become indispensable.

A second Two blind spot is also evident in this example. Twos may ask questions and then, for a number of reasons, lose interest in the conversation. When this occurs, their attention shifts away from the other person dramatically. Terry was not fully interested in the answer to her opening question, "How are you?" Once she heard the answer, Terry did not focus on Michael's sorrow and anger, but instead concentrated on what she perceived to be the potential repercussions for the instructor.

Distorting Filters

Whether the other person likes them • Whether they like the other person • Whether they want to help the other person • The degree of influence the other person has • If they feel the other person plans to harm someone they want to protect

This story also shows Twos' distorting filters. Near the end of the second phone call, Terry asked Michael, "Do you still like me?" The filter of whether the Two likes the other person and whether the person likes the Two was entangled with another common filter: when the other person is criticizing someone the Two likes or holds in high esteem. In this case, Terry believed her colleague was attacking an instructor who was respected in his field and whom Terry regarded highly.

How Threes Communicate

Thomas gets upset and perplexed when anyone tells him that he comes across as cold, abrupt, or insincere.

Thomas was focused on accomplishing a successful training program when Katherine, his co-trainer, asked to speak with him during the break. She said, "This session does not

Enneagram Style ③
PERFORM

seem to be going well, and there is another problem. The company vice president, a participant in the session, asked me out on a date. He wants me to come to dinner tonight while his wife is out of town. What should I do?"

After a moment's hesitation, Thomas responded, "Let's talk about this after the session is over." However, what he was really thinking was this: *Why is she coming at me like this? We still have four more hours of training, and we have to keep focused on making this go well. I can't do anything about this anyway!*

Katherine, bewildered and anxious, thought, *Didn't he hear what I just said? I need help!*

Speaking Style

Clear, efficient, logical, and well-conceived • Quick on their feet • Avoid topics in which they have limited information • Avoid topics that reflect negatively on them • Use concrete examples • Impatient with lengthy conversations

---

Thomas's response was delivered in the speaking style of a Three—logical, efficient, and to the point (no missing words here!). His intention was very clear: he did not want to talk about the issue now. Katherine's comment that the session was not going well could not, to his way of thinking, help him get the session back on track. The fact that the company vice president had made sexual overtures to Katherine could only hurt their continued work in the company. He did what came naturally to him as a Three, which was to become impatient with a problem he knew very little about and could not solve. Thomas was also eager to avoid discussing a topic that could derail his success.

After the session ended, Katherine approached Thomas again about her concerns. Thomas listened for a few minutes, only partially interested in the conversation, and then proceeded to list in sequential order the exact times during the session when Katherine had not performed at her best. With the thought-out words of a Three, Thomas presented the information in a highly logical and rational way.

Body Language

Look put together • Appear confident • Breathe deeply into their chest area • Keep shoulders high • Actions may appear staged for effect • Look around regularly to check the reactions of others • Let others know when their time is up

---

Thomas's body language also illustrated the way Threes often project confidence. Although Thomas had his own doubts about how well the training event was going, no one would ever have guessed that he was worried. In addition, no one would have known that he was thinking through what he would say to Katherine about the sexual overtures. With his shoulders high and his breath deep in his chest, he looked very poised and comfortable.

When talking with Katherine, both at the break and after the session, Thomas made it very clear to her that he had limited time and patience for the conversation. He did 95 percent of the talking, and once he had finished expressing his thoughts to Katherine, he quickly turned away to do some preparation and gather his materials.

Blind Spots

Impatient when they perceive others as not capable • Avoid discussing their own failings • Appear driven • Seem to rush or dismiss others • May appear abrupt or insincere

Katherine had unknowingly triggered one of Thomas's blind spots. Threes become impatient when others do not appear capable or confident, and Katherine was showing her anxiety; in Thomas's view, her lack of confidence reflected poorly on him and did not bode well for the success of their joint training effort. He also had difficulty hearing Katherine say that *his* training was not going well. This demonstrates a second common blind spot for Threes—difficulty discussing negative issues, particularly those that suggest the Three may be failing.

Katherine perceived Thomas to be cold and abrupt, and she wondered whether he sincerely cared about her or her feelings. Under other circumstances, she had found Thomas to be personable and supportive, so this shift in his behavior puzzled her.

Distorting Filters

Whether the information will make them look good • Whether the information will interfere with their goal achievement • The apparent confidence and competence of the other person

Thomas's distorting filters interfered with his being able to hear Katherine's actual message. She wanted to collaborate with him to improve the session, and she wanted his support in dealing with the vice president. Thomas, however, heard her say that the group did not like the training, which threatened his view of his own performance. Most Threes filter out any data that suggest they could fail.

In addition, Katherine appeared frazzled when she approached Thomas; Threes tend to discount information when it comes from people who do not appear confident, generally preferring to distance themselves from individuals who come across in this manner. That is exactly what Thomas did to Katherine.

How Fours Communicate

Enneagram Style
MOOD

Fritz feels hurt and angry when his behavior is misinterpreted or when he is told that he is overly sensitive.

Fritz, an architect, was quite upset when he called his mentor, Marsha, but he struggled not to show it. Fritz had been feeling increasingly dissatisfied with the lack of developmental opportunities that he had expected Marsha to provide for him. In preparation for this call, Fritz had spent time mulling over what he might say. He weighed various approaches to find a way to get his message across to Marsha without unduly distressing her. When Fritz finally had what he thought was the right approach, he called Marsha and said, "I want to talk to you about our working relationship. I really want to continue working with you. I just think that the terms of our working contract need to be clarified. I had a similar situation with someone I worked with, and I just want to make sure those things don't happen between us."

"How are you, Fritz?" Marsha replied. "And what is it about our working contract that you want to discuss?"

Fritz said, "Uh, well, I, uh . . ."

Speaking Style

Use words like *I, me, my,* and *mine* frequently • Talk about self
• Discuss feelings • Share personal stories • Ask personal questions
• Word choice may be deliberate

In this simple telephone conversation, Fritz revealed the multiple characteristics of the Four speaking style. Fours tend to use words like *I, me, my,* and *mine* more often than any other Enneagram style. Fours also tend to share personal stories and engage in "trouble talk"—that is, the discussion of incidents that have caused them distress. The frequent use of both personalized language and the sharing of personal experiences often has the effect of drawing the conversation away from the other person and toward the Four. For these reasons, the speaking style of Fours is sometimes described as "self-referencing."

As a Four, Fritz also paid close attention to his word choice. In his attempt to express himself, his language became deliberate and self-conscious. Because Fours want to be understood in exactly the way they intend, they spend time in advance thinking through alternative dialogues, then choose the approach they think most accurately expresses their intention. Fours also seek to draw the other person into the conversation—hence Fritz's choice of such words as "our working relationship" and "our working contract."

Body Language

> Intense • Urgent • Appear to be focused inward, as if analyzing the words they say • Communicate that they want undivided attention • Eyes may appear moist or sad

Fours often approach important concerns with intensity and urgency, conveying this message through their direct and prolonged eye contact, the palpable concern on their faces, and a laser-like focus on what they want to say. Fritz started the conversation by getting right to the point, bypassing such pleasantries of telephone etiquette as "How are you?"

When Fritz said, "Uh, well, I, uh," he was communicating three things simultaneously: revealing his surprise and hurt that his mentor did not know exactly what he was feeling; that he was grasping for what to say next; and that he wanted Marsha to continue focusing her attention on what he was about to say. Feeling hurt is common among Fours and is often evidenced by their perplexed facial expressions and a wet glisten in their eyes. Although Fritz was feeling hurt and sad in this situation, many Fours may look sad even when they are not because of a perpetual look of moisture in their eyes.

Blind Spots

> Pull the conversation back to themselves using self-referencing behavior • Need to fully complete a conversation even when the other person no longer wants to discuss an issue • May appear dramatic or contrived

Fritz has no idea that his speaking style and body language have the effect of drawing attention to himself; he thinks that his personal references make the conversation more real, and thus more interpersonally engaging. This behavior of Fours is one of their blind spots.

In addition, Fours frequently feel the need for continued interpersonal interaction until they feel finished. Fritz continued talking to Marsha for forty-five minutes, never asking whether she had the time or desire to continue the conversation. Fours like to discuss emotions and moods, and they seek emotional closure; they believe that others share this preference, or should. Because of this, others may perceive Fours as dwelling too much on feelings and as being overly dramatic or contrived.

Distorting Filters

Personal rejection • Being slighted or demeaned • Not wanting to appear defective • Being misunderstood

The Four's distorting filters are illustrated by Fritz's reaction to Marsha's question, "And what is it about our working contract that you want to discuss?" Fritz interpreted this question to mean that his mentor did not share his concern about their working relationship, and as a consequence he felt hurt. This misinterpretation arose from common Four distorting filters—fear of rejection, of being slighted, and of feeling defective. Because of his Four sensitivities, Fritz distorted the meaning of Marsha's question and felt demeaned. He also felt misunderstood by his mentor, another Four distorting filter. Fritz wanted Marsha to know how much he valued her, but he assumed from her words that she only wanted to talk about their working relationship. For Marsha's part, she was simply responding to the topic that Fritz had initiated.

How Fives Communicate

Enneagram Style
5 KNOWLEDGE

Frank is taken aback when someone says that he is aloof and acts superior, and he can't understand how anyone could perceive him that way.

In a business course on the Enneagram and communication style, Frank explained why the speaking style of Fives tends to be either minimalist, with few words and short sentences, or lengthy, almost to the point of a dissertation or treatise. "It's simple," he said. "It depends on whether a Five knows a lot about the subject or not!"

Speaking Style

> Speak tersely *or* in lengthy discourse • Highly selective word choice
> • Limited sharing of personal information • Share thoughts rather
> than feelings

The manner in which Frank spoke in this instance shows multiple aspects of the Five's speaking style. In this situation, Frank's answer was concise and careful, and his words were carefully selected. He gave an answer in general and objective terms rather than through personal phrasing (which could have been, for example, "I speak at length only when I know a lot about the subject"). In public settings, Fives usually talk about thoughts, rarely feelings. In Frank's comment, he made no mention of the feelings associated with his thoughts, such as "Fives feel anxious when they do not know the answer" or "I feel very ill at ease when I'm put on the spot without knowing the information requested."

Body Language

> Express thoughts with limited emotional content • Appear
> self-contained and self-controlled, with unanimated body language

When Frank shared his insight, he also displayed body language that is characteristic of most Fives. With an unanimated face and a very still body, he reported his information as though he were an objective journalist or someone who was watching his own thoughts from the outside. Often Fives look as though they exist more in their heads than in their bodies; for this reason, Fives are sometimes referred to as "talking heads." If you observe Fives closely, it may sometimes seem that they are speaking from only a portion of their head, or even that they are watching themselves from behind as they talk.

Blind Spots

> May not exhibit warmth • May appear aloof or remote • May say too
> much and lose listeners • May use too few words and so might not
> be understood by others • May appear condescending or elitist

One of the Five's blind spots is that an emphasis on the cerebral often comes at the expense of warmth in interpersonal relationships; the perceived lack of warmth can discourage dialogue. Fives may *feel* warm and compassionate, but they tend to keep such feelings inside. Fives have developed the capacity to detach from feelings in the moment; they revisit these feelings at a later time, when they are ready and feel more comfortable. This separation of thought and feeling can lead others to experience Fives as aloof or remote.

After Frank had expressed his thoughts about why Fives sometimes say a lot (and possibly lose their listeners) and sometimes only a little (and may fail to be understood by others), the audience laughed in a way that was clearly appreciative of this gift of insight. Frank's response to their laughter was non-verbal—he gave a wry smile, as though he were amused by the group's reaction. Much to the surprise of Fives, they may be perceived by others as acting elitist or superior. Members of the audience read Frank's wry smile to mean, "You didn't know this?" In actuality, his smile revealed his emotion of that moment: *I feel delighted to shed light on the inner life of the Five.*

Distorting Filters

Demands and expectations • Feeling inadequate • Overwhelming emotions from the other person • Trust in the other person to maintain privacy • Physical proximity that feels too close

---

The facilitator of the session at which Frank spoke understood Fives' distorting filters, and she was therefore careful to ask questions of Fives in ways that did not activate their filtering process. Because Fives tend to close down and remain silent when they believe someone has expectations of them or when they anticipate feeling inadequate, the facilitator asked the question in this general and emotionally neutral way: "Is there a Five in the group who can explain to us why Fives tend to speak in these two different ways?" With this phrasing, no individual participant was put on the spot to give a response.

In addition, the facilitator did not move from where she was standing, so that no Five in the audience would feel as though his or her personal space was being invaded. Many Fives filter out messages from someone whom they perceive to be too physically close to them.

How Sixes Communicate

Sam reacts very strongly when people tell him he is pessimistic; after all, he keeps most of his negativity to himself and tries to be constructive.

Sam must speak with his boss about a promotion and possible raise. He is worried. He goes into the office to make his request, but he has already had this conversation countless times in his mind. Concerned that his boss will not remember their appointment, Sam has called him several times as a reminder. Thinking that the boss might be late, Sam has prepared himself for this scenario so that he will not be disconcerted.

Should he start with what he wants from his boss, or should he lead into the conversation by detailing what he has accomplished? These possible choices and many others have been running through Sam's mind.

Speaking Style

Start with analytical comments • Alternate syncopated, hesitant speech with bold, confident speech • Discuss worries, concerns, and "what-ifs"

When Sam arrived in his boss's office, he began by talking about his accomplishments, sounding bold, yet warm. Partway through his speech, Sam began to worry about whether his boss agreed with what he was saying. His speaking became hesitant, and he asked his boss, "Is . . . is . . . is this what you think, too?" Sam's style shows the alternating speaking style of a Six—sometimes clear and confident, sometimes anxious and uncertain.

When Sam's boss mentioned a few areas in which he disagreed with Sam, Sam felt distraught, but he kept this to himself (or attempted to do so).

When Sam finally asked for the promotion, he began by saying, "Well, you might not want to do this, because . . ." Sixes often anticipate negative possibilities and then present ways to overcome these problems. It is akin to making a preventive strike and combining it with a practical solution.

Body Language

Eyes may be bold and direct • May appear warm, engaging, and empathic • Alternatively, eyes may dart back and forth horizontally, as if scanning for danger • Face shows worry • Quick nonverbal reaction to perceived threats

When Sixes feel courageous, as Sam felt at the beginning of the conversation, their body language shows this. They lean forward, eyes looking straight ahead, and they often give the impression that they can accomplish anything. At these times, Sixes can appear warm, engaging, and empathic. But when they feel apprehensive, Sixes can move back suddenly, as if under siege. At such times, their eyes may dart back and forth horizontally, and their facial muscles may become tense. Under great stress, they may look like a deer caught in the headlights. All of these nonverbal reactions are involuntary.

Blind Spots

Negative scenarios appear to others as negativism, pessimism, and a "can't-do" orientation • Self-doubt and worry can cause others to question the Six's competence • No matter how hard the Six tries to mask the worry, it is still apparent

While Sam works hard not to show discomfort, his blind spots are readily apparent to others. Others know when Sixes are worried, even when they try to hide it. As brave as Sixes may seem at certain times, their palpable worry can make others wonder about their competence. Sam's boss may start to wonder, for example, *If Sam doesn't think a promotion will work out for him, maybe I shouldn't, either.* Sixes also tend to create worst-case scenarios, which can also give others the impression that they are negative, pessimistic, or have a "can't-do" attitude.

Distorting Filters

Whether others' use of authority is proper or improper • Projection of thoughts and feelings onto the other person • Issues of trust related to the other person

Sam went into the meeting with his boss with his distorting filters already at work. Sixes, like the other two mental Enneagram styles (Five and Seven), are sensitive to authority. The Six filter regarding authority concerns whether the person in power can be trusted to use his or her authority properly. To the Six, "properly" means fairly, justly, and *in a way that will not hurt the Six.*

A second distorting filter of Sixes is projection. When Sam perceived that his boss was not agreeing with his self-assessment, he began listing the reasons why a promotion might not be considered a good idea. Sam was actually projecting his own fears onto his boss, assuming that because his boss disagreed with him in a few areas related to his accomplishments, the boss would never give him a promotion. Sam was doing more than developing worst-case scenarios; he was projecting that his boss had the same doubts about him that he had about himself. Sam's projection that his boss had concerns about his ability magnified the third distorting filter of the Six: wondering whether another person can be trusted. In this case, Sam grew concerned that his boss could no longer be trusted to promote Sam's career.

How Sevens Communicate

Sonia gets distressed when she discovers that she is not taken seriously at work; in her view, she has more ideas and knows more about most topics than other people do.

Speaking Style

Enneagram Style
OPTIONS **7**

> Quick and spontaneous, with words released in a flurry
> • Tell engaging stories • Shift from topic to topic
> • Upbeat and charming • Avoid negative topics about
> themselves • Reframe negative information

Why is it that many Sevens work so hard at what they do yet are often questioned, often implicitly, about their depth of knowledge and experience? Spontaneous in their speaking style, Sevens often release a quick flurry of information. Sharing stories to make their points and quickly shifting from one idea to the next, they tend to be upbeat and engaging until they hear something negative coming from another person. Then, Sevens tend to reframe this negative information into a positive context. If that does not succeed, the Seven may criticize the other person, usually because the Seven feels criticized.

Sonia and a colleague, George, were on the way to a meeting with a prospective client to whom they wished to sell a project. George had received the client referral from a friend and had invited Sonia to work with him. Because he had been working in this subject area for twenty years, George had developed the presentation materials. Sonia had completed a smaller, but similar, project two years earlier, and she felt well versed in the subject area. As George drove, Sonia scanned the twenty-page presentation document. After five minutes or so, she felt ready to discuss the upcoming meeting and suggested a number of new ideas to change the project's focus. Some of her ideas were valuable, but others were impractical. When they arrived in the parking lot, George stepped out of the car and asked whether Sonia needed more time to review the documents.

"I've already read them," Sonia answered.

"You could really read them that fast?" George asked.

Sonia, smiling and bright-eyed, answered quickly, "I took speed-reading when I got my degree from Harvard! It was part of our course of study, required of every student." Internally, Sonia was fuming; externally, she started pacing beside the car. She wondered, *Why is he presuming I have not read the materials? Why read something word for word when you can get the same information by scanning?*

Sonia's Seven speaking style, spontaneous and fast-paced, reflects the way her mind works, moving quickly from idea to idea and being quick to react. The Seven's style is also illustrated by Sonia's behavior after she scanned the presentation. She created multiple new ideas, starting with one thought and then moving rapidly to another in quick succession. This process is akin to brainstorming with oneself.

Sonia's reframing—that is, giving a positive context to a potentially negative comment—is seen in her interpretation of the word *scanning*. To most people, scanning is not really reading, but rather a quick and cursory way to get an overview of information. To Sonia's way of thinking, however, scanning *is* reading and offers a far more efficient and effective way to absorb material than would reading something word-by-word.

Body Language

Smiling and bright-eyed • Sharp tone of voice when angry • Highly animated face and numerous hand and/or arm gestures • May walk around and/or pace while speaking • Easily distracted

Sonia believed that George was being critical of her, and this interpretation was implicit in her body language. When Sonia commented that she had taken a speed-reading course, she mentioned that she had gone to Harvard. This was her way of communicating the fact that she was highly educated. Sonia was angry, although her feelings seemed ambiguous to George. While Sonia's tone of voice was sharp, suggesting that she was upset, her eyes were bright and she was smiling; however, Sevens also smile and appear very alert when they are happy, so this aspect of their body language can be confusing to others.

Sevens often walk around or pace when they speak, as Sonia did right after George parked the car. Sevens tend to demonstrate active body language in a variety of situations, so their actions do not specifically correlate to any one feeling. For example, the tendency to move around and pace or to become distracted by a thought or an external stimulus may indicate that a Seven is feeling excited, but it can just as easily reflect feelings of agitation, anxiety, or anger.

Blind Spots

They may not have absorbed all the information and knowledge they believe they have mastered • Fail to see that their own behavior causes others to take them less seriously • Constant shifting of ideas and animated body language is distracting to others

The interaction in this example also demonstrates the Seven's blind spots. Initially, George was merely asking Sonia a question of fact. He was not familiar with people who could scan and absorb information as quickly as Sonia felt she could. However, George also perceived some of Sonia's follow-up ideas to be impractical or to show a lack of experience with the topic. He began to wonder about Sonia's ability. George then became concerned about whether Sonia had really absorbed all of the presentation information, and he began to worry that she might not have the depth that he needed in a collaborator. Sonia's pacing near the car also distracted him from what she was saying at that moment.

Distorting Filters

Having their competence demeaned • Think they know what the other person is going to say, so they stop listening • The possibility of having limits placed on them • Being forced into a long-term commitment they do not want

Sonia's distorting filters were working when she reacted to George's question, "Do you need more time to review the documents?" Sonia believed that by asking this question, George was expressing a negative opinion of her, and she interpreted the question as a challenge of her competence.

In addition, a second Seven filter was operating: Sonia assumed what George was saying and meaning before he had even finished talking. In this situation, she also assumed that George was saying that he was more competent than she.

Sonia's two reactions led her to believe that George had the ulterior motive of intending to take control of the project. When Sevens believe that someone else is attempting to take control of a situation or is acting as an unauthorized authority figure in relation to them, they often become alarmed and fear that the other person is trying to limit their options. From George's perspective, however, he *was* in charge of the project; the client had contacted him, and he knew he had far more experience than Sonia in the area of the project. For her part, Sonia was becoming increasingly concerned that she would be asked to make a commitment to a large project about which she had serious reservations—namely, George and his leadership.

How Eights Communicate

Eric tries hard to contain himself, so he feels distraught when hearing, yet again, that he overwhelms others.

Speaking Style

8   Enneagram Style   CHALLENGE

Bold and authoritative • Big-picture and strategic • Statements designed to structure or control a situation • Impatient with detail • Raise the intensity of their language until they get a response from the other person • May display anger directly • May use profanity or body-based humor • May say very little • Blame others if they feel blamed

Eights love challenges, but they do not appreciate unexpected challenges from other people. Because of this, their speaking style may vary depending on the situation. Typically, their speaking style is one of commanding authority, and they often speak about the strategic big picture, attending to details mainly as a means to achieving a greater end. Their high energy levels match their forceful personalities, and they will continue an important conversation until they feel the other person has met their own intensity level.

In situations in which they are not sure what to do, however, Eights can be quiet. At these moments, they usually become very serious while they consider their next moves. When an Eight feels blindsided, the other person may get the full force of the Eight's wrath. In situations that are unimportant to them, Eights may amuse themselves by making comments to themselves about the events or by engaging in conversation about what they are observing, sometimes using profanity or body-based humor. If they become bored, they may disengage altogether and think about a completely different topic.

Eric worked as a line manager for a firm that was being acquired by another company. He was given the thankless job of telling numerous people from his company that they were not going to be hired by the new organization. He had no influence over the decisions being made, and the information he received from the new company was constantly changing. For four months, the following crucial elements were unclear: who would be hired, with what start dates and compensation packages; and who would be terminated with what severance dates and packages. Eric felt frustrated about the incompetence and injustice with which the transition was being handled. His boss, a director in the new company, knew as little as Eric.

While waiting for the elevator one day, Eric ran into Denise, the new company's division manager, and blurted out the following: "How can we expect employees to be loyal to us when we break up long-term working relationships, when we can't even provide offices for people to work in, and when you keep changing the compensation packages we're offering?" This chance encounter was the first time Eric had seen Denise in two months. Denise stood in stunned silence. There were three other people standing nearby, one of whom happened to be the company president.

With such important issues at stake, Eric, like many Eights, took the challenge head-on. Offering no preamble, and disregarding the fact that he had only a limited relationship with the division manager, Eric went ahead and said what he thought needed to be said. He followed his impulse because his frustration had been building over several months, and he simply let his anger burst out.

While Eric was no doubt correct in his assessment of the issues, he realized after the encounter that his timing and phrasing could have been more effective. When Eric's new boss criticized him later for what he had done, Eric's momentary chagrin was quickly replaced by harsh words about the division manager's incompetence and lack of compassion. When they feel blamed, Eights tend to blame others.

Body Language

Have a strong physical presence, even when they are silent
• Modulate voice tone for maximum impact • Give intense
nonverbal cues

Eights typically have strong body language, which remains strong even when Eights moderate their words. Eric's speaking style and body language were so strong in his elevator confrontation with Denise that news of the encounter spread quickly throughout both companies. Eric became part folk hero and part villain.

When Eights walk into a room, people often sense their authoritative presence. When they speak, Eights typically know how to alter their voices for impact. Even when Eights are silent, others are aware of the strong energy that emanates from the Eight through his or her nonverbal cues.

Blind Spots

Many people, not just timid individuals, become intimidated by them • Their energy is far stronger than they realize, even when they are holding back • Not everyone is capable of grasping the big picture as quickly as Eights can • Their vulnerability may show at times when they are not aware of it

Eric was surprised to learn that Denise was intimidated by him. He assumed that because she was a high-level manager, she would not feel unnerved by their encounter. This was due to his blind spot—a lack of awareness that even non-timid people can feel threatened by the Eight's passionate assertiveness. From Eric's perspective, he works hard to control his intensity; others actually see only about 60 percent of what he actually feels. Eric also wants other people to match his energy level. However, he is unaware that others interpret his behavior as aggressive, and assume Eric is trying to force them to back down.

Eights can also be surprised to learn that their vulnerability, which they work hard to keep hidden, actually shows through in their quieter moments. At these times they may be reflecting on something that has just happened or anticipating a future difficulty. While Eric did not show this side of himself to the division manager, he did reveal his concerns and anxieties later in discussing the incident with a colleague.

Distorting Filters

Protecting others who the Eight believes truly need protection • Weakness in others • Control • Truthfulness • Being blamed

Eights have strong distorting filters. They dislike weakness in others, but at the same time they feel compelled to protect those who cannot defend themselves. The Eights' issue with weakness reflects their unconscious denial of their own vulnerability. When Eights interact with someone, they assess whether that person is weak or strong and whether the person is attempting to exert control over the situation. If the individual appears weak, Eights disregard both the person and his or her message. If the person tries to dominate the situation, Eights will usually ready themselves for a counteroffensive. In cases where the person is asserting control but in an inept manner, Eights often become dismissive and take charge of the situation. However, if Eights feel that the person truly needs their protection, they will charge forth and defend.

Eric saw Denise, the division manager, as incompetent, controlling, and weak, and he also viewed the employees as needing him to defend them. In addition, Eric did not trust Denise, because he thought she had lied when she gave him information about the compensation packages. Eights also filter what they hear from others depending on whether they think a person is truthful and whether they feel that they, the Eights, will be blamed for something. Eric believed that Denise had intentionally given him misinformation for which the departing employees would eventually blame him.

How Nines Communicate

Natalie gets confused and then quietly angry when others do not consider her polite requests and suggestions.

Natalie had run a successful business for over twenty years and was now a member of the governing committee of a statewide agency. The agency met monthly via conference calls and only met face-to-face twice a year. The following

Enneagram Style ⑨
HARMONY

sequence of events took place through conference calls or individual telephone conversations during a six-month time period.

The agency was unhappy with its current public relations firm and wanted to switch to another company. The committee chair recommended a telecommunications firm that was seeking to expand its business into public relations and suggested, as a backup, a firm that had prior experience in public relations.

During the committee discussions about which of the two firms to hire, Natalie participated by helping the group examine the strengths and weaknesses of both firms. In addition, she prepared a comprehensive list of the expectations and tasks that would have to be within the capabilities of the chosen public relations firm. During one of the group discussions, Natalie suggested that the committee choose the firm that had a proven track record in public relations.

Instead, the governing committee decided to go with the committee chair's preference, the telecommunications firm. Three months later, this firm failed to deliver on what it had been contractually obligated to do; its principals neither understood what was involved in public relations nor had staff with the appropriate technical expertise. The statewide agency had to find a new firm to handle its public relations work. Natalie's initial assessment had been correct.

Natalie was quite angry and said to a colleague on the committee, "This is the most dysfunctional committee I have ever seen. There is no tolerance for differences of opinion!"

Speaking Style

Give highly detailed information in a sequential style • Make the effort to be fair and present all sides • May say *yes* but mean *no* • Use agreeing words, such as *yes* and *uh-huh*

Nines often give detailed information, usually in sequential order, and they try to harmonize relationships by presenting all sides of a problem. Natalie did exactly this in her work on the governing committee. While other committee members did remember that she had suggested choosing a firm with public relations experience, no one remembered exactly what she had said. Their lack of a collective memory on this was partly the result of the way in which Natalie had presented her information.

To Natalie's way of thinking, she had shared a list of the public relations tasks and responsibilities and then presented the pros and cons of both firms. In her view, it should have been obvious to the rest of the committee that the telecommunications firm lacked the required competencies. In addition, Natalie had actually suggested to the others that they hire the agency with prior public relations experience.

The committee, however, did not perceive Natalie's behavior in the same way. During the meeting, Natalie had actually sounded as though she supported choosing the telecommunications firm. When the time came to vote, the committee chair asked whether the telecommunications firm was acceptable to everyone; Natalie had appeared to agree when she said, "Uh-huh." To Natalie, "Uh-huh" meant that she was following and understanding the conversation—the verbal equivalent of a head nod when someone is listening closely to someone. It does not necessarily mean agreement, although it is often misinterpreted in this way. No one knew that Natalie actually had a strong opinion about not choosing this firm. Natalie, however, felt puzzled and resentful that no one had listened to her.

Body Language

Easygoing and relaxed • Smiling • Few displays of strong emotions, particularly negative feelings • Face rather than body is animated

Natalie's body language added to the other committee members' misinterpretation of her meaning. Nines are usually easygoing and relaxed, and they typically show few overt emotions. They smile frequently when they are feeling positive or neutral. When they disapprove of something, their disapproval is evident more from the looks on their faces than from their verbal cues. Because the governing committee's discussions about the public relations firm were not done in person, the other committee members could not read the cues from Natalie's face.

Blind Spots

Prolonged explanations that cause the listener to lose interest • Present multiple viewpoints, which negatively affects their degree of influence and possibly their credibility • Fail to make true wants known to others

Natalie finally became angry, but she did not focus her anger on the issue of whether her opinions had been ignored. Instead, her negative feelings were focused on the group and how it functioned. This refocusing of anger is frequently seen when a Nine blind spot is impacted. Natalie was unaware that her detailed explanation of public relations tasks did not hold the attention of other committee members. She was also unconscious of the group's reaction to her tendency to take multiple points of view; when she did this, the others wondered whether she really knew the best answer, because she seemed to see many alternatives. Her lack of a clear position hurt Natalie's ability to influence the committee. Although from Natalie's point of view she had been very clear, her message had been delivered too indirectly for her colleagues to understand what she meant.

Distorting Filters

Demands on them to change or do something • Being criticized, ignored, or put down • Someone having an opposing view to their own • The possibility that anger from another person will be directed at them

Nines are especially sensitive to being ignored, and this distorting filter was illustrated in Natalie's angry reaction toward the governing committee: "This is the most dysfunctional committee I have ever seen. There is no tolerance for differences of opinion!"

Nines also tend to be sensitive to being criticized or put down, and they often feel this to be occurring if someone else strongly disagrees with their opinions. Natalie felt that the whole committee disagreed with her, and her distorting filter prevented her from hearing that several members actually did agree with her.

Two additional distorting filters were in evidence when Natalie made her comment about the committee's being "dysfunctional" to another committee member. This person disagreed with Natalie and tried to get her to change her perception about the group. When Nines feel a demand to do something or change something, they often become resistant. Natalie dug in her heels when she heard her colleague disagreeing with her perceptions about how the committee functioned. When Nines become stubborn, they may block out some of the message that the other person is sending. In this situation, the committee member was trying to tell Natalie that he had actually agreed with her that the telecommunications firm was the wrong choice from the beginning, but that he disagreed with her that the committee was dysfunctional. Natalie only heard his statement of disagreement about the committee.

Another Nine distorting filter may emerge when Nines fear that someone may be angry with them, because Nines so fervently desire harmony in their relationships. After Natalie had criticized the governing committee to her colleague, she realized that she had made this remark to the committee's vice-chair. She began to feel that the vice-chair might become angry with her for criticizing the group; from the point at which this possibility occurred to her, Natalie heard very little of what the vice-chair said.

Improving Your Communication

As natural and as much a part of us as our Enneagram communication styles may seem to be, they *can* be changed. Following are some suggestions for change strategies that really work. These strategies involve removing your Enneagram style distortions. When you do this, you are free to say what you mean, and clear to hear what you receive.

- **Change one behavior at a time.** It is most effective to work on changing one behavior at a time. Trying to change everything at once can be overwhelming; also, changing one particular behavior will cause other aspects of your style to change. It is recommended that you work on changes to your communication style in the following sequence:

1. Speaking style
2. Body language
3. Blind spots
4. Distorting filters

It is easiest to change the behaviors of which we are most aware, and the sequence here represents the most common order of awareness, from most to least.

- **Increase your awareness.** Increase your knowledge of the ways in which you distort both giving and receiving messages.

  1. For one week, spend fifteen minutes at the end of each day thinking about the communications you have had with other people that day. Answer this question: *How did my Enneagram style influence my communications with others?* Write down your answers so you can remember them.
  2. After following Step 1 for one week, look over your notes and try to identify the patterns in your communications.
  3. For the next week, simply observe yourself behaving in the ways you identified in Step 2.
  4. At the end of the week for Step 3, select *one* behavior you want to change. Then, for the next week, observe all the times you exhibit this behavior. If you can, try to notice yourself doing the behavior when you are right in the middle of doing it.
  5. Finally, you are ready to change your behavior. For one week, *change this one behavior*. You can either change it right when you are about to do it, or you can change your behavior when you catch yourself in the middle of it. Either way is effective.
  6. Continue the process from Step 4, selecting a new behavior to change; repeat the process as needed, working through one behavioral change at a time.

- **Solicit feedback.** Ask others, including coworkers, for feedback on your Enneagram communication style; select people who know you well and whom you respect.
- **Audiotape or videotape yourself.** Audiotape your side of a telephone communication with someone else; review it several times, and ask other people to listen and give you their impressions. Videotape yourself during

a meeting or when giving a speech, and review the tape multiple times to observe your Enneagram style behavior.

- **Listen actively.** Use active listening to decrease your receiving distortions; paraphrase both the content and feelings you hear from the other person so he or she can give you a reality check on the accuracy of your listening skills.
- **Use a coach.** Use an executive coach who knows the Enneagram, and ask the coach for feedback. (See the Resources at the end of this book.)

Chapter 3

Giving Constructive Feedback

he term *feedback* refers to the direct, objective, simple, and respectful observations that one person makes about another person's behavior.[1] Along with lack of performance expectations and lack of skills, lack of feedback has been identified as one of the top three barriers to effective work performance. Unfortunately, most organizations and individuals are feedback-averse. Many people either do not understand the importance of feedback or do not feel that they possess the necessary skills to provide feedback to others. Some shy away from giving feedback because of their own discomfort— for example, they fear that they will hurt the other person's feelings and/or make the situation worse. The following story illustrates what can go wrong in the attempt to give effective feedback.

Frank planned to give Oliver feedback in an objective, fact-based manner, getting to the main issue early in the conversation. *A half hour*, Frank thought, *is plenty of time to get my point across. I'll give him one specific example and then give him time to think about it. We can set up a later meeting to discuss what he wants to do about the information.*

As Frank considered his approach, he decided to say the following: "Oliver, it's not that you're doing a bad job or that you aren't capable of doing the job. You just need to spend more time on your client relationships, even if that

---

1. The concept of feedback originally appeared in *Frontiers in Group Dynamics: Concept, Method and Reality in Social Sciences*, by Kurt Lewin (1947). Numerous authors have offered further refinements, in particular, *Learning Through Groups: A Trainer's Basic Guide*, by Phil Hanson (1981), and *What Did You Say? The Art of Giving and Receiving Feedback*, by Edie and Charlie Seashore (1992).

means spending less time on preparation. I can give you more details about this if you like. Two clients complained that they felt rushed during their meetings with you. Why don't you think about this, and is it possible to get together again later in the week to discuss this in more detail?"

The meeting between Frank and Oliver resulted in a disaster. Frank, a Five, gave Oliver feedback in the way that *Fives* like to receive it—briefly, logically, and unemotionally, with a limited amount of time for interaction. Giving Oliver additional time alone to reflect and deliberate, in Frank's opinion, was allowing Oliver time to prepare his part of the discussion. But Oliver, a One, became angry upon hearing Frank's remarks. Although Frank had the best of intentions, his attempt to give Oliver useful feedback actually made the situation worse.

Oliver and other Enneagram style Ones respond best to precise and accurate feedback. However, what Frank gave was not specific information; it was actually his own impressions and opinions. In addition, the specific example Frank offered concerned a situation about which Oliver disagreed.

Ones dislike feedback that contains right/wrong judgments. Frank implied that Oliver had done something wrong, with words such as "bad relationships" and "You need to spend more time on your client relationships." To Oliver, *bad* implied *faulty*, and *need to* suggested that Oliver had done something wrong.

Ones generally respond well when feedback begins with an honest compliment. Frank thought he was doing that when he said, "It's not that . . . you aren't capable of . . . ." This is known as a backhanded compliment, with something positive framed in a negative way. Oliver also doubted Frank's sincerity when Frank said, "You just need to . . . ." To Oliver, this sounded like a disclaimer. Used after an introductory phrase, words like *just* and *but* often discount the words that precede it (as in "I like you, but . . .").

Ones want feedback that is objective but that is given with warmth. They sense empathy through the other person's body language and tone of voice. While Frank may truly have felt concern for Oliver, his rational, concise style lacked the palpable concern Oliver needed in order for the feedback to be effective.

While we all want some degree of influence when we interact with others, Ones, in particular, like to feel in control of a situation. When Frank decided both to keep the meeting short and to meet with Oliver later in the week, Frank was doing something that *he*, as a Five, would prefer, because Fives like to have time to think through their feelings before they respond. However, because Ones react more quickly, Oliver was angry, perceiving Frank's decision to split the meetings as a unilateral decision, and one that left him no time to tell Frank how he felt at that moment.

Giving effective feedback is difficult to do for three basic reasons: (1) we do not understand how our own Enneagram style interferes when we give feedback; (2) we may be lacking in basic feedback skills; and (3) we may not know how to adjust our approach to the Enneagram style of the other person, both in terms of what we say and how we say it. This chapter addresses all three reasons why we do not give effective feedback. Because it is more difficult to deliver a negative message than a positive one, the examples provided focus on the conveying of negative information (sometimes called "constructive" or "corrective" feedback). However, the same principles apply whether you are saying something positive or negative.

The first section of the chapter provides examples of how individuals of each Enneagram style may err when giving feedback to someone else, regardless of the recipient's Enneagram style. Along with these examples are notes that will serve as key concepts for you concerning the ways in which your Enneagram style behaviors can impede your delivering a message. Because you know your own position on the Enneagram but may not know the other person's, the best place to start is with yourself. As you become aware of your own Enneagram style tendencies when giving feedback, you can then work to minimize the specific behaviors that can reduce your effectiveness.

The second section of the chapter provides a simple and effective technique for giving feedback to *anyone*, regardless of Enneagram style. This approach is called the Feedback Formula. If you master this method, you will double your chances of getting your message across successfully. As with any skill, the more you use it, the better at it you will become.

Finally, the chapter reviews how to adjust the Feedback Formula to individuals of each Enneagram style. The example at the beginning of this chapter—a problem regarding client relationships—is repeated throughout the final section, showing how the strategy and wording can be changed based on the Enneagram style of each person. Again, along with the examples are notes that will serve as key ideas for you to remember.

How to Manage Your Own Enneagram Style Behaviors When Giving Feedback

Some people are naturally effective at giving feedback; these people come from all nine Enneagram styles. Unfortunately, most of the rest of us would have made some mistakes were we in Frank's role, and many of these errors would have been linked to behavioral tendencies of our Enneagram style.

Even with the best of intentions, we tend to communicate a message according to our particular Enneagram style preferences, often delivering a message in the way we ourselves would like to receive it. When our best attempts at giving feedback do not work very well, we are surprised.

Interestingly, we sometimes are least effective when providing feedback to someone with our same Enneagram style. We may find the behavior of someone similar to us especially annoying because we are actually reminded of ourselves. The feedback we give in such situations may have a negative edge, which the other person intuits and then reacts against.

Following are descriptions of the involuntary, yet common, errors that people of each Enneagram style tend to make when giving feedback to others.

Ones Giving Feedback

Enneagram Style
DILIGENCE

In the same situation as that at the beginning of this chapter—with feedback being given to Oliver regarding his client relationships—if a One were to err, it would not likely be by giving too few examples. Instead, a One might typically go astray by reciting multiple examples from numerous clients, as if providing a long list of corroborating evidence. Oliver might hear, "This client said . . . ," "That client said . . . ," "And another client said . . . ," or "There is a pattern to this feedback that is . . . ." Because they are prone to diligent preparation, Ones can overload the recipient of their feedback.

Ones tend to prescribe and suggest what another person should and should not do. When specific solutions are combined with the *should/ought* language that is characteristic of Ones, the other person can feel unnecessarily criticized. For example, suppose a One told Oliver, "You really should call them, and this is what needs to be said. Then you should . . . ." Oliver, already feeling beleaguered by negative comments from his clients, may just hear this as more criticism.

Ones value honest communication and thus want to get their message across accurately. The result can be clear, clean, and effective feedback that is very helpful. Conversely, if Ones either dislike the other person or have strong

REMINDER FOR ONES

As hard as you work to make your own behavior impeccable, the feedback recipient may not want your help in becoming perfect.

negative feelings about the issues raised, their disapproval often shows, no matter how hard they try to hide it. In the above situation, Oliver might see a frown, a shaking back and forth of the head, or a stern look on the face. The words can be perfectly chosen, yet the tone of voice may be sharp. However carefully worded the verbal feedback may be, Oliver is likely to react more to the nonverbal elements.

Feedback Tips for Ones

- Utilize your skill at being very specific, but avoid being too detailed or picking on too many small items.
- Keep your capacity to generate ways someone else can improve, but work very hard to control your use of explicitly or implicitly judgmental language.
- Maintain your truthfulness, but resolve any residual anger or resentment prior to having the feedback conversation so your feelings do not show through your body language.

Twos Giving Feedback

Enneagram Style ②
GIVING

A Two talking to Oliver about his client relationships would not likely come across as too critical, but rather too positive. Twos, unless they feel unappreciated or called upon to protect someone else, are more likely to not want to hurt the feedback recipient's feelings.

In this situation, Twos might do one of three things:

1. Sugarcoat the negative feedback, making it sound less important than it is: *The clients said this, but they really aren't very upset about it.*
2. Explain away the feedback, thus unintentionally condoning the behavior: *The clients said this, but I know how busy you are, and you've always had a good relationship with them.*
3. Avoid giving any negative information at all: *I spoke with two of your clients. How has your work with them been going?*

Because they are so attuned to other people's reactions, Twos giving feedback in this particular situation might watch Oliver's nonverbal behavior closely in order to intuit how he is responding. The Two observes—often unconsciously—others' movements, facial expressions, tone of voice, and other body language, and then responds accordingly. If Oliver were to become angry about what he hears, Twos might take this personally, as if Oliver were angry

REMINDER FOR TWOS

As much as you want to give to others and to share your insights, keep in mind that the feedback recipient may not want your help and may know him- or herself the best course of action to take.

with them. They might also become self-critical and conclude that they must have done an inadequate job of communicating.

Sometimes Twos do act judgmental, particularly if the Two has been harboring unexpressed feelings about the feedback recipient. The Two can become not only critical but also inferential, drawing a conclusion that may or may not be accurate. The Two may infer from Oliver's behavior that he does not care what his clients think, and so might say, "Your clients think you don't care about them, and you may want to consider this!" All of us, at some time, create imaginary scenarios about other people; Twos however, are particularly prone to making such inferences, because they consider themselves proficient at reading people. No matter how perceptive a Two may be, it is still preferable for him or her to refer to specific events when providing feedback, rather than offering personal insights or interpretations.

Feedback Tips for Twos
- Maintain your positive regard for the other person, but not at the expense of avoiding the negative information.
- Consider the other person's feelings, but do not "fog over" the issues to keep the feedback recipient from feeling bad.
- Pay attention to the recipient's reaction, but take neither a positive nor a negative response personally.
- Maintain your perceptiveness, but remind yourself that your insights may not be accurate, especially when you are angry.

Threes Giving Feedback

Enneagram Style
③ PERFORM

When Threes need to give feedback, they usually prefer not to do so! They often fear that conveying information that includes a negative component will elicit an unpleasant reaction from the other person. Threes, typically uncomfortable dealing with other people's sad, angry, or fearful feelings, have a particularly heightened aversion when the unpleasant reaction is directed at them. The desire to avoid the distress of others, combined with the Three's tendency to focus on tasks, usually results in Threes giving feedback that is straight to the point, often without much room for discussing feelings. Giving feedback to Oliver, a Three might say, "Two of your clients called. They said they are unhappy with their meetings with you. You need to call them as soon as you can. Will you do that?"

The delivery in the example above is so direct that it may feel abrupt or unfeeling to the person who hears it, even if the Three actually feels empathic. The efficient style common to Threes, which often promotes their success in the business environment, can also interfere when they give negative feedback to someone. When Threes consider what it might feel like to be in the shoes of the other person, their style often softens, and the message still gets across.

Like Ones, Threes giving negative feedback may also err through over-preparation—for instance, having lists of many examples to support the main point. The body language of a Three tends to be less critical than that of a One, with the Three's nonverbal message tending more toward insistence or impatience. A Three may keep adding examples until the other person responds in agreement. At this stage in the meeting, the person who received the feedback may feel bombarded and/or incompetent. Thus, fewer examples are preferable. Instead of providing a great number of supporting references, which can overwhelm or confuse the other person, the Three needs to remember that a few well-chosen examples usually make the point more convincingly. If Threes do not get concurrence from the person to whom they are giving feedback, Threes may act as though they are finished with the conversation. The recipient of the feedback may then feel discounted or dismissed.

Feedback Tips for Threes
- Maintain your focus, but also allow room for feelings, particularly those of the other person.
- Be clear, honest, and remember to be gentle.

REMINDER FOR THREES

Other people may not drive themselves as hard as you drive yourself, and they may not identify with work as completely as you do, but this does not mean they do not value achievement or do not want to improve.

- Keep focused on the desired result rather than using too many small examples that may derail your main point.
- Be patient.

Fours Giving Feedback

Enneagram Style
④
MOOD

Fours try to be genuine and empathic when giving feedback, and this combination can be effective. Nevertheless, sometimes Fours may think they are placing themselves in someone else's shoes when, in reality, they are just conjecturing how they might feel in that same situation. The problem arises when the other person responds very differently from the way the Four would react were he or she receiving the same feedback.

For example, a Four with a personal concern about being rejected and misunderstood may begin the feedback to Oliver this way: "Please do not take this personally. I'm sure the clients hold you in high regard and have no desire to hurt your feelings." The person receiving the feedback may, in fact, agree with the factual information about to be described and would not take it personally; however, because of the introductory remarks used by the Four, the feedback recipient may wonder what horrible news is forthcoming and begin to act defensively before he or she has heard the actual information.

Fours value truthfulness and sometimes say exactly what is on their minds, particularly when they think the other person really needs to listen. Some people appreciate this, but for others this feedback style may be too blunt. A Four might say to Oliver, "You are really having trouble with your clients!"

Fours usually focus on what is not working well in a situation, and their feedback may highlight the negative without offering the counterbalancing positive; the message may thus take on a gloomier cast than it really deserves. With Oliver, for example, a Four might spend more time on the negative client feedback than Oliver needs to have in order to understand the issue. Or, the Four might use wording such as "I'm very concerned about this" or "This really needs to be taken care of," either of which could make Oliver feel quite anxious and thereby hinder his ability to take quick remedial action.

The Four also pays close attention to the other person and likes meaningful interaction. There is a tacit presumption among Fours that others do or should want this intense level of interpersonal contact. Consequently, the Four may attempt to draw out Oliver's deeper feelings, asking questions such as "How do you *really* feel about this?" Fours also ask these types of questions

REMINDER FOR FOURS

Even with your best efforts to be genuine, truthful, and empathic, your intentions will, at times, be misunderstood.

to make sure the feedback recipient understands both the message and the Four's intentions. Sometimes this line of questioning helps the other person to become more introspective; however, it can also have the opposite effect and feel intrusive.

Feedback Tips for Fours
- Be empathic, but be careful not to get your own feelings so involved that you presume you know what the recipient may feel.
- Maintain your truthfulness, but add a positive tone and include positive comments.
- Pay attention to the other person, but try to match his or her intensity, mood, and energy rather than trying to get the other person to match yours.

Fives Giving Feedback

The story at the beginning of this chapter describes how Fives tend to give feedback. In this interaction, Frank, a Five, is precise and concise, but his delivery style failed to get a positive response from Oliver. Fives, however, may also err in an opposite way. As seekers of knowledge, Fives can overprepare, gathering so much data that they give the other person too much information. Frank could just as easily have spent time communicating every single aspect of Oliver's client problem;

Enneagram Style **⑤**
KNOWLEDGE

had Frank done this, Oliver would have likely heard only about one-tenth of what Frank said.

The initial story of the interaction between Oliver and Frank also illustrates the Five's tendency to focus on the facts and to separate them from emotion, as seen in Frank's suggestion that they delay their discussion of the feedback given. Fives may also show through body language their desire not to discuss feelings and to focus only on the facts. Receptive body language

REMINDER FOR FIVES

The feedback recipient may not want a clearly defined, logical approach and may prefer an integrated, thinking-feeling interaction.

such as smiling, deep breathing, and direct eye contact tend to invite emotional responses from others. Fives, however, may look serious, take short breaths, or cast their eyes away from the other person in anticipation of a strong emotional reaction. The Five's implicit message may be this: *Tell me what you think, but not what you feel.*

Feedback Tips for Fives
- Keep your precision, but do not be so concise that the other person does not understand what you are saying.
- Continue to rigorously think through your approach, but be careful not to overload the feedback recipient with information.
- Keep being clear about your task, but also invite an emotional response from the other person.

Sixes Giving Feedback

6 Enneagram Style
DOUBT

Sixes may have a plan for giving feedback to someone like Oliver, but their tendency to doubt will fill Sixes with angst as they approach the encounter. They may worry that the session will not proceed well, agonize over which approach to use, or become concerned about their own delivery.

The Six may thus approach the meeting with a level of anxiety that is palpable to the other person—and also contagious. Oliver may sense the Six's anxiety and begin to feel unnerved himself. The Six's anxiety may also show through in the use of highly detailed examples. This is a by-product of the elaborate thinking and preplanning Sixes do to assuage their nervousness. However, the possible result may be that Oliver feels confused, disagrees with the details, or misses the essence of the feedback altogether.

Alternatively, because Sixes anticipate things that can go wrong, a Six might highlight for Oliver what could go wrong if he does not improve his client relationships. For example, the Six might say, "If the relationships aren't

REMINDER FOR SIXES

Once you have given the feedback, allow the feedback recipient to take responsibility to achieve a positive outcome, instead of believing that the burden of resolving the situation is on your shoulders.

repaired, these clients may never use our services again or may speak poorly of us to others." Oliver may then feel overwrought or defensive and begin to counter with reasons why these possible consequences are unlikely.

The opposite may also occur when Sixes give feedback. Aware that they are overly focused on negative outcomes, Sixes sometimes overcompensate and intentionally delete negative information that might actually be helpful to provide. In this situation, the feedback recipient may not fully understand the issues, nor know what action to take.

When Sixes do give feedback, they can be extremely insightful. However, their vivid imaginations can trick them so that what they perceive as insights may really be projections of the Six's own worries, needs, fears, motives, and so on. Sixes may have difficulty discerning the difference between an insight and a projection. For example, suppose that a Six giving feedback to Oliver said, "The reason you move too quickly through your meetings with clients is that you don't care about the client" or "I think you don't like your job, and that is why the clients complain." These comments may be accurate, *or* they may be projections of the Six's own feelings: perhaps the Six does not like the client or is thinking about other job possibilities. When giving feedback, it is safest to avoid making interpretations and to stay with actual events, working later in the conversation to interpret the information in collaboration with the feedback recipient.

Feedback Tips for Sixes

- Planning is crucial, but work to calm yourself before the feedback discussion.
- Details are important, but keep sight of the big picture.
- Thinking about possible scenarios is helpful, but try to balance the negative possibilities with positive ones.
- Honor your insights, but avoid assuming that your thoughts are accurate; treat them as hypotheses, and seek the answers from the feedback recipient.

Sevens Giving Feedback

Enneagram Style
OPTIONS

Sevens will often give feedback if they must, but they do not relish discussing negative issues, particularly those that may cause either themselves or the other person pain or discomfort. Preferring to avoid negative feelings and thoughts themselves, Sevens tend to assume that others do also (or should). Consequently, Sevens often use an optimistic approach when they deliver bad news. In the conversation with Oliver, a Seven might start with how well things have been going, and then add, "There's a little issue that I'm sure can be handled very easily."

Sevens are often adept at reframing issues by putting a problem in a different, positive, and often larger context. In the conversation with Oliver, a Seven might reframe the client concerns as a client skill deficiency, saying, "These clients are new at their jobs and may not grasp what is being covered in the meetings." Or, the Seven might reframe the issue as uncertainty in the client organization and say, "Both clients work in organizations that have mergers pending in their companies, so *this* may be their focus, not what you are covering in the meetings." While the reframing perspectives described above may be accurate and useful to Oliver, they can also obscure the central point, thereby letting Oliver off the hook. Oliver may feel the clients' concerns are their own responsibility, and so may believe there is nothing he can, or should, do differently.

A third way in which Sevens may err when giving feedback relates to how their minds work. Thinking of idea after idea, Sevens may tend to jump around from example to solution, then to a rationale for what caused the client reaction, and finally to more examples. While Sevens can follow their own multifaceted line of thinking, many of the rest of us cannot; Oliver may be deep in thought about one important issue that has been raised, but the Seven will already have covered three more topics—none of which Oliver has heard.

REMINDER FOR SEVENS

Although you can think fast and are able to multi-track, the feedback recipient may need to focus on one topic until it has been discussed completely before moving to another topic.

Feedback Tips for Sevens

- Maintain your optimism, but be careful not to let that obscure what the feedback recipient needs to hear.
- Use your ability to provide context and perspective carefully so that the central issue does not get lost.
- Do bring in related information, but keep your focus so that the feedback recipient does not get sidetracked.

Eights Giving Feedback

Although most Eights are ordinarily not shy about saying what they think, they may not relish giving structured feedback. In fact, many Eights spend a lot of time anguishing over how to say something important to someone else. They'll ponder the main issues in an effort to make certain that what they plan to say will get the other person's attention.

Enneagram Style CHALLENGE (8)

Eights also preplan because they know that when they have something negative to say to someone, they can be so honest, direct, and quick to react that the other person may find the experience too threatening. An Eight who had done no prior planning might say to Oliver, "These are our most important clients, and they are dissatisfied. They need to be taken care of. Call them!" While all of the above may be true, a more considered approach to giving Oliver feedback is likely to be more effective. Part of the consideration would include how to solicit Oliver's ideas for what to do prior to the Eight making suggestions.

In the above approach, what cannot be read in the words but can be seen when observing the interaction is the intense energy an Eight often brings to challenging situations. Eights can appear very intense, and they may move physically close to the other person; this physical proximity can feel particularly intimidating to someone receiving bad news. Even if the Eight maintains spatial distance or tries to remain low-key, the other person may still sense the Eight's energy and drive.

In their effort to be truthful and honest, Eights can forget to show positive regard for the other person, even if the Eight truly feels respectful. In some situations, Eights may not respect the other person; from an Eight's perspective, respect is earned, not simply given. When providing feedback, it is important that Eights make sure to show some degree of positive regard for the person—for example, through warm eye contact, smiling, or making supportive comments—and that they do so even if they do not like him or her.

REMINDER FOR EIGHTS

While you like to deal with issues head-on as they occur, the feedback recipient may want to deal with the issues in his or her own time frame and way.

When talking with Oliver, the Eight could add, "We know you can do it, because you've always come through in the past!"

Feedback Tips for Eights

- Maintain your ability to keep focused on the key points, but do so in a receptive way.
- Consider in advance what you want to say.
- Have some ideas about what to do, but allow the feedback recipient to make the first suggestions.
- Keep your skill in steering your full attention to the task, but downplay your energy level so the other person does not feel overwhelmed.
- Smiling, making easy jokes, and waiting patiently for a response are helpful.
- Retain your truthfulness, but include a positive component.

Nines Giving Feedback

When giving feedback, Nines are prone to delay the task, particularly if they expect conflict. Eventually, however, the need to share the constructive feedback can build up, so that the Nine may finally feel compelled to say something. The most common approach taken by Nines is to try to create rapport and maintain harmony between themselves and other people. To accomplish this mutual accord, a Nine may avoid mentioning the negative client comments at all to Oliver. Going into the meeting, the Nine may have fully intended to tell Oliver what the clients said, but somehow, as the conversation developed, it never seemed like the right time to deliver the message. Alternatively, the Nine may have fully intended to say something at the meeting, but then simply forgot to do so.

When a message is delivered, Nines most typically will present multiple viewpoints on the matter. To Oliver, a Nine might say, "This is how the client sees it, but I think your other clients don't feel rushed at all. As your boss, I understand how busy you are, and I know that your peers are all under the same time constraints as you are." While all these viewpoints may be correct and useful, they can have the effect of derailing Oliver from the central issue—which is that two of his clients report they feel rushed during their meetings.

At the point when Nines really must say something—particularly if they are agitated about, and agree with, the content of the message—they tend to speak in paragraphs rather than sentences. This lengthier discourse is a by-product of their having held something in for so long. The Nine may include additional issues that appear related; with Oliver, a Nine might add, "And you haven't been coming to work on time, and you need to start getting your expense reports in." To the Nine, these issues do seem connected to the original focus of the meeting (Oliver's rushing through work-related details). Oliver, however, may not know which item mentioned is the most important, or which discussion to pursue.

Feedback Tips for Nines
- Keep creating rapport and maintain your kindness, but also deliver a clear message.
- Retain your capacity to understand a situation from many viewpoints, but stay focused on your main point.
- Think of other issues that may be related, and save them for further discussion; try to keep your feedback focused on one issue at a time.

How to Give Feedback to Anyone: The Feedback Formula

Once you understand your own Enneagram tendencies and can manage them when giving feedback to someone else, it will be helpful for you to learn and practice the basic skills of giving feedback. In this section, you will learn how to give feedback to anyone, regardless of the recipient's Enneagram style; you will then learn how to use these basic skills in conjunction with your knowledge of each Enneagram style so that you can tailor your feedback to individuals of each style.

FIGURE 3.1 **The Feedback Formula**

Observable Behavior	Impact of the Behavior	Preferred Behavior

"When you . . ."	". . . the impact was . . ."	"I would prefer it if you would . . ."

Use this three-part method with everyone.

The Feedback Formula is a simple, time-tested way to give positive and negative messages (see Figure 3.1). Mastering this method will help you to improve both how you give feedback and, subsequently, how well the other person will receive it.

The Feedback Formula follows a three-part sequence:

1. **Observable behavior.** You begin by providing a clear, data-based statement about the recipient's concrete, observable behavior, presenting it in a factual way. Starting with several concrete examples of observable behavior (with which both you and the other person concur) gets some early agreement and reduces defensiveness in the other person.
2. **Impact of the behavior.** In this step, you tell the person why the information is important to him or her, to the organization, and to you. Done effectively, this second step motivates and provides the rationale for the change.
3. **Preferred behavior.** In the final step, you offer the feedback recipient some ideas about alternative behaviors; this helps the person think about additional choices he or she may not have considered. This step takes the guesswork out of the requested behavior change.

Feedback Formula Example

Following is an example of how to apply the Feedback Formula. The example involves the same situation presented at the beginning of this chapter, that of giving feedback to someone about how client meetings have been perceived by two different clients. The feedback scenario is divided into the three different parts of the Feedback Formula—observable behavior, impact of the behavior, and preferred behavior.

Observable Behavior

I hope we can spend some time on an issue. Is this a good time? [Listen] *Two of your clients* [name the clients] *have called me and said they perceived their most recent meetings* [give exact times] *with you to be too fast-paced. Do you agree?* [Listen]

Impact of the Behavior

The clients wondered if you were listening to their points of view. It would be a shame if they wanted to work with someone other than you because of this. We value your work, and as a company want to keep the clients with you rather than switch them to someone else. I was not there, so I do not have firsthand information, which makes for an awkward situation. What do you think? [Listen]

Preferred Behavior

In general, it would be helpful if you asked the clients periodic questions during your meetings and then listened fully to their responses. In this instance, you might want to call them directly to have them clarify what their feedback means. If you do this, please be cautious not to explain why you did or did not do something. Although you may want to tell them, they are likely to respond to this as though it means you are not listening to them. What do you think you want to do? [Listen]

Using the Feedback Formula together with the hard work of removing your own Enneagram-based barriers will make your feedback more effective most of the time. If you want to become even more proficient, you can make subtle adjustments to your approach and delivery, taking into consideration the Enneagram style of the other person if you know it.

The following sections provide examples of using the Feedback Formula to give feedback to people with each of the nine Enneagram styles. The recipient's name changes from example to example, but the situation depicted is the same that has been used throughout this chapter. Recommended changes in the wording for feedback recipients with each Enneagram style are indicated in bold type.

Giving Feedback to Ones

Enneagram Style
(1) **DILIGENCE**

Observable Behavior

Start with a sincere compliment • Be accurate and detailed with examples • Get the recipient's concurrence

Oliver, you seem to work so hard, and your conscientiousness is truly appreciated. *I hope we can spend some time on an issue. Is this a good time?* [Listen] *Two of your clients* [name the clients] *have called me and said they perceived their most recent meetings* [give exact times] *with you to be too fast-paced. Do you agree?* [Listen] ***This is exactly what they said to me.*** [Give details] ***Is this what you remember from the meetings?*** [Listen]

Impact of the Behavior

Avoid words that imply right or wrong • Come from the heart

The clients wondered if you were listening to their points of view. It would be **unfortunate** *if they wanted to work with someone other than you because of this. We value your work, and as a company want to keep the clients with you rather than switch them to someone else. I was not there, so I do not have firsthand information, which makes for an awkward situation.* ***How do you feel about what I've said?*** [Listen]

Preferred Behavior

Help the feedback recipient feel in control of the outcome

What are some ways you think this can be handled? [Listen to what he or she says, and then try to integrate his or her solutions with your suggested options] *In general, it would be helpful if you asked the clients periodic questions during your meetings and then listened fully to their responses. In this instance, you might want to call them directly to have them clarify what their feedback means. If you do this, please be cautious not to explain why you did or did not do something. Although you may want to tell them, they are likely to respond to this as though it means you are not listening to them. What do you think you want to do?* [Listen]

Giving Feedback to Twos

Observable Behavior

Sound friendly and optimistic • Make certain there is absolute privacy • Give more details only if asked

Enneagram Style ②
GIVING

Hi, Terry, how are you? [Listen] *Has everything been going well?* [Listen] *I hope we can spend some time on an issue,* **and I wanted to make sure we have the privacy to do that.** *Is this a good time?* [Listen] *Two of your clients* [name the clients] *have called me and said they perceived their most recent meetings* [give exact times] *with you to be too fast-paced. Do you agree?* [Listen] **Do you have any questions about these meetings or the clients' comments?** [Listen and respond if requested]

Impact of the Behavior

Reinforce the value the recipient places on positive relationships • Smile, and maintain a positive attitude • Emphasize the impact of the behavior on others • Ask about the Two's feelings

The clients wondered if you were listening to their points of view. **I know how important client relationships are to you!** *It would be a shame if they wanted to work with someone other than you because of this.* **It is my impression that they want to continue working with you and hope to work out their concerns. What do you think they might be feeling?** [Listen] *We value your work, and as a company want to keep the clients with you rather than switch them to someone else. I was not there, so I do not have firsthand information, which makes for an awkward situation.* **I even wish I didn't have to tell you about this.** *What do you think* **and feel about this situation?** [Listen]

Preferred Behavior

Make it clear that you stand by the feedback recipient • Reinforce your positive regard for the person

How can I be supportive of you to help you work through a solution? [Listen] *In general, it would be helpful if you asked the clients periodic questions*

during your meetings and then listened fully to their responses. In this instance, you might want to call them directly to have them clarify what their feedback means. **I think they would appreciate the direct contact from you.** *If you do this, please be cautious not to explain why you did or did not do something. Although you may want to tell them, they are likely to respond to this as though it means you are not listening to them. What do you think you want to do?* [Listen]

Giving Feedback to Threes

Enneagram Style
PERFORM
(3)

Observable Behavior

Make sure the time and place are convenient
• Contextualize the feedback as a way to help the
recipient become even more successful • Let the
recipient know precisely what was said and who said it; if possible,
pick examples from clients he or she respects • Get his or her
agreement early on about the examples you have used

Thomas, *I hope we can spend some time on an issue.* **When would be a good time for us to get together without interruptions?** [Listen] *Two of your clients have called me and* **given some feedback that we may not agree with, but if you work with it to understand their points, it can probably increase your effectiveness with them. They were** [name the clients], **and both of them said that** *they perceived their most recent meetings* [give exact times] *with you to be too fast-paced. Do you agree?* [Listen] **They may have felt this way because your schedule has been so busy lately; I know you barely have time to breathe! What do you think about what the clients said?** [Listen]

Impact of the Behavior

Reinforce the person's desire for goal achievement • Highlight the
difference between intention and impact • Utilize the Three's
competitive instinct

I'm sure this wasn't your goal. All your good intentions aside, *the clients wondered if you were listening to their points of view.* **We wouldn't want them to prefer working** *with someone other than you because of this. We value your work, and as a company want to keep the clients with you rather than switch them* *to someone else. I was not there, so I do not have firsthand information, which makes for an awkward situation. What do you think **about this?*** [Listen]

Preferred Behavior

Keep the conversation upbeat • Take a problem-solving approach • Be concrete and practical • Let the Three know you trust him or her to take effective action

---

Let's problem-solve! I have some ideas that may work, and I'm sure you do also. What are your thoughts? [Listen and use the recipient's ideas, if possible] *In general, it **might** be helpful if you asked the clients periodic questions during your meetings **and even spent an extra fifteen minutes with them at meetings for the next few months to fully listen** to their responses. In this instance, you might want to call them directly to have them clarify what their feedback means. If you do this, please be cautious not to explain why you did or did not do something. Although you may want to tell them, they are likely to respond to this as though it means you are not listening to them.* [Listen] *What do you think you want to do **next?*** [Listen]

Giving Feedback to Fours

Observable Behavior

Develop rapport with the recipient • Use personal words like *I*, *me*, and *mine* • Be careful not to accuse the person of anything • Be clear, direct, and honest • Ask about the recipient's feelings, and listen until the person indicates that he or she is finished talking

Enneagram Style ④
MOOD

Fritz, how are you doing? [Spend time listening to him first; also tell him how you are doing] *I received some feedback from two of your clients and wanted to share that information with you. I wasn't there when these events occurred, so I feel somewhat uncomfortable having to share their concerns with you. Is it okay to discuss these with you now?* [Listen] [Name the clients] ***told me** they perceived their most recent meetings* [give exact times] *with you to be too fast-paced. **Do you have any thoughts about why they would think that?*** [Listen first, then add some of your own ideas after he or she has completed his or her thoughts] ***How do you feel about all this, Fritz?*** [Listen]

Impact of the Behavior

Make the recipient feel you understand him or her • Use "feeling" statements • Show your care and empathy

---

Although I'm sure this isn't what you meant, the clients wondered if you were listening to their points of view. It would be **hard on all of us** if they wanted to work with someone other than you because of this. We value your work, and as a company want to keep the clients with you rather than switch them to someone else. **As someone who cares about both you and the clients, I feel awkward about this, because I wasn't there. How do you feel about this, Fritz? I'm sure this isn't easy to hear.** [Extend your listening time and be very receptive]

Preferred Behavior

Make the recipient feel the choice of response is his or hers to make • Maintain attention to the person's feelings throughout the conversation

---

What are you thinking we should do about it? What do you feel like doing? [Listen] *I had some thoughts about what you could do.* In general, it would be helpful if you asked the clients periodic questions during your meetings and then listened fully to their responses. In this instance, you might want to call them directly to have them clarify what their feedback means. If you do this, *it might help to be careful* not to explain why you did or did not do something. Although you may want to tell them, they are likely to respond to this as though it means you are not listening to them, **and I know you wouldn't want them to feel that way.** What do you think you want to do? [Listen]

Giving Feedback to Fives

Observable Behavior

State clear expectations for the time required for the meeting • Be very specific and fact-based • Give the recipient the space to consider what has been said

---

⑤ Enneagram Style KNOWLEDGE

Frank, we scheduled this time to review some feedback. Is this still a good time? [Listen] *There are forty-five min-*

utes blocked off for this meeting. Does that work with the time you have available? [Listen] **Within the last two weeks,** *two of your clients* [name the clients] *have called me and said they perceived their most recent meetings* [give exact times] *with you to be too fast-paced. Do you agree?* [Listen] **They said they didn't get all the information they needed, and they thought the meetings were too short. What do you think about that?** [Listen]

Impact of the Behavior

Define what is going to be discussed • Be clear about what you say
• Discuss thoughts; let the recipient be the one to bring up feelings

---

Let's talk about the potential impact of this. *The clients wondered if you were listening to their points of view. It would be a shame if they wanted to work with someone other than you because of this. We value your work, and* **don't want to** *switch them to someone else. I was not there, so I do not have firsthand information, which makes for an awkward situation.* **It is, however, what they think.** *What do you think?* [Listen]

Preferred Behavior

Give the recipient time alone to reflect on feelings and thoughts, if
that is the person's preference • Explain the rationale behind the
potential actions you're recommending in order to gain the
person's understanding

Would you like to discuss now what could be done about this, or would you prefer to discuss it later in the week? [Listen; if the person would prefer a later meeting, schedule it. If the person's preference is to discuss the options now, proceed.] **What ideas do you think would work?** [Listen, and decide whether the person's ideas seem feasible enough for the development of a plan. If you think they are not, explain why the ideas might not work, and then proceed.] **Here are some other ideas.** *In general, it would be helpful if you asked the clients periodic questions during your meetings and then listened fully to their responses. In this instance, you might want to call them directly to have them clarify what their feedback means.* **By your doing this, they would know you are concerned, and the information they provide might be helpful to you.** *If you do this, please be cautious not to explain why you did or did not do something. Although you may want to tell them, they are likely to respond to this as though it means you are not listening to them.* **That isn't what we want them to think.** *What do you think you want to do?* [Listen]

Giving Feedback to Sixes

6 Enneagram Style
DOUBT

Observable Behavior

Be concrete and specific • Give reassurance about the magnitude of the problem • Give tentative suggestions early on so that the person can foresee a positive outcome

Sam, I recently received some feedback from two of your clients and wanted to talk about it with you. I don't think there is any cause for alarm—it's data we can work through. Is this a good time to talk? [Listen] *Two of your clients* [name the clients] *have called me and said they perceived their most recent meetings with you* [give exact times] *to be too fast-paced. Do you agree?* [Listen] **They may simply need the meetings to be longer and the conversation to move at a slower pace. What was your sense of these meetings?** [Listen]

Impact of the Behavior

Create an empathic atmosphere • Help the recipient to not "catastrophize"

*The clients are wondering if you were listening to their points of view. It would be **disappointing** if they wanted to work with someone other than you because of this, **but this is definitely not the case at this stage.** We value your work, and as a company want to keep the clients with you rather than switch them to someone else. I was not there, so I do not have firsthand information, which makes for an awkward situation, **as I am sure you can appreciate.** What do you think?* [Listen]

Preferred Behavior

Let the feedback recipient know you support him or her • Assure the person that his or her concerns are normal • Provide the recipient with more than one idea so he or she can choose from among the alternatives • Be aware that you may need to review the data with the Six multiple times

I want you to know that I will help you in any way I can as you work on this. Please let me know any thoughts you have about what you want to do about this. [Listen] *Here are some additional ideas. In general, it would be helpful if you asked the clients periodic questions during your meetings and then listened fully to their responses. In this instance, you might want to call them directly and have them clarify what their feedback means. I'd be willing to review the conversation with you before you phone them if you like. If you call them, please be cautious not to explain why you did or did not do something. Although it is natural to want to tell them, they are likely to respond as though it means you are not listening to them. What do you think you want to do, and how can I help you do it? I would also be happy to review all of this information with you again once you've thought about it more.* [Listen]

Giving Feedback to Sevens

Observable Behavior

Position the critical feedback between two positive comments • Generate ideas from the recipient first • Use the recipient's own ideas whenever possible • Keep your attitude upbeat

Enneagram Style ⑦
OPTIONS

Sonia, I hope we can spend some time on an issue. Is this a good time? [Listen] *I know you have been having great success with your most recent project! However, I wondered if you noticed any issues with two of your other clients?* [Name the clients] [Listen] *They called me and said they perceived their most recent meetings* [give exact times] *with you to be too fast-paced. Do you agree?* [Listen] *What ideas do you have about why they might have perceived things this way?* [Listen] *These ideas are certainly possibilities. Here are some additional thoughts I had about why they might have this perception.* [Tell your ideas] *I know you'll be able to turn around their impressions!*

Impact of the Behavior

Keep the person involved in thinking the problem through • Use *I* statements • Frame the issue in a larger context • Do not act like you are the boss, even if you are

What do you think is the impact on you? [Listen] **What about the impact on our organization?** [Listen] *The clients wondered if you were listening to their points of view. It would be a shame if they wanted to work with someone other than you because of this. We value your work, and as a company want to keep the clients with you rather than switch them to someone else.* **I know that everyone is overloaded because we have many more clients than we expected, and I know you are especially busy!** *I was not there, so I do not have firsthand information, which makes for an awkward situation. What do you think* **about this so far?** [Listen]

Preferred Behavior

Use positive reinforcement • Give the person
his or her choice of options

I'm sure you have some constructive ideas about how to handle this. What are you thinking? [Listen] **Here are some other ideas, so you can pick what you think will work best.** *In general, it* **might** *be helpful if you asked the clients periodic questions during your meetings and then listened fully to their responses. In this instance, you might want to call them directly to have them clarify what their feedback means. If you do this, please be cautious not to explain why you did or did not do something. Although you may want to tell them, they are likely to respond to this as though it means you are not listening to them.* **Many of these ideas we've generated here sound as though they will work.** *What do you think you want to do?* [Listen]

Giving Feedback to Eights

⑧ Enneagram Style
CHALLENGE

Observable Behavior

Be brief, direct, and truthful • Give the big picture
• Let the feedback recipient respond as often as he or
she wishes

An issue has been brought up by two clients that is something I thought you'd want to know about. The clients I've heard from are [give names]. **Although they are only two of your many clients, both have the potential to create large revenues for the firm. They called to**

say *they perceived their most recent meetings* [give exact times] *with you to be too fast-paced. Tell me what you think about this.* [Listen and be prepared for either lengthy or terse comments]

Impact of the Behavior

Indicate your belief in the person's ability to handle the situation • Subtly indicate that there is backup strength in support of him or her • Demonstrate that you are not taking sides, and that you will be fair • Help the person to focus on what is and is not true

Do you have a sense of the impact or would you prefer that I share what I heard from them? [If the person says yes, ask him or her to share this understanding with you. Listen. If you agree with his or her assessment, proceed to the following paragraph, "Preferred Behavior." If you disagree with the assessment or if the person says he or she does not understand the impact, proceed with the wording that follows.] *The clients wondered if you were **truly** listening to their points of view. **Because they do have a choice of whom they work with, no one here wants them** to work with someone other than you because of this. **You know your work is valued here, and we know you're capable of working this through. Not having been there,** I do not have firsthand information **with which to tell you anything more.** What do you think **about this situation? What of their feedback might be accurate, and what is not?** [Listen]

Preferred Behavior

Let the person feel in control • Keep your comments straightforward and well considered

What do you think should be done about this? Do you want some suggestions? [Listen] *Here are some ideas that might be strategic and effective. In general, it could be helpful if you asked the clients periodic questions during your meetings and then listened fully to their responses. **This is simple, and it usually works.** In this instance, you might want to call them directly to have them clarify what their feedback means. If you do this, please be cautious not to explain why you did or did not do something. Although you may want to tell them, they are likely to respond to this as though it means you are not listening to them. What do you think you want to do?* [Listen]

Giving Feedback to Nines

Enneagram Style
9
HARMONY

Observable Behavior

Develop rapport • Be as nonjudgmental as possible • Try to elicit the Nine's thought process

Naomi, how are you doing? How are your projects going? [Listen] *With so many projects going on simultaneously, you must be tired.* [Listen] *An issue came up, and I was hoping we could talk about it.* Is this a good time? [Listen] *Two of your clients* [name the clients] *have called me and said they perceived their most recent meetings* [give exact times] *with you to be too fast-paced.* **What insights do you have about this?** [Listen]

Impact of the Behavior

Try to see the situation from multiple points of view • Give the larger context of the situation

The clients wondered if you were listening to their points of view, **which I know you usually do. They just didn't perceive it that way.** *It would be a shame if they wanted to work with someone other than you because of this. We value your work, and as a company want to keep the clients with you rather than switch them to someone else.* **That would be hard on everybody, and you have a long-term relationship with them.** *I was not there, so I do not have firsthand information, which makes for an awkward situation. What do you think?* [Listen]

Preferred Behavior

Add your ideas, but do not demand that the Nine take a particular action • Help the Nine feel comfortable with the action he or she decides to take

There are many things we could do about this. What ideas do you have? [Listen] *In general, it* **could** *be helpful if you asked the clients periodic questions during your meetings and then listened fully to their responses. In this instance, you might want to call them directly,* **if you are comfortable with this,** *to have them clarify what their feedback means. If you do this, please be cautious not to explain why you did or did not do something. Although you may want to tell them, they* *are likely to respond to this as though you are not listening to them,* **which I'm sure you wouldn't want. What ideas do you have about what** *you want to do?* [Listen]

More Tips for Giving Feedback

Here are some additional tips for giving feedback to everyone. These ideas are useful both in planning the feedback session and in conducting it.

- Think about what you want to say before saying it.
- Give feedback on areas the person can change.
- Make sure your intent is to help, not to hurt or to force change.
- Pay attention to your nonverbal communication.
- Give feedback in private.
- Be direct and respectful simultaneously.
- Be sure the other person is in an emotional state in which he or she can hear you.
- Give positive as well as negative feedback.
- Resist the temptation to interpret the other person's behavior.
- Make sure the conversation is a two-way dialogue.
- Role-play the meeting with someone else first, for practice and obtaining suggestions.
- **Remember:** No one changes another person; people change themselves.

SUMMARY

- Keep your own Enneagram style tendencies from interfering with your delivery.
- Use the three-part Feedback Formula.
- Tailor your approach to the other person's Enneagram style.

Chapter 4

Managing Conflict

*C*onflict is one of the most stressful aspects of organizational life. People clash about everything—resources, strategy, decisions, goals, roles, rewards, culture, power, leadership style, inclusion, personality—the list could go on indefinitely. Unresolved conflict usually damages both the individuals involved and the organization.

Although most people don't like it, conflict is part of life, and this includes life in organizations. While conflict avoidance and aggressive confrontation are certainly options, it is far better to prevent conflict when possible, de-escalate it once it emerges, and deal with it constructively under all circumstances. In this chapter, you will learn to do all three in the context of the Enneagram.

Which of the pictures in Figure 4.1 most accurately reflects your view of conflict? The images are arranged in order from the most negative to the most positive. If you selected the most negative picture of conflict, the boxing gloves, you may think of conflict as a struggle that ends with a winner and loser. If you chose the storm, perhaps you view conflict as something that is tumultuous, unpredictable, and intense, yet has an ending.

The two middle images—the bridge and the theatrical masks—are the most neutral of the six choices. If you selected the picture of the disconnected bridge, this suggests you may think of conflict as a situation in which something has been sharply disconnected or severely damaged, but can be repaired. Perhaps you chose the masks representing tragedy and comedy. This choice may mean that you perceive conflict as an emotionally mixed experience, containing both difficulties and positive possibilities.

The two remaining pictures represent the most optimistic views of conflict. If you chose the two people shaking hands, you may perceive conflict as

FIGURE 4.1 Images of Conflict

something that can be resolved effectively when people talk through their differences. Or, you might have selected the image of the bright sun. Perhaps you have observed some exceptional growth and development emerging from the heat of conflict.

Very few people select the bright sun; most people pick one of the negative images, such as the boxing gloves or the storm. There are two reasons for this. First, conflict usually elicits strong emotions, such as anger, fear, and sadness; most people view these feelings as negative and prefer to avoid them. Second, few people have learned how to deal with differences constructively, so their actual experiences with conflict have been negative.

Through a series of stories, this chapter will show you (1) how to markedly improve your ability to manage your reactions during conflict to prevent most interpersonal conflict from escalating, and (2) how to tailor your conflict resolution approach to the Enneagram style of the other person.

Certain work situations are likely to agitate anyone—for example, situations involving lying, cheating, and stealing—although how people react at these times will be different based on their Enneagram styles. There are also specific anger triggers for each Enneagram style—that is, certain situations that will invariably ignite anger in a person of one style, yet may not affect someone of a different style. The nine case studies in this chapter were specifically selected because they describe and explain conflict situations unique to each style. This helps answer the question that people often ask when observing another person who is angry: *This wouldn't have bothered me, so why is he or she so upset?* The behavior patterns that individuals exhibit when they are angry will be similar to those of other people with the same Enneagram style, regardless of whether the stimulus for the anger is a universally agitating event or a situation that contains a specific Enneagram style anger trigger.

When people work together, minor disruptions inevitably arise. One person may do something that violates another person's expectations. Because these expectations are not usually discussed in advance, the transgressor has no forewarning that his or her behavior will, in fact, be offensive. When these transgressions occur, the offended party feels an anger trigger, or "pinch." Pinches, which are typically knots in the stomach, can also be small jolts in the head or pangs in the chest. Along with the pinching sensation comes a thought—an internal voice that says, *This person should not have done that!*—and a feeling of anger, hurt, or fear.

When we feel a pinch, most of us do not say anything to the other person directly. We either hope the other person's behavior is a one-time offense, or we speculate that the sharing of our displeasure will only make the situation worse—that is, it may create a conflict, hurt the other person's feelings, or both.

As pinches begin to accumulate, however, they morph into a conflict reaction, or "crunch"—the time most people label as conflict.[1]

During the crunch, our feelings become more heated, our sensitivities become heightened, and the risk of discussing the brewing conflict rises exponentially. This is the time when one of two things usually happens: an argument takes place, or the individuals avoid each other. Sometimes both occur. While it usually takes three pinches to make a crunch, sometimes it only takes one or two, as you will see in this chapter.

Pinches and crunches provide excellent opportunities for our own growth; in fact, our pinches and crunches often say as much or more about us than they say about the situation or the other person. The following ideas show you how to use your pinches and crunches for your own development:

1. **Share your pinches with others at the beginning of your working relationship.** Early on in a working relationship, engage the other person or persons in a conversation about your newly formed working relationship, including both your and their working styles. During the working-

---

1. Pinch-crunch comes from a larger conceptual model called "Planned Renegotiation: A Norm-Setting OD Intervention," developed by Jack Sherwood and John Glidewell (1973).

FIGURE 4.2 Pinch-Crunch Conflict

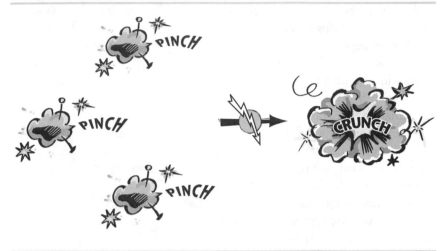

styles discussion, both of you can highlight the types of behaviors in others that tend to pinch you.

2. **Say something as soon as you are aware of feeling pinched.** Sharing a pinch as soon as it is felt creates the opportunity for a reasoned conversation with less emotional intensity than occurs after pinches begin to accumulate. The Feedback Formula from Chapter 3, "Giving Constructive Feedback," provides a structure for giving feedback about what caused the pinch, the impact of the pinch, and the preferred behavior. Additional information from the same chapter—how to manage your own style when giving feedback to others, and how to adjust your delivery to the Enneagram style of the recipient—is also extremely helpful.

3. **When you start behaving in ways that indicate you are feeling pinched, do something physical if you can, such as working out or taking a walk.** When we begin to feel angry, we typically become physically tense, and our muscles tighten automatically. Simultaneously, our mental processing and emotional reactivity become heightened. Engaging in a physical activity interrupts this cycle, and we often perceive what has occurred in a new and constructive manner.

4. **When you feel a pinch, answer this question:** *What does my reaction to this situation or to the other person's behavior say about me in terms of my Enneagram style and about the areas in which I can develop? How can working on my pinches and crunches help me to bring out the best in myself?*

This is undoubtedly the most constructive and useful way to understand and work with your pinches and crunches. All it takes is a frame of mind that has you say the following to yourself: *I just had a strong negative reaction to this event. What can this teach me about myself? How can I use this experience to experiment with a very different reaction, including my mental interpretation of events, my particular emotional responses, and the way in which I am now behaving?*

As you read the following nine stories demonstrating the pinches and crunches unique to people of each Enneagram style, keep in mind both your own Enneagram style and the styles of other people with whom you have had conflict. The chapter describes the most common pinches for individuals of each Enneagram style, how people of each style tend to behave when they feel pinched, and how to approach individuals of each style during conflict. Following the section covering the pinches and crunches for each Enneagram style, you will find suggestions for using conflict as a way to work with your own pinches. The suggestions take the four preceding ideas about how to work with yourself—discussing your pinches at the beginning of a relationship, sharing a pinch soon after it occurs, engaging in physical activity, and using your pinches for your own self-development—and customize these ideas to each Enneagram style.

Ones: Pinches and Crunches

Enneagram Style **1**
DILIGENCE

Directly after Olivia, a One, and a colleague, Jan, had completed a successful business presentation, they sat down to discuss their assessments of the meeting. This discussion included their views of what had gone well during the meeting, what they would have changed about their presentation, and what they would do as a follow-up. After this, they sat back in their chairs to relax and started a casual conversation. Jan, pleased with how the meeting had gone, highlighted the parts she had enjoyed most. She said things such as "This part was challenging" and "I especially enjoyed that!"

Olivia became quiet, and her body language quickly revealed her anger. She clenched her jaw, sat farther back in her chair, and closed her arms tightly around her body.

What had upset Olivia? Jan felt perplexed and tried to get Olivia to talk about her concerns. After several minutes, Olivia sputtered, "You're bragging!

And what's more, you didn't do exactly what we planned at the end of our presentation. And furthermore, who gave you the right to act like the leader during the meeting?"

Common One Pinches

Being criticized • Another's lack of follow-through • Another's noncollaborative changes to a plan • Feeling deceived

Although Ones often judge and criticize others, they are simultaneously highly sensitive to being criticized themselves. Olivia interpreted Jan's comments to be self-congratulatory, and she was particularly vexed that Jan made no mention of Olivia's contribution to the success of their presentation. In Olivia's mind, the absence of positive comments from Jan about Olivia's performance was the same as criticism. Olivia felt a pinch right in the middle of her stomach.

Olivia had already felt agitated by something that had occurred during the session itself. Jan, speaking during the middle of the presentation, had changed the agenda by talking about a subject that was not part of the original plan. Although Jan did this spontaneously in response to a question from the group, Olivia felt that Jan was not demonstrating the proper follow-through and was not staying with the task. She was also bothered by Jan's unilateral change of plan.

The final transgression was the most difficult for Olivia to discuss; at this point, her pinches had accumulated and transformed into a crunch. Olivia believed that Jan had been too assertive during both the presentation and their postpresentation discussion. The working agreement going into the meeting had been that they would be equal partners in the presentation. Jan had violated this agreement by fielding a majority of the questions and by her display of personal confidence. In Olivia's mind, Jan was acting as though she were the lead presenter.

When Jan heard how distraught Olivia felt, she was dumbfounded, because she believed that either of them had been free to voice an opinion, answer a question, or change the agenda.

How Ones Behave When Pinched

Curt statements • Accusations related to other issues • Nonverbal cues of anger • Saying nothing

When Ones feel pinched, they become resentful, which they usually experience as annoyance or irritation. When they feel resentful, Ones may do one of three things: say something to the other person, show their displeasure through body language, or keep their irritation completely to themselves.

When Ones do say something when they feel upset, they are likely to communicate their displeasure in one of two ways:

1. They may say something about what the other person has done in a quick and curt manner, and as a result the person on the receiving end may feel stunned and/or figuratively slapped.
2. Alternatively, Ones may make an accusatory comment about something else they think the other person has done wrong; the other individual may be quite surprised by the accusation.

In addition, Ones may show their distress nonverbally, through a sharp tone of voice or through tense body language. In this case, the other person can sense the One's displeasure but may not understand the cause of the anger. In the story above, Jan sensed that Olivia was angry with her during their casual postpresentation conversation, but this was based on Olivia's nonverbal cues rather than on what Olivia actually said. It was only after Jan asked Olivia what was bothering her that she understood what had generated Olivia's hostility toward her.

How to Approach Ones in a Crunch

Take a problem-solving approach • Allow them time to think through their feelings • Provide some structure to the conversation • Let the One talk first • Use nonjudgmental language

Although most Ones are willing to deal with conflicts directly, more often Ones prefer to avoid such situations. Because they typically work very hard to be self-controlled and self-managing, for Ones, the thought of dealing with anger and conflict directly raises the fear that either they or the other person may lose control of their feelings. In addition, Ones typically acknowledge feelings of resentment far more easily than feelings of deep anger, because they tend to believe that outrage and fury are "bad" emotions that must be contained. Consequently, Ones usually need to believe unequivocally that their anger is both righteous and just before they are willing to express it directly.

Two alternative approaches may be effective when trying to resolve conflicts with Ones. If the conflict is of low to moderate intensity—for example, it is of short duration and the One does not seem extremely agitated—a problem-solving method is the preferred approach. This involves getting the

One's concurrence that there is a problem, his or her agreement to meet at some point to discuss the concern, and a modicum of structure to the actual discussion. A sincere overture to the One, such as "I've wondered if something might be bothering you and was hoping you'd be willing to talk with me about it sometime," gives assurance to the One that the conversation will focus on fact-finding and will not be a direct confrontation. A possible time delay—the suggestion that the discussion does not have to be held immediately—allows Ones the opportunity to consider what is at the root of their anger. When the actual conflict discussion does take place, Ones usually appreciate some, but not too much, structure to the conversation—for example, a format that allows fifteen minutes for each person to articulate his or her concerns. A discussion with no structure may feel too disorganized and too risky for most Ones.

The second approach is to sit down as soon as there is an indication of a problem and immediately deal with the issues. This method works effectively in high-intensity conflict situations because it is already quite obvious that there is a problem that must be addressed. The first step is to let the One speak first, without interruption, by saying something forthright such as "You are clearly very upset about something. Please discuss this with me so we can get the issues on the table." When Ones do take the risk of expressing their anger directly, they may need some support in order to feel comfortable sharing everything they are thinking and feeling. Thus, saying something such as "I didn't know that this behavior affected you in this way. This is very useful," can encourage Ones to say even more. After Ones have had the opportunity to express all of their feelings and thoughts, they usually become far more open, relaxed, and engaged. Consequently, they are more receptive and responsive to what the other person has to say.

When sharing your issues with a One, it is crucial to use the least amount of critical language, because a perceived judgment or condemnation from someone else activates the One's own inner critic. Ones can be very tough and demanding on themselves; in many instances, they are far harder on themselves than they would be with another person. When Ones become highly defensive during a conflict discussion, they are often protecting themselves not only from another's criticism, but also from their own self-recrimination.

How Ones Can Manage Their Own Pinches and Crunches
1. **Share your pinches with others at the beginning of your working relationship.** Use the pinches for Ones listed in this section as a starting point and add any others that you choose. Please give details and specific

examples of these pinches so that the other person knows exactly what you mean. For example, "another's lack of follow-through" can mean many different things such as not meeting long-term deadlines, not doing tasks immediately, or not returning a phone call within twenty-four hours.

2. **Say something as soon as you are aware of feeling pinched.** Ones may not be aware of feeling pinched yet may exhibit pinched behaviors, such as making curt statements. You can use the list under "How Ones Behave When Pinched" as cues for determining that something is bothering you. Then ask yourself, *What is upsetting me?* Additionally, because Ones tend to display their critical reactions through their nonverbal behavior, when sharing your pinches with the other person, try to keep your body language neutral so that the other person will react more to your words than to your nonverbal cues.

3. **When you start to behave in ways that indicate you are feeling pinched, do something physical if you can, such as working out or taking a walk.** For Ones, this is particularly important, because it tends to put them back in touch with their physical sensations and feelings. Because of this, Ones may more easily recognize the deeper causes of their anger, some of which may have very little to do directly with the pinch they have just experienced.

4. **When you feel a pinch, ask yourself:** *What does my reaction to this situation or to the other person's behavior say about me as a One and about the areas in which I can develop? How can working on my pinches and crunches help me to bring out the best in myself?* This exploration of their behavior can lead many Ones to become self-critical; consequently, it is best done through a more open-ended inquiry. Examine multiple ways of considering the situation that has caused you duress, using different perspectives. For example, you can ask yourself the following sequence of questions: *As I think about three different people I know and respect who are all very different from one another, how would each of them perceive this situation? What can I learn from each of them?*

Because Ones tend to suppress their anger, it often becomes bottled up and leads to an explosive reaction over a less significant event. Pay special attention to this aspect of your anger and ask yourself this question: *What am I truly angry about?* In addition, the One's anger may be connected to deeper issues, such as feeling "not perfect enough" to be valued, or perceiving that others are not working as hard or as well but are getting away with this. Other areas of deeper issues to consider involve the One's desire to keep circumstances under control, or the One's competing with others—for example, by having the right answer, demonstrating the best behavior, being the most intelligent, or being the most perfect. An underlying sense of losing to the competition is sometimes a deep source of anger for many Ones; understanding this often takes a profound level of self-reflection.

Twos: Pinches and Crunches

Enneagram Style
GIVING

Ted, a Two, lived and worked on the West Coast. When his client needed an East Coast–based consultant for a small project, Ted referred the work to a colleague, Anna, whom he knew by reputation only. Over a six-month period of time, Ted learned from both Anna and the client that the project had gone well. One month after the project had ended, Ted and Anna spoke on the phone.

Ted fumed as he said, "I am extremely angry with you, and we need to talk about this!"

Stunned, Anna asked why he was angry. Ted replied, "I gave you this piece of work, and you never thanked me for it!"

Anna reviewed the times that she believed she had already thanked Ted. "What about the time I told you how much I enjoyed the project? Or the time I asked your advice and thanked you for it?"

Ted's response was immediate: "You never thanked me for giving you *this* piece of work."

Common Two Pinches

Being taken for granted • Feeling unappreciated • Not being heard

Anna had unknowingly pinched Ted where Twos feel it most intensely—being taken for granted. Because Anna had not explicitly said, "Thank you so much for giving me this project," Ted had felt unappreciated and had become indignant. Although Anna thought that she had thanked Ted, from his point of view these thank-yous, being indirect, were inadequate.

When Ted shared his anger with Anna, she asked him why the ways in which she believed that she had thanked him did not feel like thank-yous to him. Ted became even more incensed; he was furious that Anna did not understand instantly why he was so angry. In this situation, it took only two pinches for Ted to feel crunched.

Twos have a tender spot that gets touched when they feel that the other person is not hearing what they are saying. This soft spot can ignite into anger, particularly when Twos are trying to do the very difficult task of expressing their own desires, feelings, and needs. Because Twos tend to focus so extensively on other people's needs, when they do muster their inner resources and try to articulate a personal request, Twos expect the same courtesy that they believe they deliver—the other person's full attention and understanding. When this does not occur, Twos can become furious.

How Twos Behave When Pinched

Keep feelings to themselves for long periods of time • Intensely emotional when they do say something • Think through what they will say in advance, which will include how they feel, why they feel that way, what they believe the other person has done wrong

---

When Twos become angry, it is usually because their feelings have been building up over a long period of time. Expressing dissatisfaction directly does not come easily to Twos, who generally prefer to show a more optimistic and likable persona. However, others may sense the Two's unhappiness and displeasure through inference. For example, the Two may have been friendly and receptive but may suddenly change demeanor and appear cool and indifferent. However, cues such as these may also be ambiguous, because Twos can also act aloof when something else is bothering them or when they feel fatigued.

Eventually, however, Twos may mention their discontent directly to the other person, particularly when they anticipate an extended relationship with that individual or simply want to bring the conflictual situation to closure. Twos usually plan what they want to say well in advance and then either wait for or create an opportune moment in which to have the conversation. What they say is often a montage of thoughts, feelings, events, and inferences about the other person's behavior and motivation; it is as if the Two has already drawn a conclusion about the conflict before the other person may even be aware that a problem exists. In the story above, a long conversation followed Ted's opening remarks, with Ted going on to tell Anna that he thought she was ungrateful, ambitious, and out for herself, and that he knew she was completely unaware of these qualities.

How to Approach Twos in a Crunch

Let them talk extensively • Ask clarifying questions • Share your perspective • Make sure to validate their perspective • Discuss feelings and thoughts

As noted above, Twos usually prefer to discuss conflicts at a time and place of their choosing. Here, the challenge is how to approach someone who may prefer to initiate the conversation. The entry point is that Twos often appreciate having someone notice and care about their feelings, as long as this is done in an unobtrusive way. While many Twos will appreciate this overture, others may feel put on the spot, and it is difficult to predict which reaction you will receive.

However, even if a Two feels put on the spot to deal with an issue that he or she is not ready to discuss, the Two will more than likely think about it later and get back in touch with the other person. Simply saying, "I've noticed that you seem less relaxed than normal and wondered what might be causing it. I'd be very open to discussing this, or to just listening to you if you'd like to talk sometime," can allow the Two to discuss concerns when he or she feels ready.

When a Two is ready to discuss a problem, his or her behavior is relatively predictable. At this time, the Two will have a lot to say; listen intently to what he or she is saying, without commenting on whether or not you agree. After the Two has completed his or her thoughts, ask a few questions to help clarify what has been said. Questions and statements such as "What made you feel that this is what I was doing?" and "Please help me understand what occurred that caused you to interpret my behavior in this way," work very well with Twos. Twos are often very receptive to what the other person has to say after they have had the opportunity to express their thoughts fully.

After Twos have expressed their concerns, they often respond well to the following question: "Is it okay with you for me to tell you how I perceived the situation?" Twos will almost always answer yes to this question, providing they feel you have listened to them and understood what they have said. If a Two says no, it usually means that he or she has not finished talking. If the answer is no, ask the Two, "What else is on your mind?"

When Twos are ready to listen, they usually do so with their full attention. During this time, they will be most receptive if the other person frames what he or she says in the context of "From my perspective . . ." and "During this time, this is what I was thinking and feeling . . . ," Using this method works well with Twos because it does not invalidate their opinions and feelings but does create a desire in the Two to be empathic.

With many Twos, an honest airing of feelings in a context of mutual respect often resolves a conflict. There may be specific behaviors that require changing on both your parts, but these can be addressed once rapport has been reestablished.

How Twos Can Manage Their Own Pinches and Crunches

1. **Share your pinches with others at the beginning of your working relationship.** The pinches for Twos bear a striking similarity to each other; essentially, Twos like to be needed, acknowledged, and appreciated. However, because they tend to do things for others in what appears to be an effortless way, such as rising to meet a need and offering assistance, it can appear to others that Twos enjoy giving for its own sake. People often do not realize that Twos want to be explicitly thanked.

   Most Twos would not be able to tell someone else, particularly in a new working relationship, that they want to be appreciated and thanked. To say this might be embarrassing because of its personal tone in a business context and the perception of their being "needy." However, these Two pinches can be effectively communicated through anecdote and story. For example, after encouraging the other person to discuss his or her pinches, Twos can frame their pinches in this way: *One of my key values is that every-one gets treated with courtesy and respect. That means using "please" when ask-ing someone to do something, and explicitly saying "thank you" to someone for a job completed or something he or she has done. I behave toward others this way and want to be treated this way myself. Once, I recommended a colleague for a project, and this person never explicitly said thank you for it. This is one of my core pinches.*

2. **Say something as soon as you are aware of feeling pinched.** Twos may worry that if they raise the fact that they feel pinched, the other person may feel hurt or angry; Twos rarely want to elicit either reaction. The fol-lowing perspective can be invaluable to Twos: when you share a pinch soon after it occurs, you are truly helping the other person to learn something about the impact of his or her behavior and you are helping your mutual relationship to grow. In addition, when you are forthcoming about feeling pinched, you are also helping yourself by learning to express your own needs early in a relationship.

3. **When you start to behave in ways that indicate you are feeling pinched, do something physical if you can, such as working out or taking a walk.** Physical activity serves Twos well because when they do something physical that they enjoy, they are actually doing something for

themselves rather than focusing their attention on the needs of others. When Twos care for themselves, they often need less affirmation and appreciation from other people.

Twos often find that physical activity helps to "ground" them during times of emotional duress. The act of doing something physical focuses their concentration on their bodies rather than on their emotions or thoughts; this distance from their reactions often allows new perspectives on their pinches and crunches to emerge.

4. **When you feel a pinch, ask yourself:** *What does my reaction to this situation or to the other person's behavior say about me as a Two and about the areas in which I can develop? How can working on my pinches and crunches help me to bring out the best in myself?*

This question makes Twos focus on themselves rather than the other person. The issue becomes not what the other person needs to learn, but what the Two needs to examine about him- or herself. This change of attention can startle many Twos, and they may need to ask themselves the above question multiple times. The answers Twos most often give are these: *I need to be appreciated or I needed to be needed and I'm not getting that response from this other person.* Whatever the initial answer to this question, it is very helpful for Twos to deepen their level of self-exploration and ask themselves these questions: *Why is appreciation so important to me? How would I be different if I didn't need to be needed and appreciated?* This line of questioning often leads Twos to explore the issue that they are usually giving to others in order to get something in return. It is the tacit expectation of something given back to the Two—for example, being honored, being indispensable, being praised, or even being revered—that is referred to by the term "manipulation." Although many Twos do not like this term applied to them, the word *manipulation* means getting someone else to do something or shaping someone else's behavior without their explicit knowledge or consent. It is sometimes said that Twos give to get, under the guise of looking as if they are giving to give. This awareness can be both troubling and enlightening for most Twos.

Threes: Pinches and Crunches

3 Enneagram Style
PERFORM

Trevor, a Three, was given the job of team leader as a reward by his boss, Roseanne, for his hard work and outstanding achievement. In addition, Roseanne knew that Trevor had earned the respect of the other team members. Roseanne reasoned, *This is a perfect job for him. The team members have variable talent, but what they lack most is focus. Trevor will be a terrific role model for them, and he will appreciate being acknowledged for his efforts. This is a win-win situation for me as their boss. Because this team lasts for only six months, it will also give me time to groom Trevor for a bigger position within the organization.*

However, Trevor was neither excited nor enthusiastic when Roseanne approached him. When Roseanne said, "I want you to be the team leader for this team. I know you will do an excellent job," Trevor was taken aback. Although he was somewhat flattered, this sentiment faded quickly as he thought about the challenge ahead. He knew his nine teammates very well. In Trevor's estimation, two of them were both skilled and motivated, five were skilled but lacked initiative, and two were motivated but lacked the basic skills to do the job.

Trevor did his best to set goals and organize this team. However, only half of the team members worked very hard. The other half seemed more interested in socializing than in accomplishing anything. They knew how to do the work—Trevor had even shown them how to do it—but they just didn't take their jobs very seriously. In the end, Trevor and four other team members did most of the work.

Common Three Pinches

Being put in a position of likely failure • Not looking good professionally • Being blamed for the poor work of others • Not receiving credit for their work

Although Roseanne's intention was to honor and reward Trevor, she actually unnerved him. Because of the way in which Roseanne offered him the position of team leader, Trevor did not feel he could refuse. When she said, "I want you to be the team leader for this team. I know you will do an excellent job," Trevor believed that if he declined the offer, it would be the same as saying that he was not interested in advancing himself. Had Roseanne asked him, "Do you want this position?" Trevor would have said, "Sometime in the future would be far preferable. The timing is not good right now." To Trevor, Roseanne was not asking him to take the job; she was telling him that he *was* the team leader.

Trevor did not find the team leader role attractive because he had already sized up the team members and believed that only a few of them were both willing and capable of achieving excellent results. In Trevor's view, the rest were likely to end up making him look bad; he could not imagine anything he could possibly do to get them all to perform well. Trevor was thinking not only of how he, as their leader, would look in Roseanne's eyes, but also about

the larger organization; Threes usually avoid situations in which they anticipate that they will not look good professionally.

In Trevor's view, the situation raised the possibility that he would be
blamed, or at least held accountable, for the poor work of other people.
Because of his concerns about the team's overall capability, combined with his
self-awareness that he would *never* let the team fail, Trevor anticipated that he
would end up doing most of the team's tasks.

In his mind, Roseanne had offered him a role that would only inundate
him with work. Further, these were tasks for which he would never receive
the credit. In this situation, the first pinch Trevor felt—Roseanne's expectation that he would take the team leader position—transformed immediately
into a crunch. Trevor felt he was in a double bind: he would fail with the team
if he said yes, but fail in the organization if he said no.

How Threes Behave When Pinched

Ask a short sequence of structural questions • Unlikely to say that
they are upset • Body language unlikely to give clues • Over time,
tone of voice becomes sharp • Over time, sentences become clipped

Roseanne had no idea that Trevor was upset. When she offered him the position, he merely listened intently to her and then asked her a few questions
related to the team's deliverables and timetables. She did sense that Trevor had
some concerns, but she attributed these to his conscientious attitude about
doing the task well. Trevor gave her no direct data that he was displeased. Like
many Threes, he was adept at masking his apprehensions by displaying a calm
and confident demeanor.

During the time the team worked together, Trevor neither complained to
Roseanne about the team members nor expressed any unease about his ability to lead them. Roseanne did notice that Trevor began to appear unusually
tired, particularly during the last two months of the six-month project.
Because she was concerned, Roseanne decided to watch the team in action,
and she then spoke to Trevor: "It seems that part of your team is working
hard, but the other part is not taking the work very seriously. Can you tell me
who is contributing and who is not?"

Trevor surprised Roseanne when he answered, "Everyone is contributing
to our goals," and he proceeded to list what each team member had accomplished. Although Trevor was highly frustrated with several of his team members, under the circumstances he would never have mentioned this fact to
Roseanne. First, she had asked him this question within earshot of several of
the team members. In Trevor's estimation, the team members would have

become demoralized, angry, and even less motivated if they heard him say that several on the team were not contributing.

Second, he assumed that any team members he mentioned would be upset at him for betraying them to their supervisor, and they would disrespect him for displaying behavior unbecoming of a leader; both reactions would hurt his ability to lead them. Third, Trevor knew that he would not want someone else to make disparaging remarks about him to Roseanne, and he assumed that his team members would feel the same way. Because Roseanne had asked him this question in a public setting, he felt she had put him on the spot once again.

Had Roseanne asked Trevor privately what she could do to help him get the low performers to work more productively, Trevor might have welcomed the question. Or, if she had asked him how he was enjoying being the team leader, he might have shared his frustrations with her or even told her why he would have preferred to not be this team's leader.

Because Trevor's negative suspicions about the team members were confirmed by their later performance, his feelings of frustration and anger only grew. If at some later date Roseanne were to appoint him to be the leader of another questionably competent team, she might be startled by his reaction, as Trevor would be likely to blurt out a short, sharp, and highly negative response. Only then would Roseanne know that something was terribly wrong.

How to Approach Threes in a Crunch

Be kind and clear • Make sure there is no excessive work pressure • Do not use an intensely emotional tone • Use a rational, problem-solving approach

When Threes clearly exhibit anger or distress, it is reasonably safe to assume that it has been building up over a period of time. A kind and clear inquiry about what may be upsetting them can open the door to an honest dialogue, as long as this is done in private and at a time when the Three is not distracted by intense work pressure. It is likely to be embarrassing to a Three to be asked publicly about what might be bothering him or her, because it threatens the common Three desire to show a positive public face. When Threes are busy with work, deadlines, and other pressures, they will often not want to take the time for an emotional discussion. The other person can instead choose an appropriate time and setting and say something like, "It appears as though something may be bothering you. If it's something I did, I would very much like to hear about it."

In response to this request, some Threes may not want to admit that something is bothering them, while others may acknowledge the problem, but prefer not to discuss it immediately. However, even if they prefer not to discuss the matter at all, most Threes will usually start to think about the issue in more depth. Their self-reflection will pave the way for a productive conversation at a later time. They may bring up the subject themselves, or the other person can raise the issue in a week or so by saying something like, "The other day when I asked if something was bothering you, you said no. I'm still thinking that you may be upset and was hoping you'd talk with me about it."

When Threes are angry, some may be fully aware that they feel angry, while others may feel only mildly perturbed but not understand why. Still other Threes may be so busy and active that they may not have realized that something is upsetting them. Thus, a simple overture without any pressure for an immediate response gives Threes the time to reflect on their own feelings. Once they have made this self-assessment, Threes may suggest a follow-up discussion. If they do not, the other person can bring up the topic again by saying, "I was wondering if we could talk about what is on your mind." If two or three overtures like this receive no affirmative response, it is a clear message from a Three to stop asking. A Three who does not want to talk about a problem can become quite agitated.

However, most Threes will discuss a conflict if they believe a solution is possible. Consequently, a problem-solving orientation, with an emphasis on the word *solving*, optimizes the chances of a positive outcome and works far better than an emotional approach. For Threes, a problem-solving orientation focuses on three things: first, the impact of the problem from the perspective of results; second, the basic causes of the distress, discussed in a nonemotional manner; and third—and most importantly—what can be done to resolve the issue. An emphasis on the solution aspect of the problem suits the Three's "can-do" stance quite nicely.

To more clearly understand the way to best approach Threes, the following example shows two different ways of dealing with a situation in which a Three has not included another team member in an important client meeting. In the first version, the excluded team member takes an emotional approach when confronting the Three colleague:

When you met with the clients yesterday and did not let me know about the meeting, I was very angry about being excluded. These clients are both of ours, not just yours. It affects my ability to work with them and undermines both the project and our relationship. What were you thinking or feeling that led you to do this? If there are some issues between us, let's get these on the table now. Once we are completely honest with each other, I am hopeful we can work things out.

This approach may cause the Three to shut down his or her feelings or become defensive and accusatory. Although many Threes do appreciate directness and honesty, an emotional approach contains an implicit demand that the Three engage in an intense emotional discussion about the relationship. Threes usually prefer to get a problem solved quickly and to move on to a more productive working relationship. Thus, they may shy away from a discussion that requires them to examine their deeper feelings. This does not mean that they will not discuss difficult feelings under certain circumstances, but that they will most often discuss feelings when *they* feel the need to do so, rather than as the result of a demand from another person.

Threes are also highly sensitive to being blamed for something that has not worked effectively. In the example of the emotional approach, there is the implication that the Three has done something wrong—in this case, not inviting a colleague to a meeting. The exclusion of the colleague may have been an inadvertent mistake by the Three, but it also may have been intentional. In either case, most Threes would become defensive upon hearing the other person's remarks.

Using the second option, a problem-solving approach, the person excluded from the meeting might say the following to the Three:

When you met alone with the clients yesterday, it may have given them the impression that they do not have a team behind the work we're doing for them. They may have inferred that there are tensions within the team; if so, the clients could lose some confidence in us. Perhaps it was an oversight, and that can be easily remedied. Or perhaps you have some issues with my performance, and I would invite you to talk with me about any concerns, should that be the case. Whatever the cause, I am as committed as you are to a quick and effective solution. What do you think?

The above example is phrased in a more objective manner; it invites the Three to say as little or as much as he or she desires. With an open invitation to solve a problem, most Threes will explain their thoughts, feelings, and behavior and will make suggestions to remedy the situation.

How Threes Can Manage Their Own Pinches and Crunches
1. **Share your pinches with others at the beginning of your working relationship.** At the beginning of a working relationship, engage the other person in a conversation about how you can both contribute to an effective and successful relationship. A helpful way to begin is to make an opening statement like, "Because we're just starting to work together, it would be really helpful for me to know about your preferred style of working with others,

especially your likes and dislikes. That way, I can adjust my behavior accordingly when possible. I'd also like to share my preferences with you."

When it is your turn to share pinches, you might say, for example, "I work best with people who are highly capable and responsible. What I mean by highly capable is that people are highly skilled, and they work constantly to improve their performance and achieve high-quality results. I personally believe that what each of us accomplishes reflects positively or negatively on all of us. I dislike work situations in which I have to kill myself to get the job done, look around, and not see others putting in the same effort."

2. **Say something as soon as you are aware of feeling pinched.** As busy as a Three may be and as difficult as it may feel to discuss a pinch with someone, it is well worth the time. In fact, it will take less time and require less ongoing attention when pinches are discussed soon after they occur. A kind and straightforward introduction such as "Do you have a minute to talk about a minor event that happened?" usually paves the way for a fruitful discussion.

3. **When you start to behave in ways that indicate you are feeling pinched, do something physical if you can, such as working out or taking a walk.** Physical activity has a major benefit for Threes—the focus on work ceases momentarily. However, to take full advantage of this "time-out" moment, try to engage in a physical activity that allows some time for self-reflection, such as walking, hiking, or yoga. Threes may be tempted to engage in highly competitive physical sports, such as tennis or basketball, but these sports may be so absorbing that there is little time left for feelings to emerge. Strenuous sports may also release so much of the anger that Threes no longer feel any need to deal with the issues. This may feel like a relief in the moment, but does not really resolve the situation or give you the opportunity to take a look at yourself.

4. **When you feel a pinch, ask yourself:** *What does my reaction to this situation or to the other person's behavior say about me as a Three and about the areas in which I can develop? How can working on my pinches and crunches help me to bring out the best in myself?*

For Threes, it can be helpful to consider how the other person's behavior relates to the Three's ability to succeed or fail; this issue is often the basis of a Three's negative reaction to others. Some related areas to examine include: looking bad in front of others; feeling competitive with someone else; appearing less than fully competent; and disliking others who appear to be failures in some way (for example, people whose projects haven't succeeded or whose personal styles do not exude confidence). Questions for Threes to ask themselves will include these: *What is it about appearing to be successful that is so important to me? If this were not my ongoing intention, how would I be different, and how would my thoughts, feelings, and behavior change? What would happen if I were not so focused on impressing other people?*

Fours: Pinches and Crunches

Carl had not heard back from his colleague Bart for two weeks, despite having sent Bart three e-mails and having left two messages on his voice mail. Carl's intention had been to make contact about their joint project and to ask how Bart was doing. After two weeks of waiting for a response, Carl was becoming agitated, angry, and hurt.

Enneagram Style ④
MOOD

Carl began to wonder what he might have done to anger Bart. At the same time, he began reflecting on their relationship. He remembered two instances in which Bart had seemed distant, as well as several times when he, Carl, had been unhappy with Bart. For example, he thought about a time when Bart had suggested that they use another colleague's materials for a presentation because it would save them preparation time. However, Bart did not want to give credit to the colleague, because he believed that doing so would undermine their credibility with the client. Besides, Bart had reasoned, they all worked for the same firm, so no harm would be done.

Carl also realized that he was angry that Bart seemed so highly regarded at the firm. Carl wondered, *Why is Bart given high-level assignments when his work is not consistently excellent? Don't the higher-ups realize that Bart seems to be more out for himself than supportive of the growth of others in the firm?*

At the end of three weeks, Carl finally received the following e-mail from Bart:

Carl—Sorry to have taken so long, but work has been at a frenzied pace here. Will be back in touch with you next week.

Common Four Pinches

Being ignored or slighted • Being asked to do something contrary to his or her values • An event that elicits his or her envy

Carl already felt pinched before he received Bart's e-mail. However, after Carl read Bart's e-mail, he was so hurt and angry he felt crunched. Carl felt slighted and ignored because Bart had not responded quickly to his multiple overtures for contact. Fours have a tendency to personalize situations in which they reach out to others; it is as though they interpret an immediate affirmative response to an overture as personal acceptance, but a delayed or nonaffirmative response as personal rejection. When others do not respond immediately and affirmatively, Fours often begin to wonder what they themselves have done wrong.

Carl's strong reaction to Bart's lack of responsiveness illuminates the Four's sensitivity to rejection; it is this area in which Fours frequently feel pinched. When Fours reach out to others, they are often simultaneously hopeful about connection and anxious about rejection. When the other person does not reciprocate in the manner desired by the Four, Fours often begin blaming themselves, as Carl did in the above story. After this initial self-recrimination, however, Fours often move to finding fault with the other person; this is fundamentally a hedge against their anticipated rejection. As this inner process of shuttling between hurt, self-deprecation, and blame continues, Fours often become both agitated and remorseful.

When Fours find fault with the behavior of others, it is common for them to interpret the other person's actions in a values-based way. Fours tend to read meaning into their interactions with others; a difference in values provides the explanation and rationale for their being deeply upset with someone else. Fours also try to act in ways that are congruent with their values and become quite agitated when they have to interact with someone whose values they deplore or when they are required to behave in ways that are inconsistent with their value systems. In the story above, Carl began to doubt Bart's integrity—for example, Bart's willingness to use a colleague's material without assigning credit.

Bart's e-mail also provoked feelings of envy in Carl. Envy refers to the feeling *others have something that I am missing*, as opposed to jealousy, which connotes *I want to take something that the other person possesses*. Envy is more of an invidious comparison of oneself to others; though often unconscious, envy is fundamental to the Four's personality. When Carl, while waiting for a reply, began to blame Bart for past transgressions, envy was an implicit subtext in his internal monologue about the high degree of respect Bart commanded in the firm. The implication was, *Why Bart, and not me?*

How Fours Behave When Pinched

May say something in a blunt way • Become extremely quiet
• Experience multiple feelings simultaneously and intensely
• Excessively analyze the situation in order to understand
• Hold on to feelings for long periods of time

When Fours feel pinched, they may either say something in a blunt way—for example, "Why did you do that?"—or they may become quiet. However, when the pinches build into a crunch, Fours often become distraught; at these times, they often become tense and intense and say very little. Fours may close out their external worlds and become submerged in the internal world of feelings. A multitude of emotions, such as distress, sadness, fear, and anger, may occur together and ricochet off one another. After the onset of strong feelings, Fours often begin an elaborate process of mental analysis, moving from one plausible interpretation of what has occurred to another. This analysis is often subjective rather than objective, and its central purpose is to offer the Four some understanding of what has taken place. At some point in this analysis, the Four's feelings will reemerge, often with greater intensity than before. After this resurgence of feelings, the analysis and development of multiple interpretations may begin again.

When a Four is deeply distressed, he or she will typically discuss these feelings and events with other people. These conversations have a threefold purpose: (1) to gain emotional support, (2) to gain the perspectives and interpretations of these other individuals, and (3) to explore additional avenues for action. Once Fours believe that they understand their own feelings and have thoroughly analyzed the situation, they may be ready to take action. Action for Fours usually entails the full expression of their feelings in an authentic and passionate way.

How to Approach a Four in a Crunch

Offer an open invitation to express his or her feelings • Listen until the Four is completely finished • Paraphrase the Four's feelings, thoughts, and meaning • Do not suggest that the Four is being overly sensitive • Be careful not to act blaming or accusing

The best approach with Fours is to allow them to express themselves fully, even in situations in which their behavior and reactions may appear unreasonable. Fours feel their emotions intensely and have a need to express them outwardly. The Four responds favorably when the other person is receptive, empathic, and honest. For example, the following conversation starters work well with Fours: "Please tell me what upset you," or "I can tell you are distressed about something, and I would really like to know what is on your mind."

On the other hand, some opening statements almost never elicit a positive response from a Four. Statements such as "You are overreacting," "You are being overly sensitive," or "I feel I have to walk on eggshells around you" will invariably pinch Fours and cause them to feel hurt, to shut down emotionally, or to become furious. The reason for these defensive reactions lies in the way in which Fours relate to their emotional lives. Fours often identify so strongly with their feelings that they can have great difficulty seeing troublesome situations from a more objective perspective. Because Fours often believe that they *are* their feelings, a criticism of a Four's feelings may be taken as a criticism of the Four as a person. In addition, Fours yearn to be understood; statements that discount their feelings make Fours feel deeply misunderstood, and as a consequence they often become angry.

However, given a genuine invitation to share their feelings, most Fours will open up, particularly if they have already sorted through their myriad of emotions and thoughts. If they have not yet done this and prefer to discuss the situation at a later date, they may say, "I am not ready to talk." Or, they may be quiet, yet their hurt and anger shows in their body language. When they are ready to talk, Fours will often initiate the discussion, because they like to reach emotional closure. If they do not broach the subject within a week of the initial overture, a simple statement such as "Are you ready to talk yet?" will usually receive a welcome response.

During the conversation, it is best to allow Fours to purge themselves of thoughts and feelings. If the Four begins to repeat things he or she has already said, this is often a clue that the Four is not sure that he or she has been understood. It can be helpful to paraphrase what the Four has just communicated, and to then ask for confirmation or disconfirmation. Paraphrasing involves stating a summary of what the Four has said, and it is most effective when it includes the Four's thoughts, feelings, and perceived meaning.

Once Fours feel heard by the other person—and paraphrasing often accomplishes this goal—they are usually ready to listen. Often, they will be open to what the other person has to say as long as they do not feel blamed or criticized. An effective way to accomplish this is to use introductory phrases such as "I know this must have felt like that to you, and my experience of the same situation was this."

It has been said that Fours may or may not forgive, but they certainly do not forget. Their memories of feelings can become lodged in their minds and bodies; consequently, while an open conversation may help them express their feelings, they may maintain their sensitivity to the issues that caused the crunch in the first place. Time, combined with a series of positive interactions, will often lessen the Four's reactivity.

How Fours Can Manage Their Own Pinches and Crunches
1. **Share your pinches with others at the beginning of your working relationship.** Because Fours like to establish a connection early in a work-

ing relationship, it can be quite easy to add the topic of pinches into these early conversations. A Four might say, "Something I find very helpful in a relationship is for both of us to be honest about what we know from past experiences that has and has not worked well. That way, we can get to know each other better and learn what to do and what not to do. I'd be happy to go first." When discussing such pinches as being slighted or feeling envious, Fours are likely to feel that this is too personal and revealing at the early stages of a working relationship. However, a Four can say, "I tend to work well with others when I feel respected and included in conversations or meetings that directly or indirectly affect my work. The other thing that means a lot to me is responsiveness. When I send an e-mail or call someone, I really appreciate a prompt response—within a day or two. I know this is not always possible, but even a quick response such as 'I am really busy and will get back to you later this week' is very helpful."

2. **Say something as soon as you are aware of feeling pinched.** When they feel pinched, Fours tend either to say nothing or to say something quite spontaneously. It is almost impossible, even for them, to predict which will be the case. Because Fours are so sensitive to pinches, it is important for them to express feeling pinched as soon as possible. However, this needs to be done in a way that does not put the other person on the spot. For example, a Four who is asked to do a task without financial compensation may say in a blunt manner, "What about me? What do I get out of this?" While this is certainly an honest response, it can be off-putting to some people. Another way to say the same thing without creating an adverse reaction might be, "Although I understand why you are asking me to do this, I feel uncomfortable about being asked to do something like this without any compensation. Can we discuss some alternatives?" To avoid giving a response that may be perceived as too aggressive, Fours can use the age-old technique of taking three deep breaths. This gives them a chance to regroup and decide what to say about the pinch. Alternatively, Fours may prefer some time away to think before they say something. This is fine, but they should not let too much time go by, lest another pinch occurs and builds upon the first one.

3. **When you start to behave in ways that indicate you are feeling pinched, do something physical if you can, such as working out or taking a walk.** Many Fours find the thought of an impending conflict to be discouraging and depressing. As a result, lethargy may set in, with Fours concentrating their attention on the reverberations of their feelings and the related mental analysis of why a particular thing has happened. Even when Fours exercise regularly, they may put this aside during moments of distress. Giving yourself the message to take care of yourself can be helpful,

with some form of physical activity included as part of this. Exercise also serves to keep the Four's feelings and thoughts moving and flowing, countering the Four's tendency to recirculate the feelings and thought patterns of the upsetting experience.

4. **When you feel a pinch, ask yourself:** *What does my reaction to this situation or to the other person's behavior say about me as a Four and about the areas in which I can develop? How can working on my pinches and crunches help me to bring out the best in myself?*

Fritz Perls, the father of Gestalt therapy, explained that depression is often caused by anger that is turned inward. Fours can benefit from this concept, because depression—from mild to severe—is a familiar feeling for most Fours. When Fours become depressed, it can be extremely helpful for them to ask themselves, *If my depression is masking my anger, what am I really mad about?* When Fours pursue this question in depth, the answers can be illuminating and enlightening. What frequently emerges are issues related to rejection, envy, and feelings of being defective in some way.

Growth for Fours does *not* come from the outside—for example, getting others to be less rejecting, reducing the immediate feeling of envy by increasing one's credentials, changing one's image, or encouraging others to treat the Four as special in some way. While these tactics may reduce a Four's anxiety momentarily, they do not support genuine long-term growth. For Fours, real growth occurs when they explore their sensitivity to rejection, understand the role that envy (continuous invidious comparison) plays in their lives, and accept that everyone is special and no one is any more defective or flawless than anyone else.

Fives: Pinches and Crunches

Enneagram Style
KNOWLEDGE

Peter's company had recently hired an accounting firm to handle the company's financial records, which had been in disarray for two years. The need for accurate record keeping and financial reporting was critical and daunting. In his role as the company's chief operating officer, Peter was responsible for defining the accounting firm's tasks, roles, and accountabilities.

Over a three-week period, Peter had spent considerable time developing a positive working relationship with the accounting firm's owner, Martha. The initial work product from the accounting firm was not acceptable. However, Peter believed that his rapport with

Martha was strong enough to enable them to resolve the work-related difficulties, which he attributed to the challenges of starting a new business relationship.

During a meeting among the senior executives of his company to discuss the problems with the new accounting firm, Peter defended both Martha and her firm and put forward the steps he planned to take to resolve the accounting problems. During a break in the meeting, one of the other executives casually asked him, "Are you really sixty-five years old?"

Startled by this question, Peter responded, "How did you hear that?"

"Martha mentioned this to me," was the reply.

Peter said, "She did what? That conversation was just between the two of us!"

After learning that Martha had disclosed this information, Peter withdrew all of his support from her and her firm. Within one month, Peter's company terminated its contract with Martha's firm and retained the services of another accounting company.

Common Five Pinches

Breaking confidences • Being surprised • Dishonesty
• Out-of-control situations • Overwhelming tasks

Peter's trust in Martha evaporated the instant his colleague reported that Martha had disclosed information about Peter's age. As is typical of most Fives, Peter carefully guarded his privacy; personal information such as his age was simply that—personal and private. Peter had shared his age with Martha during a one-to-one conversation because she had asked him this question, and he believed that sharing this information would further their rapport. When Peter learned that Martha had shared his confidence with another person, he was outraged. The fact that Peter was older than he looked and preferred not to tell others his age lest he be treated differently was only a small part of his anger. The primary issue for him, as it would be for most Fives, was the invasion of his privacy and the subsequent loss of his trust for Martha. After this event, whenever Martha's firm was discussed, Peter always brought up the issue of her having shared the information of his age with other people. As troubling as many of the accounting errors from her firm were, Peter was adamant that this violation of his privacy had been the worst offense. For him, this pinch was so serious that it bordered on being a crunch.

Peter was upset not only because his confidence had been breached, but also because Martha's indiscretion came as a surprise. If Martha had told Peter that she had shared this private information, he would have felt angry, but he would have gotten over it. However, because he learned about Martha's lapse in a semipublic situation—and from someone with whom he would not have chosen to share his age—he had been caught completely off guard. Peter was doubly troubled and feeling crunched.

Peter now perceived Martha as dishonest. While he had never explicitly asked her to not reveal the personal information he had shared with her, he had assumed that there was an implicit agreement between them that should not be violated—they would keep the content of their private conversations to themselves. Most Fives share private information with very few people and only confide in those whom they trust. Thus, when Martha revealed his age, Peter concluded, "If she doesn't respect my privacy, how can I trust her with anything?"

The pinches described in the above paragraphs would have been sufficient grounds for Peter to feel enraged. However, what made the situation even worse was the organizational context in which the events had occurred. Fives usually detest circumstances they perceive as being out of control. They also become quite tense in situations where they find the tasks to be overwhelming. The financial accounting systems of Peter's company were in a threatening state of disorder. Up until this point, Peter had trusted Martha to take charge of the situation and remedy it. His faith was based on their mutually respectful relationship and on his belief in Martha's positive intentions and her capabilities. However, when he no longer trusted Martha to do the work, he realized that he himself was now 100 percent responsible for addressing these tremendously complex issues.

How Fives Behave When Pinched

Say little • Pull back, but may not show this outwardly • Retain the experience mentally • May express anger as outrage during an intense pinch or during a crunch

When Fives feel pinched, they often say nothing to the other person, but the violation usually becomes lodged in their memories. Fives may also subtly pull back, moving away from the person who offended them. Their withdrawal may not be perceptible, however, because many Fives take a figurative or literal step back from other people under nonconflict conditions as well.

When Fives perceive a breach to be extremely serious, or when several pinches accumulate, they may either withdraw entirely or, conversely, erupt in outrage. When Fives become highly withdrawn, they will not say or do anything, and they may go so far as to avoid all contact with the other person.

This can include not attending meetings, not returning phone calls or e-mails, or arriving quite late for appointments without offering an explanation.

During this time, the exterior coolness of Fives may mask their highly active, intense, and strategic mental processing. Fives can spend hours hypothesizing about the aberrant causes of someone else's unseemly behavior and conjuring up various alternative actions in response, some of which can be quite aggressive. The Five's behavior may seem similar to the Six's preplanning and prevention method of handling anxiety-provoking situations that is described in the next story; however, when Fives engage in extensive analysis and planning, it usually occurs *after* rather than before something negative has happened. As part of this accelerated mental activity, Fives often become the judge, jury, prosecuting attorney, and victim all rolled into one. Although individuals of all nine Enneagram styles tend to believe that what they think is actually true, often without hearing alternative points of view, Fives tend to do this in a more extreme way, particularly when they become highly enraged and embittered.

A less common behavior for Fives is to erupt with rage in the presence of the person with whom they are angry. The Five may be furious, but in this case he or she is highly engaged in the situation rather than detached from it. An incensed Five who is willing to communicate his or her feelings directly can be articulate, powerful, and quite persuasive.

How to Approach Fives in a Crunch

Give advance notice that you wish to speak to the Five • Allow him or her to select the time and place for the discussion • Give the initial discussion a clear and agreed-upon time frame • Allow the Five to share his or her feelings and thoughts first • Give the Five an abundance of physical space • Maintain a rational approach to the problem • Keep your feelings low in intensity so that the Five does not feel emotionally overwhelmed

---

As noted earlier, Fives tend to keep their anger to themselves. While it might be difficult to determine when Fives are upset, it is a good idea to approach them upon observing the first signs of withdrawal or coolness. This allows them less time to hypothesize, conjecture, and draw firm conclusions; consequently, they are likely to be more open to what the other person has to say.

Try to find a private moment with the Five, inviting him or her to discuss the situation by saying something such as, "Would it be possible to meet for half an hour to discuss a few issues?" Giving Fives the choice of time and location helps them feel in control of the interaction; they also appreciate not having to discuss the issues immediately. An e-mail or voice message that requests some time with the Five can be effective, since this removes the element of surprise; many Fives feel put on the spot when a request of this sort is made in person. An e-mail or phone message prevents the Five from having to deal with the need to hide his or her initial reactions. If the first overture produces no response, one or two more requests, spread out over several days, may get the Five's attention.

While a thirty-minute meeting may sound very short to many of us, the brevity can be reassuring to a Five, who may not want to commit to an intense and lengthy emotional interaction. If the initial conversation goes well, Fives will often extend the meeting or reschedule for further discussion.

At the first meeting, encourage the Five to share what he or she believes has caused the problem. In order to draw out the Five's feelings and thoughts, consider using an indirect yet clear approach. While a direct statement such as "You seem angry and I want to know why" may work, it can also backfire and cause the Five to become even more distant. An indirect approach tends to be more effective—for example, "I was hoping you might discuss some concerns that I sense you may be having." Should the Five say that he or she has no concerns, it can be useful to give a specific example of what in the Five's behavior indicates that there is a problem. For example, a comment such as "I've noticed that you don't seem to solicit my input as often as you used to," may encourage the Five to be more forthcoming.

Once the conversation has started, listen to the Five and affirm the fact that he or she has taken the time to speak about these issues. This approach tacitly acknowledges that the Five is spending time doing something that he or she probably finds quite draining.

As noted, enraged Fives will sometimes say exactly what is on their minds. It is important for the person on the receiving end to appreciate that when Fives do this, they are either taking an enormous risk—that of being fully connected to their feelings in the present moment—or they are so infuriated that the intensity of their emotions overrides their long-practiced ability to separate from, and thereby control, their feelings. When Fives seem to be finished talking, a simple request such as "Please tell me more so I can fully understand" often encourages them to share even more.

Whether they are withdrawn or forthcoming, Fives strongly prefer ample physical space between themselves and others, and particularly so when the conversation is about conflict. Every culture has its own definition of the personal space that people are expected to maintain when engaged in interpersonal interaction. In the United States, the appropriate and expected physical space between people is twelve to eighteen inches. For Fives, however, comfortable physical space is between eighteen and twenty-four inches under normal circumstances. Under duress, Fives prefer twenty-four to thirty-six inches of physical distance. Similarly, most Fives dislike unsolicited physical contact, and they usually detest it when they are feeling upset.

After Fives have expressed themselves, they will often be open to hearing another point of view. A rational presentation of events, interwoven with the expression of feelings that are not communicated too intensely, usually works well. At the end of the conversation, it is helpful to end with a mutually agreed-upon solution. Fives usually appreciate a defined resolution that is practical, concrete, and mutually negotiated. Such a resolution also gives them some assurance that they will not have to go through this emotional turmoil yet again.

How Fives Can Manage Their Own Pinches and Crunches

1. **Share your pinches with others at the beginning of your working relationship.** This type of self-disclosure early on in a working relationship can be a stretch for many Fives, but it also has many benefits. The level of disclosure can be as simple as "Let's talk about how we work best with others so that our relationship begins on a productive note. There are only a few things that are very important. I like work to be well-managed and under control, and I dislike surprises. By 'surprises' I mean things like unnecessary, last-minute requests, as well as demands that I work beyond certain hours when I have already made other plans. I also don't like to be surprised by information that you may know that can help me understand the organization or the project better. I like to work with others when we keep each other informed."

2. **Say something as soon as you are aware of feeling pinched.** This is actually a great way to minimize surprises for both you and the other person. In the initial conversation to discuss working styles, simply suggest that you both agree to discuss any pinches that may occur as you work together. A simple statement such as "Let's agree to discuss any pinches or glitches as they occur so that we can continue to have a productive work relationship" will almost always be well received by the other person. With this agreement in mind, make a commitment to take the initiative and share any concern, even a small one, soon after it arises. This is not an intrusion on the other person, because he or she has already agreed to this plan. The biggest issue is for Fives to actually say something, since this means they will need to acknowledge that something has disturbed them and stay connected to their feelings, as well as assert themselves and approach the other person.

3. **When you start to behave in ways that indicate you are feeling pinched, do something physical if you can, such as working out or taking a walk.** In disconnecting from their feelings and disengaging from other people, Fives use different techniques. For example, some Fives stop breathing deeply and begin to breathe only as far as their necks. Other Fives simply focus all their attention on their minds and engage in a flurry of thought. Still others may compartmentalize a distressing event by placing it in their minds as a categorized mental idea. (Compartmentalization is described in more detail in Chapter 1, "Discovering Your Enneagram Style.") Whichever process Fives use to disconnect and disengage, their choice of technique invariably puts them less in touch with their bodies and their feelings. Physical activity of any type usually reestablishes the connection between mind and body; it often reconnects Fives with their feelings as well, because feelings correspond to sensations located in the body.

4. **When you feel a pinch, ask yourself:** *What does my reaction to this situation or to the other person's behavior say about me as a Five and about the areas in which I can develop? How can working on my pinches and crunches help me to bring out the best in myself?*

   Because most Fives crave knowledge and understanding, pursuing this type of self-discovery often suits them very well. The crucial consideration is to answer this question in both an emotional and objective way. The emotional aspect involves the exploration of feelings and the treatment of these as equal in importance to thoughts. To answer the question objectively, Fives must take stock of themselves, not only from their own perspective, but from the perspectives of others as well. A helpful question to ask is this: *I understand my reaction as a Five in this way, but how would individuals from the other eight styles perceive it? What can I learn from these alternative points of view?* Very often, the self-discovery leads Fives to understand the ways in which they disconnect from their emotional lives and disengage both from other people and from experiences.

Sixes: Pinches and Crunches

Enneagram Style
6
DOUBT

Sheldon, a Six, waited a week before finally returning the phone calls he had received from a coworker, Barry. Sheldon worked in a division located five hundred miles from the corporate headquarters where Barry worked. Over the past year, the two had been working together on several common projects. Barry had left three separate messages for Sheldon over a week's time simply to ask whether Sheldon planned to attend an important meeting for one of their joint projects. This meeting was scheduled at the corporate headquarters for the following week.

When Sheldon finally called, he felt highly agitated and acted in an accusatory manner. He began by saying, "Stop putting so much pressure on me! I haven't decided to attend this meeting. I don't want to have a fight with you, and you seem to want to provoke one with me."

Barry, who was dumbfounded, replied, "Sheldon, I just wanted to know whether you were planning to attend the meeting so I could make the appropriate arrangements for you. Why are you so agitated?"

Common Six Pinches

Pressure • Lack of genuineness • Lack of commitment • Abusive authority

---

Sheldon's strong reaction on the telephone stunned Barry. However, Barry had unwittingly agitated Sheldon multiple times. First, Sheldon was under a great deal of pressure at work, but Barry was not aware of this. Several issues had been weighing on Sheldon's mind about the meeting: (1) how he would get the pile of work on his desk completed before the meeting; (2) how he could afford the trip, given that he was already over budget; and (3) what would happen if he caught the flu and was too sick to make the trip. For all of these reasons, Sheldon worried about whether he could make the trip, and he had not yet made the decision of whether to go. From Sheldon's perspective, Barry's phone calls felt like pressure.

In the three messages that Barry had left for Sheldon, he had not mentioned anything work-related about the upcoming meeting, nor had he touched on anything about Sheldon's well-being—for example, a statement such as "I hope you are doing well." Sheldon interpreted the absence of such remarks as an indication that Barry was not committed to either their working relationship or their work-based friendship.

Finally, Sheldon felt suspicious of Barry's motives. During the previous project meeting, Barry had exerted more informal influence in the group than Sheldon had. Because of this, Sheldon suspected that Barry planned to take an increasingly larger leadership role in this project. A shift of this sort was something they had never discussed. Consequently, Sheldon began to worry that Barry was being disingenuous in their relationship—in a sense, that Barry was using their mutual work as a platform for increasing his own power.

Sixes are often highly sensitive to legitimate (that is, formal) versus illegitimate authority, as well as to the possible misuse of power by authority figures. This concern arises from the Sixes' fear of the injury that might be done to them or others by those who could potentially use power in an unfair or abusive manner.

In this story, Sheldon's pinches surfaced not because of anything that Barry did directly, but rather because of what Sheldon thought Barry had done. As one pinch began to build on another, they transformed into a crunch, as Barry found out only when Sheldon finally returned his phone call.

How Sixes Behave When Pinched

May withdraw • Engage in intensive analysis • May be highly reactive • Conjecture and project

Initially, most Sixes withdraw from the relationship for a period of time. Because their fears become ignited and their imaginations take hold when they become incensed, they often analyze and reanalyze situations in order to gain clarity and to determine alternative courses of action. This extensive analysis, combined with worry and self-doubt, often leads to procrastination and, ultimately, to delayed action or no action whatsoever. Sheldon put off contacting Barry as long as he possibly could. He was worried about calling and worried about not calling. He was anxious about going to the meeting and anxious about not going to the meeting. However, he felt obliged to make some contact with Barry before the meeting; not showing up without some explanation was *not* an option.

After extensive worry and analysis, Sixes may conclude that the other person has a threatening motive. Sixes may also conclude that they themselves are either not capable or not powerful enough to remedy the situation. When they draw either or both of the above conclusions, Sixes may never approach the other person. This does not mean, however, that the Six no longer thinks about the conflict. On the contrary, the issues are likely to remain in the Six's mind for a long time.

On the other hand, some Sixes may say something immediately when they feel angry, and they are most likely to do so when the other person is directly in front of them. Sixes usually react strongly and quickly, but they often keep this to themselves. However, when the other person is physically present, Sixes may spontaneously say something sharp and piercing. Because Sixes are often intuitive and insightful, their comments often strike right at the core of an issue. However, because Sixes are prone to projection, they may attribute to the other person what may actually be the product of their own thoughts, feelings, or behaviors. Thus, comments made by Sixes may also miss the mark entirely.

How to Approach Sixes in a Crunch

Give them space when they withdraw • Allow them to share completely • Validate their right to their perspective • Be warm and genuine • Rebuild trust

When Sixes feel agitated, indignant, or outraged, the best tactic is to approach them in a way that does not make them feel pressured. When under duress, Sixes often pressure themselves to such an extreme that even a simple request to discuss an issue may feel like a demand to them. Combining their own heavy self-pressure with the slight pressure from the other person, Sixes imagine that all of the pressure they feel is coming from the outside. This is actually an example of projection on the part of the Six.

When Sixes withdraw to analyze and process their feelings and thoughts, it can be helpful to give them all the time they need before having a conversation with them about the issue. A simple acknowledgment that you know the Six is distressed may be appreciated—for example, "I sense that something has been concerning you, and I'd be glad to discuss it with you if and when you are ready." However, a very upset Six may perceive even this overture as a threat.

When Sixes do feel ready to discuss an issue, let them fully explain their thoughts, feelings, and overall reasoning. This can require some self-restraint on the part of the listener, particularly if what the Six shares primarily involves his or her projections. Such projections can come across as accusations, and because the Six has spent time alone agonizing and elaborating on these ideas, he or she may fully believe them to be accurate representations of reality. Sixes in particular do not respond well to being told, "You are making that up" or "It didn't happen that way." It is far better to say something such as "It really helps me to understand this from your perspective" or "If I saw it that way, I would have the same reactions you're having." Using this approach allows you to validate the Six's perceptions without overtly agreeing with his or her conclusions.

When sharing your perspective with the Six, it is best to do so with genuine sincerity and warmth. Trust typically degenerates during intense conflict with anyone, but this is especially true for the Six, for whom the issue of trust/distrust is a personality cornerstone. Sixes will be listening not only to what the other person has to say, but also to sense whether trust can be regained with this person. Warmth, honesty, and forthrightness therefore go a long way in discussions with Sixes. In being honest, however, it is essential to be truthful without either accusing Sixes of wrongdoing or making them anxious that some harm will come to them as a by-product of the discussion.

How Sixes Can Manage Their Own Pinches and Crunches

1. **Share your pinches with others at the beginning of your working relationship.** This is simply a good, practical suggestion, and most Sixes recognize a good idea when they hear it. Sit down with the new person with whom you are working and talk about work in a casual manner. Toward the end of the discussion, raise the issue of mutual expectations by saying something like, "Let's talk about our mutual expectations so we can get this working relationship off to an excellent start." The discussion can cover goals, roles, accountabilities, and so forth. After discussing these topics, the idea of pinches can be introduced in the following way: "I've learned that if people discuss working issues that bother or pinch them, it can be really helpful in preventing misunderstandings. Perhaps we can share some of our pinches from other working relationships so we can understand what will work well for us here." When the time comes to share pinches, Sixes can share that they don't respond well to pressure from others (i.e., numerous phone calls to check progress) because they usually have excellent memories. Sixes can add that because they put pressure on themselves to follow through, pressure from others feels doubly stressful.

2. **Say something as soon as you are aware of feeling pinched.** Once you have both agreed to share pinches when they occur, there is little need to worry when either you or the other person initiates a conversation about a pinch. Keep in mind that the pinch will likely be a low-level frustration that can be easily remedied. Sixes can also gain some reassurance that the sharing of pinches as they occur, along with the subsequent productive conversation, builds mutual rapport, loyalty, and teamwork.

3. **When you start to behave in ways that indicate you are feeling pinched, do something physical if you can, such as working out or taking a walk.** Walking and other sorts of physical activity help Sixes to soothe their concerns and calm their active minds. In a pinch, and especially in a crunch, physical exertion serves to get the Sixes back into their bodies and away from being overly focused on thoughts and emotions. There is often a sense of relaxation and freedom that comes from physical exercise, particularly outdoor activities. When more relaxed, Sixes can often conceive of new ways to perceive and handle potentially difficult situations.

4. **When you feel a pinch, answer this question for yourself:** *What does my reaction to this situation or to the other person's behavior say about me as a Six and the areas in which I can develop? How can working on my pinches and crunches help me to bring out the best in myself?*

   Like Fives, most Sixes seek to understand themselves in most areas of their lives. For Sixes, however, the caution in answering the above question is to refrain from overanalyzing themselves and to work, instead, on simply observing their inner processes and reactions. One instructive way for them to do this is to pay special attention to both the content of their reactions and the process they go through during these times. For example, a pinched Six may focus on events that have the following underlying content: loyalty, trustworthiness, dependability, authority, or other factors. In taking note of the process by which they think about these issues, Sixes may realize, for example, that each time they replay an event, their emotions accelerate or that once their emotions become activated, they remember numerous past events that created the same feelings in them, thus agitating and heightening their feelings even more.

To take this a step further, it can be helpful for Sixes to consider what sets off their anticipation of and planning for worst-case scenarios. All repetitive behavior serves a purpose, although the exact purpose may not be obvious at first. Sixes can ask themselves these types of questions: *What function does envisioning worst-case scenarios really play in my life? What is the underlying purpose of my tendency to project onto others? What makes loyalty so important to me, and what does being loyal help me avoid feeling or having to deal with? Although I focus on trusting others, what would I learn if I focused more on trusting myself?*

Sevens: Pinches and Crunches

As she sat through the daylong meeting, Samantha said very little. She made an effort to appear interested and engaged, but ever since the first fifteen minutes, she had wondered if she could maintain this facade all day long. She thought, *Here are seven doctors, but nothing is happening. We're making no progress in developing new clients, and we keep repeating the same conversations with no resolution.* The few times she decided to make a comment, it seemed to her that none of the others responded affirmatively to her ideas, either by saying that they agreed or by building upon the suggestions she offered.

Enneagram Style **7**
OPTIONS

The other people in the room had noticed that Samantha was more subdued than usual, but they attributed this to fatigue or illness. During the afternoon break, several people asked her informally, "Are you okay? You haven't said very much today."

Samantha gave each of them the same answer: "Yes, I'm just fine."

Common Seven Pinches

Boring and mundane tasks • Feeling dismissed or not taken seriously
• Unjust criticism

Samantha, of course, was not "just fine." In fact, she was so furious that she was ready to resign from the month-old medical practice group. Samantha felt bored and very frustrated during the meeting; from her point of view, it was an endless repetition of conversations that had already taken place informally among some of the individual physicians. She saw no need to watch a rerun of an old movie.

After the meeting, she discussed her frustration with one of the other doctors. He explained that the meeting had been designed to make sure that every physician knew all the information so that there would be a common understanding within the entire group. Samantha refuted his point with the following statement: "So why take up my valuable time doing this when several of us, myself included, already know it?" Sevens often get frustrated and impatient with tasks they perceive to be mundane or repetitive. In fact, Samantha felt pleased with herself for having stayed through the whole meeting and not having created an excuse to leave early.

Samantha had also felt angered by the fact that no one had responded positively to the few suggestions she did make during the meeting. No one had said, "That's a great idea," "Yes, we could do that in this way," or "That idea makes me think of this idea." Instead, the discussion seemed to continually revert back to a slow, monotonous conversation about how they should all work together.

Further, Samantha had felt depleted by the low energy level in the room. She was usually able to add vitality and energy to the groups in which she participated; however, in this situation, she felt that all of her attempts were thwarted. Samantha was disgusted and distraught that no one had affirmed her ideas. When Sevens feel dismissed or not taken seriously, they often become hurt, then outraged. These accumulating pinches, combined with the fact that Samantha felt compelled to stay in a meeting she intensely disliked, led to her feeling crunched.

Finally, Samantha felt pushed over the edge when she was asked during the break why she was being so quiet during the meeting. Rather than interpreting this question as earnest concern about her well-being, she took it as a criticism of her behavior; what she heard was "Why aren't you contributing more?" At that point, she erupted.

How Sevens Behave When Pinched

Avoid the situation by thinking of pleasurable alternatives
• Rationalize their own behavior • Blame or condemn others

When Sevens become angry, they often react quickly. Although Samantha chose to say nothing as she sat and fumed during the meeting, her silence in itself indicated to others that something was awry. When angry Sevens are silent, their inner dialogue is usually not. Their minds may swirl, with one thought leading to another; one interpretation of events leads to another hypothesis about why something has just occurred; and one plan of potential counterattack leads to other possible strategies.

Sevens typically avoid painful situations. Consequently, when they are distressed they often react by thinking about something positive and interesting—for example, new and fascinating ideas, where they will go on their next vacation, or whom they need to call to close a new business deal.

However, when Sevens feel agitated to the point of outrage and alarm, instead of thinking about pleasurable and stimulating ideas, they tend to move to defensive and counteroffensive strategizing. Because the Seven has an agile and facile mind, once this process begins it often moves at a fast and furious pace. Sevens analyze the situation, draw conclusions about the events and individuals involved, create a plan of action, and ready themselves to execute the strategy.

Although Samantha initially tried to distract herself with her own thoughts and plans, she eventually became bored. She began to wonder how the other doctors could stand being part of this horribly dull conversation. She conjectured that their attentiveness was attributable to the fact that they were less experienced and savvy than she was. In reality, some of the other physicians had far more experience than Samantha did. Her inner process—namely, developing an explanation for why her response was the appropriate one and someone else's reaction was flawed—illustrates the tendency of Sevens to rationalize their own behavior when they feel anxious.

During the course of the meeting, Samantha's reactions became increasingly more negative. As she began to feel personally dismissed and discounted by the group, she began thinking, *What an unimaginative group! They certainly can't be very good doctors if this is all they can talk about! Not even one creative or intelligent idea has come out of their mouths!* When Sevens become increasingly agitated and rationalization no longer works to reduce their anxiety, it is quite common for them to become highly critical and blaming of others.

Once Samantha felt unjustly criticized for her nonparticipation, her criticisms turned into condemnations. She began to wonder whether some of the doctors had ulterior motives—for example, a desire to gain access to her client list. To Samantha, these colleagues were obviously not forthright individuals whom she could trust. Soon after this meeting, she severed her relationship with the group.

How to Approach Sevens in a Crunch

Make the initial overtures for conversations nonintrusive • Ask nonjudgmental, open-ended questions • Allow the Seven to fully express himself or herself • Draw out the Seven's line of reasoning • Communicate your understanding of the Seven's feelings • Validate the Seven's experience • Be sincere, direct, and nonaccusatory

When a Seven feels enraged, it can be very difficult to get him or her to discuss an issue of concern. A low-key, nonconfrontational approach may work, such as "What did you think about the meeting" or "How did you like the meeting?" If the Seven responds by saying, "Everything was fine," this may sound like *End of conversation; ask no more!* However, a personal statement from the other person may actually encourage the Seven to talk—for example, "I thought we spent too much time on some of the topics."

As Sevens begin to open up and share their interpretation of the situation, the best approach to use is a series of nonjudgmental, open-ended questions that draw out the Seven's line of reasoning. For example, once a Seven begins explaining his or her thoughts, many of which may be rationalizations, it can be helpful to ask, "Can you help me understand this more?" After Sevens have shared their thinking, they are often open to the other person's ideas, as long as these are presented in a way that does not come across as a counterargument. It can be effective to say something such as "That's very interesting. I was thinking about it in a different way."

When Sevens have reached the point of blame and condemnation, dissuading them from their perceptions and conclusions requires skill and perseverance. The best tactic is to acknowledge the Seven's apparent anger and make a genuine request that the person share what is on his or her mind. For example, you might make an overture such as this: "I can see how angry you are, but I don't fully understand the cause. Our relationship matters enough to me to urge you to please take some time for a discussion." As noted above, once Sevens begin to speak their minds, it is essential to let them fully express themselves. Once that has occurred, the next step is to communicate to them that you understand the intensity and importance of their thoughts and feelings. Statements such as "This must have caused you tremendous distress" or "I can understand how angry and frustrated you have been" will often open them up to say more; it also helps Sevens to be more receptive to what you will say later in the conversation.

If you disagree with an accusation or interpretation from the Seven, it can be helpful to add a comment such as "Because you've experienced this incident in the way you have, it's perfectly understandable that you would draw this conclusion." A sincere, direct, and validating approach to dealing with the emotional side of the Seven's distress can be very helpful later, when you both work toward a resolution of your differences.

How Sevens Can Manage Their Own Pinches and Crunches

1. **Share your pinches with others at the beginning of your working relationship.** All this requires from Sevens is taking the time to do this step, and making sure that they communicate their pinches in some detail. Although it may feel like a waste of time to go through mutual expectations before conflict has occurred, it doesn't take much time and is well worth the effort. It also provides an opportunity to get to know the other person better.

   When you discuss your pinches, make sure you are highly explicit. Sevens often talk quickly and may leave out certain details that seem obvious; consequently, slowing down the pace of discussion can be helpful to the other person. It is safest to assume that nothing is obvious. In a new work relationship, even the obvious is worth stating clearly.

   The other caveat for Sevens during this initial conversation is to listen thoroughly to the other person and then ask for clarification of what has been said. Because their minds move so quickly, Sevens may not always fully understand what the other person means, even if they believe that they do. For instance, if the other person mentions that timeliness is one of his or her pinches, the Seven can ask, "Can you give me some examples of what you mean by timeliness?"

2. **Say something as soon as you are aware of feeling pinched.** Because Sevens often avoid situations and conversations that are either uncomfortable or possibly painful, they may avoid saying anything about feeling pinched. This avoidance may even be unconscious; Sevens may simply start thinking about something that interests them and not even be aware of feeling pinched. The first step for Sevens is to acknowledge that they are feeling upset; Sevens can usually do this if they pay closer attention to themselves. Another technique for Sevens is to try to notice when their

minds switch from topic to topic and to say to themselves, *I just changed mental gears. Am I feeling pinched or uncomfortable about something?* Once Sevens realize that something is distressing them, they need to make a commitment to say something to the other person. It sometimes helps Sevens to do this when they realize that even if the discussion may be uncomfortable, the conversation will usually be far more difficult if they wait until more pinches have built up.

3. **When you start to behave in ways that indicate you are feeling pinched, do something physical if you can, such as working out or taking a walk.** Physical activity helps release some of the anxiety and built-up energy that Sevens often experience when they feel pinched. The Seven's mental activity often increases during times of distress; physical activity helps Sevens focus more on their bodies, and therefore often slows down their thought processes and helps them to clear their minds. After doing something physical, it particularly helps Sevens to stop, be still, and focus on their feelings and reactions for an extended period of time. The following question can also be helpful: *What did the person actually do that caused the pinch, as opposed to my interpretation about what he or she did?*

4. **When you feel a pinch, ask yourself:** *What does my reaction to this situation or to the other person's behavior say about me as a Seven and about the areas in which I can develop? How can working on my pinches and crunches help me to bring out the best in myself?*

   Sevens can benefit by asking themselves the above question over and over again. The reason for this is that Sevens may start to answer the question but then do one of two things: (1) stop seeking answers after their first response because their first answer may be insightful or interesting to them, or (2) begin by thinking about themselves but then drift into thinking about what the other person did and should have done, and what might be wrong with that individual. Sometimes the first answer is the best answer; however, more often than not, continued self-questioning peels back the layers of the onion, and subsequent answers often produce deeper personal insight. Sevens also need to focus on their own issues rather than unconsciously derailing their own self-development by focusing primarily on the other person's perceived actions.

   Learning to focus is fundamental to the development of Sevens. When Sevens become aware that they are having difficulty staying focused on one idea, task, person, or feeling, it is very helpful to ask, *What am I feeling right now? Am I feeling anxious, angry, or sad? What is the real source of these feelings?* Determining the answers to such questions can profoundly affect and transform a Seven.

Eights: Pinches and Crunches

Eileen, an Eight, had had a long-standing feud with Shannon, though the two had never discussed it together. Both,
however, had given their versions of the story to numerous
other people. Five years earlier, Shannon had applied to be a
partner at the consulting firm in which Eileen was already a
partner. Shannon was told by her secretary that Eileen had
conducted an informal reference check on Shannon's performance by making a confidential call to someone she knew at
Shannon's current firm.

Enneagram Style
CHALLENGE (8)

Within consulting firms, revealing who is applying for jobs is considered a
professional transgression, because it creates the threat that the departing consultant might take his or her clients to the new firm. The interviewing consultant may not receive new firm clients and may also experience some ostracism.

Within one day of Shannon's interview, everyone at her current firm knew
that she was interviewing with other firms. Shannon was furious. On the basis
of this incident, she withdrew her name from consideration at Eileen's firm, and
she made it clear exactly why she was no longer interested in being hired there.

This story, however, is about Eileen's reaction to the event. For her part,
Eileen was also deeply angry. Five years after this incident, Eileen and Shannon involuntarily became partners in the same department at another consulting firm as the result of a large merger.

Common Eight Pinches

Injustice • Not dealing directly with the issues • People not taking
responsibility for their own behavior • Being blindsided • Another's
lack of truthfulness

It might be easy to assume that Eileen was angry because a confidential phone
call she made had become public knowledge. According to Eileen, however,
she never made the phone call. Taking into consideration this new information, it is plausible to assume that Eileen's anger was the result of her having
been falsely accused of unprofessional behavior. The truth, however, is that
while Eileen was seriously concerned about the false accusation, she was also
deeply troubled by several other factors.

Eileen learned of the nonexistent phone call from a few people in her firm
who, in turn, had heard it through the firm's gossip mill. Eileen's boss had also
not said anything to her, although he was the person whom Shannon had tele-

phoned when she cancelled her interview process. Shannon had not contacted Eileen to indicate how angry she was or to challenge Eileen's behavior. Eileen formally heard about the incident from her consulting firm's managing partner. During their conversation, he condemned what he believed was Eileen's behavior. Eileen was furious that no one with organizational authority had had the nerve or integrity to come to her directly and find out her side of the story. She was not merely pinched; she was in a crunch.

Eileen was also outraged that others did not seem to be taking responsibility for their own behavior. She knew that someone had leaked something, but that it certainly had not been her. She wondered, *Did the person I supposedly called hear about Shannon's interview from another source but blamed it on me? Did this individual want to undermine Shannon or me for some reason? Had Shannon mentioned to someone else that she was interviewing with other firms and then attributed the revelation of this information to me?* To Eileen's thinking, the real culprit was silently allowing her to take the blame.

Eileen also felt completely blindsided by this event. She found out that most of her partners had known about it days before she did yet had kept quiet about the situation. Eileen felt deeply hurt and angry that her coworkers appeared to choose either their loyalty to the firm or their fear of organizational censure over their friendship with her. Eights dislike surprises and like situations to be under control, and they count on the loyalty of those they trust. Eileen felt vulnerable and deeply alone.

In addition, Eileen was distraught that the truth could not be brought to light. The incident had occurred between people in two different organizations, and resolving this situation thus appeared daunting and fruitless. Eileen believed that she had no avenues through which to clarify what had really happened.

How Eights Behave When Pinched

Feel surges of anger that propel them to action • Sift and sort information and feelings quickly • Avoid feeling vulnerable or out of control, if possible • May withdraw entirely • Seek the counsel of individuals they trust and respect • Dismiss and discount those for whom they lack respect

When Eights become provoked, they typically react viscerally and instantly. The physical sensation is far more than a twinge or knot in the stomach; it is a deep surge of anger that starts in the belly, rises upward, intensifies, and seeks to be expressed externally—through actions, words, or both. Eileen was stupefied when she learned about what she had supposedly done, and she was further stunned by the events and accusations that followed. By the time she had sifted through and sorted out the chain of events, she was outraged, and her anger was rising.

Eileen wanted to walk into her boss's office, the head of her practice group, to tell him exactly how she felt about these false accusations. However, before she could do this, the managing partner charged into her office. It was immediately clear to Eileen that he was not fact-finding; rather, he was there to reprimand her and seemed to be trying to intimidate her. Eileen no longer had questions about why neither her boss nor the managing partner had come to her as soon as they heard about the event; they had assumed that she was guilty. Eileen felt boxed in, with no avenues of remedy in sight.

Most people like to feel that they are in control, particularly in stressful situations; however, for Eights, feeling in control of situations is fundamental to their personality structure. In this situation, Eileen felt distraught, extremely vulnerable, and powerless. Because Eights commonly avoid showing their weakness and vulnerability to others, especially when they are under extreme duress, they will often retreat. They may withdraw by minimizing their conversations with others, throwing themselves into work, closing their doors, or finding excuses not to be in the office. Eileen behaved in all of these ways.

She did, however, discuss her rage, disbelief, and anxiety with the few people in her firm whom she still trusted. During these conversations, she would replay the events as she knew them, discuss her hurt and anger, and ask for their reactions. Indirectly, she was seeking suggestions about possible alternative courses of action. Most often, Eights keep their own counsel. However, when they are uncertain about what course to pursue or do not perceive any viable alternatives, they will seek the advice of individuals whom they both trust and respect. The individuals in whom she confided tried their best to offer her support and advice, but they, too, were at a loss for viable avenues for Eileen to pursue.

She did not, of course, trust or respect her direct boss, the managing partner, Shannon, or the friend she was said to have called at Shannon's firm to gather information. These relationships were, in her mind, beyond the point of no return. In fact, she proceeded to summarily discount and dismiss all four individuals to everyone with whom she talked.

How to Approach Eights During a Crunch

Be direct • Be honest • Listen to the intensity of the Eight's feelings
• Do not act weak or uncertain • Avoid language that the Eight
might perceive as blaming of him or her

None of Eileen's antagonists—her direct boss, the managing partner, Shannon, or the friend she had purportedly called—approached her to discuss this situation. Even if they had, however, Eileen would have been highly unlikely to respond affirmatively to any of them. Because she never would have agreed to meet with them voluntarily, they would have had to go to her office without an appointment and be prepared for one of the following reactions: a chilly silence, a demand that the person leave immediately, or an intense blast of direct and honest feeling. When Eights become very angry, they often feel a fury that even they prefer not to express directly to the object of their rage.

Had anyone in the firm other than her closest confidants or her antagonists approached Eileen while she was so angry, it is hard to say how she might have reacted. It is possible that she would have been very remote and withdrawn. If she were feeling particularly distraught and frustrated, Eileen might have used the other person as a sounding board. Eileen, however, never had to deal with this situation, because no one other than her closest work friends ever initiated any conversations with her. Most of her coworkers avoided her, fearing any residual negativity that might come their way should upper management perceive them to be aligned with her.

Both Eileen's direct boss and the firm's managing partner missed an opportunity to keep this painful conflict from escalating. All they would have had to do was come to Eileen immediately after they heard about the event, tell her what they had been told, and listen with an open mind to her side of the story.

In approaching Eileen, they would have been well advised to keep four guidelines in mind—be direct, be honest, listen to her rage, and not act weak or uncertain. Because Eights are usually direct and honest themselves, this is what they expect from others. In this hypothetical conversation, the managing partner or her boss could have responded to Eileen's side of the story with a straightforward comment and question—for example, "You must be really angry! Can you even talk about it now?"

If Eileen had wanted to discuss the issue, the other person would have needed to devote 100 percent of his or her attention to what Eileen was saying and then be completely honest in return. When Eights are under duress, they are even more sensitive to forthrightness and truthfulness; it is as if they have antennae that can instinctually sense the other person's honesty and integrity. For example, if Eileen had asked a question during the conversation—for example, "Do you think I did this?"—the only way for the conversation to have continued would have been for the other person to be completely honest. The only response acceptable to Eileen would have been the truth, even if the answer to her question was "Yes" or "I don't know." Although either of these responses would likely have angered Eileen, at least she would have respected the individual for being truthful.

Once Eights begin to express their rage freely, it is best not to interrupt them until they have unleashed their full fury. This enables Eights to release the anger from their bodies. Not only does this usually make them feel better, but they are also then far more likely to listen to an explanation, to consider another point of view, and to strategize about what to do next.

When the managing partner discussed the incident with Eileen, he did not do so with an open mind. Eileen's boss never talked with her about the situation, although she never knew why. In some way, both of these individuals may have been intimidated by Eileen's forceful personality and the likelihood that she would react to these charges with outrage. If she intimidated them in any palpable way, their discussions with her may not have worked anyway. In approaching Eights, it is essential to not act weak or uncertain in their presence. Eights do not respect individuals whom they perceive to be easily intimidated, lacking in courage, or fragile, and they will often act derisively toward them.

Although Eights are often thought of as enjoying conflict, it is more the case that they appreciate truth-telling, become energized by genuine engagement between people, and feel better when they release their pent-up anger. However, they may feel guilty afterward about having expressed their rage so fully.

The situation is different when the conflict is directed toward the Eight, particularly if he or she feels falsely accused, lacking in power, or especially vulnerable. Under such circumstances, Eights have a much more difficult time expressing their feelings and thoughts. In this situation, Eileen felt all of the above and truly needed support from others in the firm, particularly her boss and the managing partner. Had they listened to her side of the story, either of these two individuals could have convened a meeting of all involved parties in order to discuss the events.

Even if it were not possible for them to get all of those involved to attend such a meeting, Eileen would still have felt markedly better. She would have thought, *At least someone has the nerve and the sense of justice to try to bring the truth to light.* Such a meeting would obviously have been an awkward situation, but the issues would have come out in the open, the parties could have confronted one another, and perhaps someone would even have stepped forward and admitted what he or she had done.

How Eights Can Manage Their Own Pinches and Crunches

1. **Share your pinches with others at the beginning of your working relationship.** Once Eights understand the value of discussing pinches early on in a work relationship, it becomes quite easy for them to start such a conversation in a natural and direct way. They may say something like,

"Let's talk about what we know bugs us when we work with others" or "We all have things we know can annoy us when we work with others, and these are mine!"

One aspect to consider is how to explain the pinches. Many Eight pinches have a moral tone to them—injustice, lack of directness, lack of truthfulness, and failure to take responsibility. When these are shared with someone else in the context of a new working relationship, however, giving examples and specifics will often be more useful than stating only the value or moral issue itself. The reason for this is that people may agree with a value but have a very different understanding of what it means or what it looks like in action. There are many kinds of injustice, for example, and one person's sense of justice may be the opposite of another's. It is therefore important for Eights to take time to discuss both their pinches and the other person's in some depth.

2. **Say something as soon as you are aware of feeling pinched.** Eights need to remind themselves to do this, and to not discount little pinches as unworthy of mentioning. No pinch is too small to share; further, sharing even small pinches has the secondary effect of helping both parties learn how to have productive conversations about their concerns. This early positive experience increases the likelihood of positive outcomes when future, and possibly more severe, pinches occur. The skills have been developed, the process for having the conversation is clear, and both parties are more likely to anticipate a constructive outcome.

   In addition, it is very important that Eights not let their displeasure build up. The force that often comes with the sharing of accumulated, unexpressed pinches can overwhelm the other person under normal circumstances. When this built-up anger or frustration combines with the typical power and intensity of most Eights, the other person can be doubly overwhelmed.

3. **When you start to behave in ways that indicate you are feeling pinched, do something physical if you can, such as working out or taking a walk.** Physical activity provides an excellent way to release some of the pent-up and rising anger that many Eights experience. Aerobic activities in particular keep the juices flowing and provide constructive outlets for the excess energy that Eights often feel. In addition, when Eights feel deeply angry and frustrated, they can become sedentary and lethargic. Exercise gets Eights up and about.

4. **When you feel a pinch, ask yourself:** *What does my reaction to this situation or to the other person's behavior say about me as an Eight and about the areas in which I can develop? How can working on my pinches and crunches help me to bring out the best in myself?*

A long, hard look at this question always gives a tremendous amount of useful information to Eights, many of whom truly want to understand themselves better. The answers almost invariably lead Eights to the territory that is most uncomfortable for them—their deep, often hidden vulnerability. Issues such as the need to control, the insistence on justice, and the desire to tackle the largest challenges and move things forward in significant ways almost always lead to this underlying issue.

In addition, the issue of intimidation is an important one for Eights to think about. Most Eights do not understand why others are often intimidated by them and do not believe that they intimidate others (at least, not consciously). It can be helpful to ask some people whom you respect why they think others might be intimidated by you, and then to ask them this: "Are you, in any way, intimidated by me?" The answers to these questions may be surprising and illuminating. Next, ask yourself this question: *Do I ever consciously try to intimidate anyone else?* For example, as you think about nonwork situations when you interact with strangers (at the gas station, grocery store, and so on), do you ever raise your voice, step forward, or engage in other assertive behaviors when you are displeased? At work, do you assert your opinions over opposing points of view—for example, speaking without waiting for the other person to finish his or her thoughts—in an attempt to have your will prevail? Try to be completely honest in answering these questions.

Nines: Pinches and Crunches

Norma had been the manager of a large office-building complex for ten years, and she truly enjoyed her job. Her responsibilities included making certain that all of the office systems—electricity, heat, and so on—were functioning properly. She also became involved in interviewing prospective tenants, planning the logistics of leasing the office space,

Enneagram Style (9)
HARMONY

as well as many other such administrative matters. Although she did not like having to be available twenty-four hours a day in case of an emergency, evening or weekend interruptions were infrequent and usually involved a lost key or a false alarm related to security. Norma enjoyed the predictability of her job and the opportunity to interact with interesting people.

One Sunday morning, the security guards from the office called Norma to tell her that a large, old tree had fallen in front of the building. No one had been injured, but the giant tree had fallen directly in front of the office's main doors. In the security guard's estimation, this created a logistical and dangerous problem because tenants would not be able to enter the building safely on Monday morning.

Once Norma had driven to the building and surveyed the situation, she realized she must take immediate action. Because she had never encountered this type of problem before, she did not know whom to contact for assistance. After making several telephone calls to get referrals for companies that could handle this type of problem, she contacted seven tree removal companies. Only one of the companies that she called actually worked on Sundays, and Norma knew that she had to get the job done immediately. She was stuck and asked them to meet her at the office building.

Several hours later, once the tree removal was complete, the individual in charge of the job walked over to Norma and asked her for payment. This took Norma by surprise, because she had assumed that the bill for the work would be sent to her by mail. When she asked him how much the job cost, the man hesitated for a moment, and then abruptly said that the fee was $4,000.

Norma asked him why the bill was so high and was told that the tree was quite large, and that there was an extra charge for weekend work. Norma wrote a business check for $4,000 and drove home. During this drive, Norma felt tense and highly displeased. "I've been taken advantage of," she thought. "Does this guy think I'm an idiot?" Over the next five days, she became increasingly angry. She knew that workers charged more for weekend work, but $4,000 seemed excessive. In her estimation, the bill should have been no higher than $3,000. She thought about stopping payment on the check, but she decided that this tactic would be too confrontational. She worried about what her boss would think when he reviewed the monthly budget but decided just to deal with that when the time came. Perhaps the boss wouldn't even notice it.

Two weeks later, Norma was still stewing about the $4,000 for the tree removal. When her boss, George, asked her about the bill during their budget review, Norma confessed that she had felt stuck and that she had been gouged. She explained that no one else would work on a Sunday, and the fallen tree had presented a serious safety problem. Besides, if the tenants had not had access to the building on Monday morning, that problem would have cost them a lot more than $4,000.

When George asked Norma why she hadn't confronted the foreman about the price gouging, Norma's response surprised him. "I did confront him! I asked him why the price was so high."

"Norma," George responded, "That wasn't a confrontation, that was a question. Why didn't you tell him that the price was so excessive that you couldn't pay him on the spot? You could have bought yourself some time, and we could have sent him a check for a smaller amount."

Norma couldn't think of anything to say in response. Finally, she said, "Well, I did the best I could." Inside, however, she was doubly furious. She was still angry with the foreman for ripping her off, and she was also angry with George for not supporting her and for putting her on the spot.

Months later, Norma was still furious with the foreman and with her boss, and she also felt angry with herself.

Common Nine Pinches

Disruption of peace and harmony • Being told what to do • Feeling ignored • Rudeness in others • Overt hostility • Feeling taken advantage of • Being confronted • Not feeling supported

After the call from the security guard that Sunday morning, Norma, who was normally even-tempered, felt distressed. Her relaxing weekend was being disrupted by an event that she had not expected and felt forced to deal with immediately. Nines commonly take great pleasure in their recreational off-hours and do not appreciate disruptions in the peace and harmony of those relaxed times. This was the first pinch.

Norma also perceived this problem to be a nonnegotiable demand on her time. Nines tend to dislike being told what to do. Though in this situation, it was the job, not a person, that demanded her time, Norma reacted as though someone had given her an unwelcome command. Again, Norma felt pinched.

From the time the tree removal company began the job until the work was completed, Norma had a limited amount of interaction with the foreman and the workers. She had expected the foreman to review the parameters of the job, clarify the amount of time needed, and discuss the bill and the billing process with her. However, all the foreman had said when he met Norma was the following, "So this is the tree?"

Before Norma could get the words out of her mouth to ask him any questions, he was off giving orders to his workers and starting up the chainsaw himself. The work was clearly dangerous, the noise was loud, and Norma had to keep a safe distance away. In Norma's mind, no other conversation with the foreman was possible until the work was done. In fact, after this initial interaction, the only other conversation they had was the discussion of the bill. Because of this limited interaction, Norma felt completely ignored, and this was the third pinch.

During the brief conversation about the bill, Norma thought that the foreman was abrupt with her. Because she could usually develop rapport with almost anyone, she was frustrated by the fact that he seemed so disinterested in any conversation. Norma also thought that his reaction to her question about the price was curt. All in all, Norma decided that the foreman was rude; this was the fourth pinch. Although it usually takes three or fewer pinches to develop into a crunch, with Nines, it may take four or five pinches before the crunch is reached.

Norma also sensed some latent hostility in the foreman. Although she had wanted to pursue the issue of the price, she did not want to get into a conflict with him. Norma imagined that if she had been more direct about his price gouging, the foreman would have become highly agitated and angry. Nines typically avoid, sidestep, or try to defuse conflict situations; in this case, Norma decided to say nothing more to the foreman.

Norma became the most angry when she thought about the price of the tree removal. It seemed outrageously high, and she believed that the foreman had taken advantage of the fact that she was caught in an emergency. Because he had hesitated slightly before telling her the amount, she believed that he had charged her the highest amount he thought he could get. While individuals of all Enneagram styles might feel taken advantage of in this circumstance, for most Nines such situations are especially distressing, discouraging, and infuriating. This was the point at which Norma felt a crunch.

The crunch was heightened when Norma's boss challenged the way in which she had handled the situation. Eight years after the incident with the tree, whenever Norma thought or spoke of it, she still said with great intensity, "I should *never* have given him that money!"

How Nines Behave When Pinched

Say nothing • Facial tension may give a slight indication of anger • May be unaware of own anger • May displace anger onto someone not involved • Anger may remain with them for periods of time

---

When they feel angry, Nines usually say nothing about it; their body language may also give little indication that they are upset, though their displeasure sometimes shows in very subtle facial tension. Their eyes may dart back and forth slightly, and their mouths may show a small grimace around the edges. Although Norma was quite angry with both the foreman and her boss, neither of them was aware that she was feeling this way.

It is often the case that Nines themselves are not immediately aware that they are feeling distressed. However, as they reflect on a situation later, Nines may become aware that they are tense or even angry. This process can be observed in Norma's response to the price gouging. Although she had every right to be angry at the time, she was not really aware of her feelings until she left the office building. The more she thought about it, the angrier she became.

The Nine's anger is often of the slow-burning variety. Sometimes, Nines may be aware of exactly what has generated their negative feelings, as Norma was in this story. At other times, Nines may know that something is agitating them but may not be aware of the actual source. A Nine who is very irritated by something a colleague has done may speak in a sharp tone *not* to this colleague but to an assistant, who may have done nothing whatsoever. Because this short-tempered behavior is so different from the everyday affability and easygoing behavior of Nines, the assistant may feel quite confused about the Nine's behavior. The Nine may not even realize that he or she has acted in a curt manner. However, if the assistant has the courage and forthrightness to ask the Nine about the situation, this can bring attention to the fact that something is bothering him or her.

Individuals of all nine styles may displace their true feelings onto someone or something other than the real cause of their emotions. Sometimes this other person has done absolutely nothing, or he or she may have done something only mildly irritating. Nines, however, tend to displace their anger more frequently than individuals of the other eight Enneagram styles because of the tendency to deny their own anger.

At the point when Nines realize that they are truly angry, they often think about these feelings in a recurring pattern: they may think about the events and conversations, mull over their own reactions, think about what they might have said or done differently, and then feel angry all over again about the incident. This cycle can repeat itself over and over for weeks, months, and even years.

Individuals of several of the other Enneagram styles may also obsess about their angry feelings; Fours and Sixes, for example, may keep repeating the same emotional material in their minds, but they tend to do so continually until they reach emotional and mental clarity. The Nine's style of dealing with anger differs from this in that while Nines use a repetitive pattern of reexperiencing and reanalyzing the event, this process is not continual. For Nines, the replay of events and experiences is usually interspersed with a variety of other activities or stimuli that command their attention. This prolonged, yet discontinuous, replay of disturbing events helps explain why eight years later, Norma was still quite angry about the situation.

How to Approach Nines in a Crunch

Ask about his or her anger in a kind and simple way • Ask about his or her anger in an indirect and low-pressure manner • Listen fully • Affirm the fact that the Nine has expressed anger directly • Share alternative perspectives in a way that still validates the Nine's feelings

A major challenge in approaching Nines is the fact that many Nines may feel deeply angry and injured, yet may not even be aware that they feel this way. In general, Nines tend to not pay attention to their own feelings, and this is particularly true when their feelings involve anger. Anger and conflict unnerve and unsettle most Nines because they threaten the harmony and interpersonal rapport that Nines so deeply desire.

Norma had conflicts with two individuals—the foreman and her boss, George. The foreman could have guessed that his behavior angered Norma, but he probably would not have cared. George, on the other hand, unknowingly angered Norma, but as her boss he would likely have been concerned had he known.

A better approach for George to have used with Norma would have been to ask her how she was feeling about the situation, but to do so in a way that would have allowed her great latitude in how she responded. For example, he could have asked, "Are you upset about this?" Although he could have substituted the word *angry* for *upset*, a word such as *upset* is slightly less direct and more likely to be perceived by a Nine as less confrontational. Even if Norma had answered a firm "No!" to the above question, a follow-up comment could have helped her explore the possibility that she was, in fact, quite angry. A comment such as "Well, your voice has a sharper tone to it than usual" or "If this had happened to me, I would have felt angry" would likely have elicited more information about how she was really feeling.

After listening to Norma's feelings, George could have proceeded to discuss the alternative courses of action that may have been available to her. This discussion, however, would be best done collaboratively, with George first asking Norma, "In retrospect, what alternatives do you think were possible that may not have been so obvious at the time, when you were under pressure to get the job done?" After Norma responded, George could have added some of his own thoughts.

Sometimes Nines will tell you exactly what they are angry about and when they do, they can be remarkably lucid and powerful. In her conversation with George, Norma would have been likely to discuss her feelings about the foreman, because she had had time to realize how furious she really was. For George to have elicited the full range of Norma's feelings, he would have had to do one thing: *listen.*

Once Nines clearly feel they have been listened to and not ignored, simply ask them a few questions to help them examine what else may be upsetting them. For example, if a Nine says that he or she is angry because work is not being accomplished according to agreed-upon deadlines, it can also be useful to ask, "Is there anything else, related or unrelated to this, that might be bothering you?"

Once Nines have fully expressed their anger directly, one particular follow-up statement can have a remarkable effect on them: "Thank you so much for telling me exactly how you feel. I applaud you [appreciate you] so much for doing this." Expressing anger directly is so difficult for Nines that the act of reinforcing them for rising to the challenge and taking this risk can have an extraordinary impact on them. It affirms them and encourages them to continue this behavior in the future. The message sent is this: *Conflict does not have to sever or strain relationships; in fact, the direct communication of concerns can bring people closer together.*

When Nines feel heard and affirmed, they are usually very open to hearing other perspectives on a situation. Sometimes a simple request such as "Can I share with you how I felt about this?" reminds Nines to be open to another viewpoint. Nines usually embrace multiple perspectives of a situation as part of their personality structure; however, in conflict situations, they tend to do so only when they do not feel invalidated themselves. This means that while it is not necessary to agree with them, it is simply important to honor their experience. This can be done with words such as "What you said was very helpful. What I meant during the situation was this, although I can understand how you heard it differently."

How Nines Can Manage Their Own Pinches and Crunches
1. **Share your pinches with others at the beginning of your working relationship.** Spending the time to build rapport at the beginning of a working relationship is something that many Nines do quite easily, even without prompting. They do, however, tend to do this in a more casual way—for example, by stopping at someone's office and schmoozing, or by going to lunch with the other person and talking about work or about things unrelated to the work environment.

   Talking about pinches, however, requires a bit of structure and focus. Offering an open-ended invitation to the new colleague works well for Nines—for example, "Would you mind taking a few minutes to talk about what each of us would like from the other to have a productive and harmonious work relationship? That could help us continue to have a smooth transition as we work together." To communicate their pinches, Nines can say, "I like to be included in decisions and conversations about work, and I like to include others as well" rather than "I don't like to be ignored." Instead of saying, "I don't like being told what to do," Nines can instead say, "When someone wants me to do something, I highly prefer that the person make a genuine request, rather than a demand or veiled expectation. In fact, it helps when I have input and influence over how and when something gets accomplished."

As a caveat, Nines need to make sure that they actually initiate the conversation about pinches. They may intend to do so, but if the conversation feels comfortable and the topic is interesting, the time may slip away before the pinch conversation can occur. Nines may also unintentionally avoid the conversation about pinches because of their general aversion to conflict. It can be helpful for a Nine to remember that the discussion of pinches is *not* the same as conflict; in fact, the conversation can prevent conflict from arising.

2. **Say something as soon as you are aware of feeling pinched.** This can be difficult for Nines, for three reasons. First, as noted earlier, Nines who may feel pinched may not even be aware that they are experiencing displeasure. However, when Nines start paying closer attention to themselves and their reactions, they become more aware of feeling agitated and angry. They do, however, need to take a serious look at what is truly causing the pinch and not direct their displeasure toward a secondary source.

Second, when Nines are aware of feeling pinched, they may not say anything for fear of creating a conflict. It can be helpful to reassure yourself that discussing pinches as soon as they occur usually decreases conflict, increases rapport, and builds trust with coworkers because of the self-disclosure that's involved.

Finally, as noted, Nines may fully intend to say something to the other person but may procrastinate about initiating the conversation. The time may never seem right, or other pressing work issues may draw their attention. Thus, Nines must make a firm commitment to raise the issue soon after the event occurs; they need to realize that while doing so may feel a little awkward, it will be far less so than the conversation that would take place after the pinches have accumulated.

3. **When you start to behave in ways that indicate you are feeling pinched, do something physical if you can, such as working out or taking a walk.** Physical activity works just as well for Nines when they feel pinched as it does for individuals of the other eight Enneagram styles. However, Nines need to make sure that they do not use walks or other forms of exercise as a way of avoiding conflict. Being in nature and engaging in physical activity often soothes Nines to such a degree that they may "space out" or forget that anything was troubling them. When they begin to diffuse their focus away from themselves toward the activity in which they are involved, they need to bring their attention back to themselves. The following structured practice can assist them in refocusing on themselves. At ten-minute intervals during the physical activity, ask yourself the following two questions: *Am I still paying attention to the issue that caused me the pinch? What am I thinking and feeling about it right now?*

4. **When you feel a pinch, ask yourself:** *What does my reaction to this situation or to the other person's behavior say about me as a Nine and about the areas in which I can develop? How can working on my pinches and crunches help me to bring out the best in myself?*

This question may be difficult for some Nines, because it requires them to really pay attention to themselves. Enneagram style Nine is known as the "self-forgetting" style, which means that Nines tend not to pay attention to what they think, feel, need, or should be doing. In this sense, Nines neglect themselves. While individuals of the other eight styles also engage in self-forgetting and self-neglect, it is not usually to the same extent as it is with Nines. For Nines to focus on themselves to the degree required to answer the above questions can be a challenge, but it can also be a transforming experience.

This is especially true for Nines, because conflict avoidance is central to the Nine's personality structure. When Nines do focus on how they deal with conflict, they often find that they feel taken advantage of or ignored, in large part because they have difficulty expressing their true feelings, standing up for themselves, and stating what they truly believe. They often discover that their way of dealing with potential conflict is to acquiesce and then become passive-aggressive, by saying or implying yes when they mean no.

More About Conflict

Most relationships, whether they are professional or personal, begin with a degree of hope for the future and goodwill on the part of the individuals involved. Even in those relationships born out of some difficulty or tension—for example, a new boss who has been chosen over an internal candidate or a coworker with a questionable reputation—most people do try to make the relationships work.

Pinches do not typically occur in the first part of a new relationship, because during the initial encounters with others, both parties are usually trying to create a good impression, develop the new relationship, and get accustomed to the changed working environment. Over time, however, pinches invariably arise because one person unknowingly offends another. As described earlier in this chapter, these violations or pinches are often connected to our Enneagram styles.

Every pinch signals the possibility of an impending disruption and is really an early warning sign. If these differing expectations are not addressed early in the relationship, a pinch is likely to become a major disruption—a crunch.

When expectations are discussed early on, the parties have more choice and control over how they react and behave when one of the members feels a pinch. When the resolution of conflict is left until the problem has reached the crunch stage, emotions and tensions are higher, more issues have built upon one another, and the situation becomes more stressful and higher-risk. Because of these factors, the resolution of conflict becomes a more arduous task for everyone involved.

Enneagram style–based pinches are not, of course, the only sources of organizational conflict. For conflict to be effectively resolved, the organizational factors causing it must also be accurately identified and discussed—for example, roles, resource allocation, coordination difficulties, information, values, organizational direction, performance expectations, culture, and power. However, no matter what the root cause of the conflict is, the Enneagram styles of the key parties involved will always be a factor in the dynamics of the conflict and its resolution. A thorough understanding of the Enneagram enables each individual involved to make conflict resolution a constructive rather than destructive experience. The more the main participants know themselves, understand their own responsibilities in the conflict interaction, engage in constructive self-management, and know how to best approach their adversaries through knowledge of the Enneagram, the greater the chances of a swift and effective outcome.

Sometimes conflict can be neither prevented nor resolved by the individuals involved. Bringing in a third party to assist in the resolution of conflict can be particularly helpful in the following situations:

- High-intensity conflict
- High-risk conflict (for example, when one person's job is at risk)
- Chronic, long-term conflict
- Those involved in the conflict have very different status levels
- Multiple individuals are involved in the conflict
- Some or all of the parties do not have sufficient emotional control to deal effectively with the conflict

Third parties can be human resource or employee assistance personnel, ombudsmen, consultants who work internally or externally to the organization, or even other individuals from within the organization, such as managers. It is important for the individual to have the necessary skills for this role, to agree to maintain confidences, and to be acceptable to everyone directly involved in the conflict.

Whatever the conflict situation, it is important that conflict resolution always be approached from a perspective of compassion and appreciation. This

WHAT TO AFFIRM IN EACH ENNEAGRAM STYLE

- **Ones:** for listening with an open mind and heart
- **Twos:** for expressing their own needs directly
- **Threes:** for disclosing personal information that does not make them look good
- **Fours:** for their objectivity and emotional balance
- **Fives:** for expressing their feelings in the moment
- **Sixes:** for differentiating between their projections and insights
- **Sevens:** for being willing to deal with and stay focused on difficult and painful issues
- **Eights:** for sharing their feelings of vulnerability and showing their softer sides
- **Nines:** for taking a clear stand on issues and expressing their anger directly

not only creates a more positive result, but it also helps those involved to grow and develop. Compassion is not sympathy, pity, or any other sentiment that elevates one person above another. In this context, compassion emerges from the following understanding: *The other person's feelings, thoughts, reactions, and behaviors are just as difficult for him or her to deal with as mine are for me; they may be different from mine, but they are just as challenging.* For example, a Six may be troubled by a One's tendency to criticize. However, if the Six can remember that not being critical is every bit as difficult for a One as not worrying is for a Six, the Six's frustration and anger can change into compassion and engagement.

It is very important to affirm individuals of all nine styles. Affirmations are of particular importance when they concern behaviors that an individual finds especially difficult to execute in a conflict situation. Remember to also affirm and reinforce yourself for your own hard work in dealing with your pinches and crunches. When individuals take responsibility for their own behavior in dealing with issues that inevitably arise in the workplace, all the parties involved in the conflict and the larger organization benefit:

- Differences between people are treated constructively, as problems that can be solved
- Employees are more cooperative and focus on work rather than on difficulties with one another
- The work environment is more harmonious
- Organizations are more productive

Chapter 5

Creating High-Performing Teams

lmost everyone who works in an organization works within a group or team context at least to some degree. In fact, most people are members of multiple work groups and teams—for example, an individual might be part of a work unit, a committee, and a project team. Working with others in a team setting is always more complex than working alone because teamwork involves a great deal of interpersonal interaction, communication, and coordination. These factors can make being part of a team challenging and sometimes frustrating, but at the same time highly rewarding; it can be said that there is almost nothing in a work setting that is as exasperating as being a member of a poor team, nor as satisfying as being part of an excellent one. When a team is not functioning well or not performing to its potential, it often requires some outside assistance, as illustrated in the following story.

Theresa, the manager of a human resources department, confided to Fred, an organizational consultant, "I'm supposed to know how to make my group get along without any outside help, but this situation is way beyond me. We're supposed to develop goals for our group and then action plans for the next year, but I'm afraid the group members won't be willing to work together. I'm just sick of listening to them complain about each other, and my conversations with each of them separately don't seem to do any good. Can you do anything to help us?"

In order to understand how to work within a team, it is important to clarify the basic distinction between a group and a team. A *group* is a collection of individuals who have something in common; a team is a specific type of group. A *team* is composed of members who share common goals that can only be reached by the interdependent efforts between and among various team members.[1] Teams have a far greater potential for high performance and member satisfaction than do groups. The team's common goals enable its members to become aligned around a common purpose, and team success usually provides a sense of collective exhilaration that is difficult to match through group or even individual performance.

The Enneagram can be extraordinarily helpful in the creation and development of high-performing teams. First, when all of the team's members know their Enneagram styles, they can use this knowledge to improve their personal effectiveness as well as to adjust their interpersonal behaviors to the styles of the other team members. Knowledge of the Enneagram also increases team members' understanding and compassion. Instead of interpreting and misinterpreting someone else's behavior based on one's own frame of reference, team members can begin to view other members from a more objective and accurate perspective. In addition, as you will see, knowledge of the Enneagram can assist both team members and leaders in developing team goals and interdependencies, as well as in expanding the repertoire of team-based roles and behaviors over the stages of team development.

This chapter offers a case study of the efforts of a real-life group to become a team during a two-day retreat. The story presented here describes not only the events themselves, but also the thoughts, feelings, and behaviors of each group member before, during, and directly after the retreat. Conflicts and other types of behaviors are analyzed according to the Enneagram styles of the participants; analyses of the behaviors of each group member are made using the insights of the Enneagram integrated with four different models from the field of organizational behavior.

Before analyzing each team member's group behavior, it is helpful to establish some understanding of how teams operate. Because teams are complex and dynamic, it is difficult to understand them from a single perspective or at only one moment in time. Teams must be considered from multiple perspectives or frameworks, including one that illuminates the team's dynamics over its life cycle. The team whose story is presented in this chapter will be analyzed from four different team perspectives:

1. Ideal team goals
2. Ideal interdependence within a team

---

1. The importance of common team goals and collective responsibility for achieving them (interdependence) is most clearly articulated in *The Wisdom of Teams* by Jon Katzenbach and Douglas Smith (1993).

3. Roles played on teams[2]
4. Behavior during the four stages of team development[3]

All of these topics will be covered in greater depth later in the chapter; for now, brief explanations are provided as a framework for exploring the dynamics of the case-study team.

Ideal Team Goals

Each of us has expectations based on our Enneagram style of what ideal team goals should be. The more our expectations are met, the greater our satisfaction with the team.

Ideal Team Interdependence

Individuals of each Enneagram style have different preferences regarding how dependent they want to be on other people's work performance. Some prefer low interdependence, akin to that of a golf team; some prefer medium interdependence, as on a baseball team; and others prefer high interdependence, as on a basketball team (see Figure 5.1).

Roles Played in Teams

Individual Enneagram behavior in teams tends to fall into two types of predictable roles: task roles and relationship roles. *Task roles* involve behaviors directed toward the work itself. *Relationship roles* involve behaviors focused on feelings, relationships, and team processes, such as decision making and conflict resolution.

Four Stages of Team Development

A team in the *Forming* stage orients itself in three areas: team goals or tasks, team membership, and leadership. After a group has formed, conflict often emerges as the team goes through the *Storming* stage. The conflict may be

continued

---

2. The classification of group roles into task and relationship roles first appeared in "Functional Roles of Group Members," by K. Benne and P. Sheets (*Journal of Social Issues*, 1948), although the roles were originally named task and maintenance roles.

3. The four stages of group development were the original work of Bruce Tuckman (1965). Tuckman added a fifth stage, Adjourning, in 1977.

FIGURE 5.1 **Interdependence**

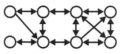

| Low Interdependence | Medium Interdependence | High Interdependence |

mild, moderate, or extreme. During this stage, tension may arise between the team and the leader or between team members regarding the team's direction and ways of structuring the work. Underlying these tensions are issues of power, influence, and control, as well as such other factors as values, perceptions, and opinions.

As teams resolve these conflicts, they evolve to the third stage, *Norming*. During this stage, teams develop consensual working agreements, or norms; these often include solutions to issues of prior disagreement. During the fourth and final stage, *Performing*, the team becomes extremely productive, displaying team synergy and high morale.

These four stages are developmental; the issues in one stage require resolution before the team can move successfully to the next stage. Teams may also revert back to a prior stage when unresolved issues arise or new challenges appear. Some teams never develop beyond the first two stages of development. (See Figure 5.2.)

FIGURE 5.2 **Stages of Team Development**

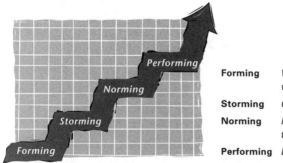

Forming	*Who are we, and where are we going?*
Storming	*Can't we all just get along?*
Norming	*How do we get out of this mess?*
Performing	*Let's soar!*

Case Study

A nine-person human resources department (see Figure 5.3), created three years ago and currently serving four thousand employees, is on a Friday-Saturday retreat with a facilitator for the dual purposes of team building and developing goals and plans for the coming year. The two-day retreat has been set up at the request of the department manager, Theresa, who has hired an outside facilitator to plan and facilitate the retreat so that she herself can participate fully. Theresa and Fred, the facilitator, have agreed that the retreat should involve an overnight stay in a location away from the work setting, thus allowing participants to be more relaxed and less distracted by work demands. Olga, the department's administrative assistant, has secured a small, attractive conference center an hour's drive from the office.

As part of the process, three weeks prior to the retreat, Fred conducted confidential, two-hour interviews with each staff member. The interviews enabled Fred to get to know each participant, to gain an understanding of the department's needs, and to identify any sensitive group issues that might need to be addressed at the retreat. Fred asked these questions:

- What is going well in the human resources department?
- What needs to be improved?
- How would you describe your department staff in terms of being a team?
- What needs to occur at the retreat so that you will feel it has been time well spent?

One week before the retreat, Fred gave a summary of the data from these interviews to Theresa. In addition, he recommended that he teach this group about the Enneagram at the beginning of the retreat, for several reasons. During the interviews, Fred had discovered that several unresolved conflicts existed within the group and that several department members were critical of Theresa's leadership style. Fred reasoned that understanding the Enneagram would help staff members discuss and resolve some of these issues. Theresa agreed; she felt that the staff would enjoy being exposed to the new information, and that it would potentially be helpful to them in building their skills as human resources specialists. Theresa later sent an e-mail to all staff members suggesting that they learn and use the Enneagram at the retreat; the responses to this e-mail were positive.

FIGURE 5.3 **Retreat Participants**

Enneagram Style	Name, Age	Role	Main issues in relation to the retreat
1	Olga, 40	Manager's assistant	Impatient and feels she does not have a real role in the retreat
2	Tammy, 30	Junior HR specialist	Wants to help but does not know the issues
3	Theresa, 46	Manager	Talented, but feels anxious, knowing she is the object of staff anger
4	Fred, 45	Facilitator	Skilled, but anxious, knowing that many of the group's issues are interpersonal and difficult to deal with
5	Faye, 50	Senior HR specialist	Wants to run and hide in order to avoid emotional attacks from her antagonist, Simon
6	Simon, 48	Senior HR specialist	Emotionally distressed and aggressive; has a lot to say, but is worried about hurting the group, other people, and himself
7	Saul, 55	Senior HR specialist	Wants to emerge from the retreat unscathed and with a promotion in hand
8	Esther, 42	HR specialist	Desperately wants to leave the department and does not respect Theresa, the manager
8	Elliot, 23	Intern	Depressed and perplexed because he feels ignored and disrespected, particularly by Simon
9	Nigel, 38	HR specialist	Totally disengaged and wants to avoid the impending conflict

The Week Before the Retreat: Individual Perceptions and Behaviors

Each member of the department had specific concerns about the upcoming retreat, and some shared their concerns with Fred and/or with coworkers. Following are glimpses into the thoughts and fears of each participant one week prior to the retreat.

Olga, the administrative assistant and a One, provides administrative support to most of the department's human resources specialists. Just prior to the retreat, she makes comments to certain members who she thinks may agree with her about various issues pertaining to the office and to the retreat: To Nigel, she says, "Can you believe that Simon is still upset with Elliot?" To Faye, she remarks, "What in the world will we do for two whole days!" And to Tammy, she comments, "Why can't Esther and Theresa just get over whatever is bothering them and just work together?"

Tammy, a junior human resources specialist and a Two who reports to Simon, recently returned from a six-month leave of absence and so has missed the work situations that prodded Theresa to hold this retreat. When she met with Fred for her interview, she had very little to say. Tammy wants everyone to be enthused about working together toward common goals, but informal conversations with Simon, Olga, and Esther indicating that a number of unresolved problems exist within the group have dampened her hopes. *What is our common purpose?* she wonders. *What can I do to help people get past their frustration with the department head, Theresa, and their distrust of one another?*

Theresa (a Three), the department head, feels perplexed as she considers both the causes of her department's problems and their possible solutions. Outwardly, Theresa appears energetic and cordial. Inwardly, she feels anxious in anticipation of what might be said during the retreat about her leadership style. A week before the retreat, after reviewing the data from Fred's staff interviews, Theresa expresses her anxiety and impatience to him: "What can we do about these issues? What can I do about these staff conflicts? Do you think the agenda for this retreat will really work? Spending our energy on these issues is not a good use of anybody's time!"

After interviewing all of the staff members, Fred, the consultant and a Four, has become more concerned about how well the retreat will go. Staff members have told him about a number of sensitive issues, including three major conflicts that, in Fred's opinion, all directly or indirectly involve Theresa. During the interviews, Fred also learned that most of the staff do not want to attend the retreat. They also told him that they hoped he would be objective and unbiased in listening to them and in facilitating the retreat. Fred is hoping to live up to these expectations. He has other concerns as well: *Will people be forthcoming when they come together? Do I have enough trust and goodwill to draw out some difficult issues? What if this retreat isn't productive? If it isn't, I may never work in this company again!*

Faye, a senior human resources specialist and a Five, feels frightened and distant as she thinks about the coming retreat. She wants to be in control of what she will say there, as well as how and when she will say it. Her preference is to say nothing, although she knows that this is unlikely. She feels agitated as she wonders, *Why does Simon make such nasty remarks about me? I work just as hard as everyone else, maybe harder. Don't clients always come first? Will Simon attack me in this retreat? How should I react if he does?*

Simon, also a senior human resources specialist and a Six, is ambivalent about this retreat. On the one hand, he wishes he could avoid the whole thing; on the other, he thinks it is finally time to get the issues on the table. As he thinks about his feud with Faye, which began eight months earlier, he anguishes, *Faye does not carry her weight in the group. She chooses to do her client work at the expense of our collective human resources projects. She misses departmental meetings and takes credit for the work done by people who report to her. No, she is not a team player! Should I say all this? Will I be forced into sharing my thoughts? What if no one else is willing to be honest? Why does Theresa keep supporting Faye? If I do have to say something, what should I say? Is our consultant capable of handling all of this?*

Saul, the most experienced senior human resources specialist in the group and a Seven, wonders if he will have anything to contribute to the retreat. He knows that he has more experience and perspective than the other department members, but he works in a completely separate business unit and rarely sees his coworkers. He thinks, *Why would I want to get involved in their mess? Besides, I could hurt my relationships, especially with Theresa. She and I get along fine. What if something negative happens at the retreat, and I'm somehow involved? I need Theresa's support for my forthcoming promotion. I guess I'll just have to look interested even when I'm not and keep a low profile!*

Esther (an Eight) has the credentials to be a senior human resources specialist, but Theresa refuses to formally raise her level or even to acknowledge Esther's experience and expertise. Esther feels angry as she thinks, *I could be the department head—at least I'm decisive! Is Theresa threatened by me?* Esther's major concern about the retreat, however, is Elliot, the department intern, with whom she is very close. She thinks, *He is more capable than most people in this department. Sure, he has a few rough edges, but I thought we were supposed to mentor him. He's a diamond in the rough, and we should be helping him! Theresa should be watching out for him; instead, she just lets Simon attack him.*

Elliot (another Eight) has been with the group for a year working as a paid intern, but everyone knows that he plans to leave in two weeks. The process of looking for a new job and separating from the human resources department has been exhausting and stressful for him. He tried to excuse himself from having to attend this retreat, but both Esther and the facilitator, Fred, have urged him to attend. Elliot worries, *Why is Simon so hostile to me? Why hasn't Theresa tried to find me a job in this group? I have no idea what I would have done all these months without Esther. Sometimes she gives me great advice. Some-*

times it's nice just to talk with her and be understood. Could I have done something to upset the others? All I've done is conduct research, make suggestions, and ask the hard questions. Mostly, they've ignored me!

Nigel, a human resources specialist and a Nine, has not been looking forward to this retreat. Although he has had a few conversations with his coworkers about the coming event, he has kept his real feelings to himself. His strong preference would be not to attend the retreat. His thoughts are these: *What a pathetic group! The personalities can be so strong and overbearing. There's so much work on my desk—how can I take two days away from the office?*

The Retreat Agenda

The following agenda was distributed to group members prior to the retreat.

FRIDAY 9:00 A.M.–12:00 P.M.
Learn the Enneagram

Lunch

FRIDAY 1:00 P.M.–5:00 P.M.
Review and discuss the data from the interviews
Prioritize the issues
Discuss and resolve issues in priority order

Group dinner and social time

SATURDAY 9:00 A.M.–5:00 P.M.
Continue discussion and resolution of issues

During the Retreat

The retreat officially begins on Friday at 9:00 A.M., although group members trickle into the room between eight-thirty and nine to have a continental breakfast and to socialize. Theresa, Simon, and Tammy are the first to arrive. Esther and Faye are the last to join the group and arrive at exactly nine o'clock. The room resembles a comfortable living room, complete with a fireplace; two couches and several armchairs are arranged in a circle. The circular seating arrangement, while inviting, surprises many in the group who would have preferred a more formal arrangement, with tables and chairs. The arrangement sends a clear message: participants will have to discuss their issues face-to-face, without the psychological safety barrier that more formal settings often provide. This factor creates a subtle tension in the group.

Fred, the facilitator, is fully aware of the effects of the room arrangement. From his past experience, however, he knows that having group members face one another directly contributes to a more honest and personal conversation between and among them, thus outweighing any concerns about increased discomfort.

ITEM 1: LEARN THE ENNEAGRAM (9:00 A.M. TO 12:00 P.M.) Fred spends the first morning of the retreat teaching the Enneagram to the group and helping members identify their Enneagram styles. Participants respond positively to the Enneagram and have no difficulty in identifying their styles. They are also relieved, because focusing on the Enneagram delays their having to deal with the difficult group problems that they all know exist. They also know that they are expected to use their newly acquired Enneagram knowledge to discuss and resolve the impending group issues. They do not, however, understand exactly how they will accomplish this task, although they trust Fred to help them do so. When they break at noon for lunch, they are all feeling more relaxed than they had at nine that morning.

ITEM 2: REVIEW AND DISCUSS THE DATA FROM THE INTERVIEWS (1:00 P.M. TO 1:45 P.M.) Directly after lunch, Fred shows the group two large charts he has created that summarize data from the individual interviews conducted prior to the retreat.

DATA ABOUT THE GROUP

Group members disagree about whether they want to be a real team. The following questions were raised during the interviews:

- What common goals should they have, given that they have separate client responsibilities?
- More interdependencies mean more work for each of them; therefore, what benefits will outweigh this increased burden?
- What is the value added to the organization if they were to become a team rather than remain a group?

Conflict exists between two group members (Simon and Faye) that negatively affects other group members.

- Simon and Faye display overt and covert hostility at group meetings.
- Conversations occur regularly (behind closed doors) about this conflict.

Elliot, the department intern, is leaving the group, but some group members feel that he has not been well treated.

DATA ABOUT LEADERSHIP

Theresa is perceived to have great leadership strengths, but significant concerns about her leadership also exist.

Strengths
- Strategic orientation
- Respected in the larger organization
- Approachable
- Intelligent
- Capable

Concerns
- Overextended
- Inaccessible
- Favors some group members over others
- Has not treated Elliot well

Fred reads these summaries aloud and asks for initial reactions. The group members respond affirmatively, saying that the information presented accurately reflects what they have told him. With this response from the group, Fred knows they are ready to prioritize the issues and then have a deeper discussion about them.

ITEM 3: PRIORITIZE THE ISSUES (1:45 P.M. TO 2:30 P.M.) After a forty-five minute discussion, the group decides by consensus on a sequence for approaching the issues. There is minimal disagreement about these choices, because the group members have fully discussed their preferences and the rationales behind them. The inclusion of the rationales influences some group members to change their choices so that a strong consensus emerges. These priorities and the rationales behind them are shown on the next page.

PRIORITIZING THE ISSUES

1. Leadership issues
   Rationale: This is the most difficult and important topic to discuss.
2. Conflict between Simon and Faye
   Rationale: If this conflict persists, group members will resist becoming a team in order to avoid one another, yet they will not acknowledge this as the reason for their resistance.
3. Concerns related to Elliot
   Rationale: Although Elliot is leaving, the group still needs to learn what went awry; how a group treats its least powerful member usually reflects an extreme version of how group members tend to treat one another.
4. Should the group become a team?
   Rationale: The discussion of common goals and potential interdependencies could then take place without being contaminated by unresolved leadership and interpersonal issues.
5. Goal development
   Rationale: Goals can easily be developed once the issue of whether the staff is a team or a group has been clarified.
6. Action plans
   Rationale: Action plans are designed after goals are clear, so this topic needs to be the last agenda item.

The setting of priorities is complete by 2:30 in the afternoon on Friday. The group spends the remainder of the afternoon discussing and resolving the leadership issues and the conflict between Simon and Faye. On Saturday, they will complete the remaining four issues from their priority list.

On Friday morning, the group had been relaxed and involved as they learned the Enneagram. This is not the case, however, as they begin the afternoon session that day; they feel anxious about what will occur next, yet they feel a little more hopeful after the positive experience of learning the Enneagram together. The following section describes key perceptions and behaviors of the team members and of the facilitator from the afternoon session on Friday through the end of the retreat on Saturday.

INDIVIDUAL PERCEPTIONS AND BEHAVIORS: FRIDAY AFTERNOON AND ALL DAY SATURDAY Olga, the administrative assistant, acts hesitant yet alert during most of this time. When she speaks, Olga most frequently asks questions that are really statements, such as, "What are we doing?" or "Why are we talking about this?" She becomes particularly impatient and agitated during the leadership discussion, and she makes comments such as, "I think Theresa has been very supportive of everyone" and "Don't you think it's time to move to goals and action planning?" During the later discussion on the topic of goals and action planning, however, Olga (a One) becomes enthused and animated. She suggests ways to meet more regularly and volunteers to take on numerous assignments.

Tammy (a Two), the junior human resources specialist who reports to Simon, asks many questions during the retreat. Some of these questions are requests for information that will fill in her six-month gap of understanding—for example, "When did this happen? What happened next?" Her other inquiries are attempts to draw out the feelings and thoughts of other group members: "What did you think when that happened? What kept you from sharing your feelings when you were upset? We all need to make a commitment to sharing our reactions, or these kinds of problems will happen again." At the end of the retreat, Tammy volunteers to work with several other team members on a number of different tasks.

Theresa (a Three), the department head, handles herself constructively throughout the retreat. She feels well prepared by Fred, the consultant, who met with her privately before the retreat in order to share the same information the group is now discussing. She starts the afternoon session on Friday by saying, "I know we have some serious issues to discuss, and my goal is to do whatever I can to help resolve them so we can keep adding value to the organization." During the retreat, Theresa decides to share her real feelings about her leadership style with the department members. She tells them, "I want everyone to be successful in this group. I'd feel terrible if anyone were unhappy. I know I've not made time for everyone, and I want to change that. Please be very honest with me when you tell me about my leadership." (See the "Analysis of the Three Leadership Issue" sidebar on the next page.)

With the leadership issues dealt with, Theresa can shift her focus from responding to questions about her leadership to helping guide the group in discussing and resolving the remaining topics. She asks open-ended questions such as these: "Are we making progress?" "Are we meeting our goals for this retreat?" "Do you think it's time to move on, or is there more to discuss?"

Fred (a Four), the consultant, feels he is really earning his money conducting this retreat. Although the first morning was relatively easy because the group enjoyed learning about the Enneagram, Fred knew that the hard work lay ahead. For the remainder of the retreat, he has to pay attention to each team member's feelings and reactions, to the group's dynamics, and to moving the agenda forward without spending too much or too little time on any one person or issue. He makes sure that the agenda still meets the group's

ENNEAGRAM ANALYSIS OF THE THREE LEADERSHIP ISSUE

During the leadership discussion, it became clear that Theresa's leadership style is largely a result of her Enneagram style. Threes often have a strategic orientation, one that can be described as a focus on goals and an ability to reach these goals both efficiently and effectively. Because Threes achieve results and are typically very competent, they often gain respect within their organizations.

Most of Theresa's staff members find her approachable; like most Threes, Theresa is optimistic and interested in people. Threes are often adept at reading other people because they want to know what it will take for them to gain the respect of others. As the department head for human resources, Theresa knows that her staff members want a positive response from her. When she is in the office, she usually greets her staff with warmth and friendliness.

Theresa's weaknesses are also a reflection of her Enneagram style. Threes often become unavailable to those with whom they work because of their tendency to overwork, overschedule, and overextend. Theresa often had limited time for her one-on-one weekly meetings with her staff, and she has often cancelled these appointments at the last minute. Theresa's tendency not to be available for these meetings has been exacerbated whenever she has been scheduled to meet with an individual with whom she feels some tension. Threes usually like to keep their interactions positive and upbeat, and many Threes prefer to avoid conversations that require them to deal with individuals about whom they have negative feelings.

Theresa and the group also gained insight into an additional connection between Theresa's inaccessibility and her Enneagram style. Threes commonly create an image of success. When they do this, they may not share their real feelings or reveal information that puts them in a negative light. The group knew Theresa's persona or image, but they did not feel they really knew her. Theresa changed this dynamic during the retreat by sharing her feelings, including her fears of failing as the group leader.

Because Theresa was so forthcoming and open about herself, the group was able to both discuss and resolve the leadership problems. This freed them to be able to move to the remaining topics.

needs by asking questions such as, "Should we spend more time on this?" "Are we finished with that topic?" "Shall we add another item to the agenda?" He simultaneously pays attention to each person's reaction to the group's dynamics. He watches each person's body language closely and asks questions such as, "Do you have something to say?" "What feelings do you have about that?" "Is there something else on your mind?"

Faye (a Five), a senior human resources specialist, says little during the leadership discussion except for supportive statements such as, "I can understand why Theresa has such limited time." She feels nervous about the time when she and Simon will deal with their conflict. She assumes Simon will launch the attack, because she has very little to say to him. In fact, her only problem with him is his negative attitude toward her. When Fred opens the discussion about the conflict between the two, Simon confronts Faye about her not being a team player. Although Faye initially becomes flustered, she regains her composure and says, "I *am* a team player, as much as anyone else in this group. I attend the staff meetings except in an emergency, and I complete every assignment requested of me. All of us are under tremendous time pressure. Isn't our individual client work our first priority?"

Simon (a Six), a senior human resources specialist, has not decided in advance whether or how he will confront Faye. When the time comes to discuss their conflict, the room is silent. Finally, Simon sits forward in his chair and begins a series of intense statements: "Faye always puts her work ahead of the group's work. She never volunteers for group projects." Fred, the consultant, asks Simon to make these three changes in his delivery: (1) talk directly to Faye, using words such as *you* rather than *she*; (2) slow down his speech; and (3) give specific examples. Simon continues by saying, "Faye, I don't think you are loyal to the team, only to yourself. I believe this because you choose your client needs over our group's needs, and you sit back when the time comes to volunteer. You may complete the few things assigned, but not always on time."

The Enneagram helped Simon and Faye understand that by their own definitions each was acting in good faith as a team player, and their conflict subsided. (See the "Analysis of the Six-Five Conflict" sidebar on the next page.) Faye agreed to volunteer for more tasks and to attend staff meetings regularly, even when she was dealing with an emergency. Simon, for his part, realized that his vision of a team was only one viable way of defining a team; not only did he relax his assault on Faye, but he also apologized to her.

Saul (a Seven), the most senior human resources specialist, says very little during any of the three heated discussions: the concerns about Theresa's lead-

ENNEAGRAM ANALYSIS OF THE SIX-FIVE CONFLICT

As the heated dialogue between Simon and Faye continued, the Enneagram provided the group with an understanding of both Simon's and Faye's perspectives about their conflict. Fives like Faye prefer teams that have a few well-chosen goals, with each team member having concrete and relatively autonomous tasks related to those goals. That is how Fives work best—with a clear focus and minimal interdependencies. Fives view an ideal team as one in which the individual can flourish. From Faye's point of view, she was an exemplary team member.

Sixes, such as Simon, have a very different ideal team in their minds. Sixes usually believe that there is individual safety in numbers and therefore prefer collective team tasks. Independent work, to most Sixes, is not teamwork. Simon's perception of an ideal team is one in which team members subordinate their individual needs for the good of the group. In the Sixes' view, team members demonstrate their personal integrity by volunteering for specific tasks and demonstrate their commitment to the team through timely follow-up. Simon was furious at Faye for not doing these things, and he perceived her as being self-serving rather than as serving the group.

ership style, the conflict between Simon and Faye, and the issues related to Elliot. Saul does, however, appear involved, as if tracking the conversations closely. Occasionally, his eyes twinkle as he makes a spontaneous joke, for example, "If our clients could see us now, they might reconsider using our services!" Everyone laughs. During the goal-setting and action-planning discussion, Saul becomes very animated, sharing ideas for strategies and bringing in ideas from his prior experiences: "If we organized ourselves along client and project lines simultaneously, we could continue our individual work and create world-class human resources initiatives. This was very successful in the engineering environment where I last worked. Here's how you do it."

Esther (an Eight), a human resources specialist, has brought some client work with her and sits far away from Theresa. She thinks that perhaps she will do some work in the event that she does not like the conversation. Esther knows that the other group members will not like this, but she doesn't care. During the leadership discussions, she watches closely but says little. She wonders, *Why are we doing this? Is this session going the way it needs to go? Is all this talk, including Theresa's apologetic response, for real?* When the agenda moves to the issues about Elliot, however, Esther initiates the discussion, saying, "We need to take a long, hard look at what we've done here. Elliot is our group intern, and what have we done? Simon is downright rude to Elliot, Theresa has done nothing visible to find him another position, and the rest of us have let Elliot get completely demoralized. Does anyone else care?"

Elliot (another Eight), the department intern, feels very vulnerable, but he is also very angry. He wants to stay with the organization and knows that burning bridges is not in his best interests; at the same time, he wants to say something. He wonders, *How much should I say?* After Esther's preamble, the group turns to look at Elliot. Elliot responds by saying, "I will continue working in the company, just in another department. This group means a lot to me, and it was my hope to stay in human resources. Simon not only does not support me, but he is openly hostile. Why? I don't know. Why, Simon? What have I done?"

Simon's answer surprises many group members when he says, "Who do you think you are to come into this group, work under me, and assume you know more about how we should do things than I do? It takes time to learn, but you just assume that you know everything. I don't care if you do have an MBA!" (See the "Analysis of the Six-Eight Conflict" sidebar on the next page.)

Nigel (a Nine), a human resources specialist, wishes all this were not happening. He is caught between wanting to avoid all the group tension and not wanting to be invisible in the group. He knows he will be ignored if he says nothing. During the discussions about conflict in the group, he steels himself and says, "Another factor to consider is Theresa's demanding international travel schedule. Have we thought through the intense pressures on us all to serve so many clients? Maybe Simon and Elliot are both concerned that with the possible restructuring, there may not be jobs for everyone. Maybe we're all worried about this." During the goal setting and action planning, Nigel becomes very relaxed and active. "This can really work. We're finally getting somewhere! We're a team!"

Fred suggests that they spend the last half hour of the retreat discussing feelings and thoughts about how the retreat has gone. During this time, everyone talks about how incredible it has been to move from dissension and conflict to the feeling of being a real team. A number of comments are made about how important it was to resolve the leadership and interpersonal issues first, because this made the goal setting and action planning go so smoothly. There is consensus that the Enneagram was very helpful in giving participants a perspective on their own behavior. Esther compliments Simon on his willingness to be honest and forthright about his feelings and reactions regarding Faye and Elliot. Elliot tells the team how emotionally touched he is that they care enough about him to deal with his concerns about the team, and he says how much he will miss them. Theresa talks about her fears going into the

ENNEAGRAM ANALYSIS OF THE SIX-EIGHT CONFLICT

Sixes and Eights have different perspectives on organizational relationships. From the perspective of a Six, such as Simon, interpersonal trust presumes organizational loyalty, and loyalty is demonstrated through personal support, dependability, and respect for roles and hierarchy. From an Eight's perspective, interpersonal trust is based on respect, and respect must be earned. While Eights do acknowledge hierarchical positions, a person's credibility supersedes his or her organizational role. For Eights, credibility comes from a combination of forthrightness, intellect, and a willingness to stand up for what is right, particularly in the face of opposition.

Simon wanted to be Elliot's mentor and expected deference from Elliot. Elliot, in Simon's mind, was disrespectful and disloyal. He did not share Simon's view of "appropriate" intern behavior and instead charged forward, sought to make a difference, and tried to earn the respect of his colleagues. Esther, seeing Elliot as a younger version of herself, became his mentor. She perceived Simon as misusing his power at Elliot's expense. Eights often become very protective of people they perceive as being victims of organizational abuse.

Because Esther, Elliot, and Simon were willing to be direct and honest with one another, and because they also used the Enneagram as a tool to aid in their understanding, Elliot and Simon were able to take personal responsibility for their conflict. The other group members were also able to look at themselves and then explicitly discuss why they had been unable to help resolve this conflict earlier.

retreat and says how much better she feels now. Finally, Fred compliments the team on their hard work.

Sometimes people also have reactions to events that they do not discuss with others, but the responses are very real and give additional insight into an individual. Following are each person's reactions and thoughts during the drive home following the retreat.

Directly After the Retreat: Individual Post-Retreat Perceptions

Olga is delighted that the air has been cleared so the team can get back to work. She also believes the retreat took longer than it needed to, but she realizes that not everyone goes at the same pace as she does.

Tammy is content both because she now knows what she missed during her leave of absence and because the team now has several common goals and a commitment to work together. She does wish that she could have been more helpful during this retreat.

Theresa is appreciative that the retreat went so well, but she feels guilty that she has not been more supportive of Elliot.

Fred feels the retreat went as well as it could. The team was feeling relieved and had found their direction. The success of the retreat means that there will probably be more work for Fred in the organization. He is feeling concerned that the conflict between Esther and Theresa was never discussed at the retreat, but he hadn't known how to raise the issues; he only heard about it from Esther, and she had told him she didn't want it brought up.

Faye feels free. She now knows why Simon has been so aggressive with her, and she is relatively confident that he will stop his verbal assaults. She thinks the two of them might even be able to work together.

Simon feels appreciative that Fred managed everyone's negative emotions so well during the retreat, and he is cautiously optimistic that the group will start to act like a team.

Saul's plan worked. He stayed active, alienated no one (at least no one of whom he is aware), and made some important contributions.

Esther feels satisfied that there is some closure for Elliot regarding how he was treated in the group. She likes the team better, but she is still not sure that she trusts Theresa.

Elliot feels exhausted and relieved. He understands more fully what happened to him and why his experience in the department was so painful, but he still thinks the team needs to reinvent the ways in which it serves clients.

Nigel thinks the time has been well spent. He looks forward to the team's continued progress.

The human resources department went on to become a high-performing team, using what they had learned and developed during this retreat as the basis for both working better together as a team and for improving their client service. Not only does this case study demonstrate how to accomplish these goals, but it also illustrates how each team member's behavior reflects his or her Enneagram style on teams. Each person's behavior will now be explained and analyzed according to the following four team frameworks (explained at the beginning of this chapter):

1. Ideal team goals
2. Ideal team interdependence
3. Roles played on teams: task and relationship roles
4. Behavior during the four stages of team development

Analysis of Ones' Team Behavior

Enneagram Style
DILIGENCE

Recap

BEFORE Olga, the administrative assistant, provides administrative support to most of the department's human resources specialists. Just prior to the retreat, she makes comments to certain members whom she thinks may agree with her about various issues pertaining to the office and to the retreat: To Nigel, she says, "Can you believe that Simon is still upset with Elliot?" To Faye, she remarks, "What in the world will we do for two whole days!" And to Tammy, she comments, "Why can't Esther and Theresa just get over whatever is bothering them and just work together?"

DURING Olga acts hesitant yet alert during most of this time. When she speaks, Olga most frequently asks questions that are really statements, such as, "What are we doing?" or "Why are we talking about this?" She becomes particularly impatient and agitated during the leadership discussion, and she makes comments such as, "I think Theresa has been very supportive of everyone," and "Don't you think it's time to move to goals and action planning?" During the later discussion on the topic of goals and action planning, however, Olga becomes enthused and animated. She suggests ways to meet more regularly and volunteers to take on numerous assignments.

AFTER Olga is delighted that the air has been cleared so the team can get back to work. She also believes the retreat took longer than it needed to, but she realizes that not everyone goes at the same pace as she does.

ONES

- **Forming.** Task-focused, with minimal need for social connection; may suggest ways to structure work
- **Storming.** Frame conflict as a problem to be solved, exert leadership to do this and grow impatient if the conflict endures
- **Norming.** Suggest rules for working better together
- **Performing.** Embrace high production of excellent quality

Olga's behavior changed throughout the team-building retreat. Prior to the session, during the leadership discussion, and during the time when the group was dealing with conflict, she criticized the group for not moving beyond their conflicts and doing their real job—developing goals and action plans. During the goal setting and action planning, however, she became engaged, excited, and initiating. She made suggestions about how the team could meet more regularly and assumed responsibility for many tasks.

Olga's shift in behavior can be explained by a number of factors. Ones prefer, even demand, *goals* that are clear, achievable, and meaningful. The initial focus of the retreat—dealing with the multiple conflicts, none of which involved Olga directly—met none of her criteria.

Ones usually prefer to work on teams that have moderate to high *interdependence*, but only when the other team members are competent, committed to the work, and complete their tasks. During the conflict discussions, Olga felt highly interdependent with other team members in working to accomplish this difficult task, but she doubted the others' competence to resolve conflict. She felt anxious and concerned about being part of a team that was high in interdependence but low in capability.

Olga's main *task role* can be observed in her attempts to structure the work for the group and her willingness to give her opinions. While most of her comments were posed as questions, questions are often opinions in disguise. For example, Olga's question, "Don't you think it's time to move to goals and action planning?" was really a statement made as an attempt to influence the group to change its direction. Olga's primary *relationship role* was to suggest norms or new ways of working together—as, for example, in her recommendation of how often she thought the team should meet. She exhibited her task role at the beginning of the session, and she switched to the relationship role near the end of the retreat.

At the *Forming* stage of a team, Ones often try to organize the work and usually have limited patience for building social connections. From the beginning of the retreat, Olga wanted to get the group organized, but she felt thwarted. Because of her role as support staff, she did not have enough clout to influence the group's direction.

Although the group was still forming, it was simultaneously *Storming*. During this stage, Olga was frustrated because there was conflict, and also because people were not dealing with the issues quickly. Ones usually treat conflicts as problems to be solved; once solutions have been found, Ones are ready to move on to the next task. When the group members engaged in discussing the conflict for what Olga perceived to be a prolonged time, she became impatient.

Ones actually prefer the Norming and Performing stages of team development. During *Norming*, they often suggest rules for better working relationships. This stage elicits what Ones tend to do anyway; they often create efficient methods for getting the work done. When a group is *Performing* at a high level of excellence, Ones experience the thrill of working on a perfect team.

Ones almost always appreciate a job well done, and Olga felt satisfied with the outcome of the team-building effort. The One's tendency to be judgmental, however, can still be seen in Olga's post-retreat thought that the session took too long. Ones can appreciate the accomplishments of the moment and simultaneously sense what can still be improved. Olga did gain some perspective on her desire to push the task along, as evidenced by her realization that not everyone moves at her preferred pace.

Analysis of Twos' Team Behavior

Enneagram Style
GIVING

Recap

BEFORE Tammy, a junior human resources specialist who reports to Simon, recently returned from a six-month leave of absence and so has missed the work situations that prodded Theresa to hold this retreat. When she met with Fred for her interview, she had very little to say. Tammy wants everyone to be enthused about working together toward common goals, but informal conversations with Simon, Olga, and Esther indicating that a number of unresolved problems exist within the group have dampened her hopes. *What is our common purpose?* she wonders. *What can I do to help people get past their frustration with Theresa and their distrust of one another?*

DURING Tammy asks many questions during the retreat. Some of these questions are requests for information that will fill in her six-month gap of understanding—for example, "When did this happen? What happened next?" Her other inquiries are attempts to draw out the feelings and thoughts of other group members: "What did you think when that happened? What kept you from sharing your feelings when you were upset? We all need to make a commitment to sharing our reactions, or these kinds of problems will happen again." At the end of the retreat, Tammy volunteers to work with several other team members on a number of different tasks.

AFTER Tammy is content both because she now knows what she missed during her leave of absence, and because the team now has several common goals and a commitment to work together. She does wish that she could have been more helpful during this retreat.

Tammy felt frustrated during the early part of the retreat because she did not fully understand the past events that had led to the group conflict. Twos like to help others but are hindered from providing assistance when they lack information and insight. There was, however, more to Tammy's frustration than her information deficit. Twos such as Tammy like purposeful *goals* that build on other people's talents. From Tammy's perspective, the group's goals were neither clear nor shared. For example, she wondered, *What is our common purpose?* In addition, Tammy had concerns about this group because she perceived everyone (herself included) to be highly talented and underutilized.

Twos like Tammy often prefer moderately to highly *interdependent* teams, but only when the team provides a safe and encouraging environment in which people feel motivated, listen to one another, and focus on the task at hand. Consequently, Tammy attempted to make the group into one in which she wanted to be a member. Almost all of her comments were made in the form of questions offering support to others for expressing their feelings and thoughts. Tammy believed that this encouragement would help others air their issues, then move on to the task of developing goals and action plans.

Tammy's primary *task role* during the retreat was one of soliciting information from other team members. She was quite active in extracting additional data from her colleagues—for example, "When did this happen?" and "What happened next?" Tammy's questions throughout the retreat also reveal the common Two *relationship role* of facilitating the process to encourage participation. She tried to draw out the feelings and thoughts of everyone in the

TWOS

- **Forming.** Encourage people's contributions; facilitate organizing group around a central purpose
- **Storming.** Assist others to express feelings toward a quick resolution; may give advice or distract through humor
- **Norming.** Push group for clear, shared agreements
- **Performing.** Like performing, particularly in support of star performers

group by focusing on implicit as well as explicit feelings. For example, she asked, "What kept you from sharing your feelings when you were upset?"

Tammy's behavior was fairly typical of Twos during the four stages of team development. When the team was *Forming* and *Storming* simultaneously, she tried to encourage other people's contributions related to the group's central purpose as she perceived it at that moment—resolving internal conflicts. At this time, she also tried to help others gain clarity about the issues. Tammy was not only seeking information, but she was also trying to understand how she might help the others resolve their issues.

During times of conflict, Twos often seek a quick resolution because they perceive conflict as an impediment that keeps people from performing at their best. Twos often take responsibility for easing edgy situations by giving advice or using humor to lighten the tension. Tammy did not exhibit either of these latter two behaviors, most likely because of her junior status in the group. Giving advice or making spontaneous jokes to ease conflict usually requires the messenger to be of a status equal to or higher than the other team members; if Tammy had made jokes or given advice to anyone in the group, her behavior would have been perceived as inappropriate.

During the *Norming* stage, Twos may assert themselves in a group by suggesting new agreements for working together. Tammy did this when she stated, "We all need to make a commitment to sharing our reactions, or these kinds of problems will happen again." This strong statement from an otherwise nonaggressive person is likely to get a response from someone in the group; most Twos will make this type of statement several times, if necessary, in order to get group agreement.

At the end of the retreat, when the group had reached the *Performing* stage, Tammy felt invigorated. She volunteered to work on several tasks, working alongside the other team members. Twos generally like high-performing teams and particularly enjoy supporting the team's superstars. They also take pleasure in the feeling of group synergy that arises when everyone is functioning at his or her potential.

Tammy tried her best to assist everyone else during the retreat. Afterward, she felt doubtful about whether she had given enough; however, she had in fact been one of the most helpful team members. It is very common for Twos to feel that they have not given enough to others, no matter how much assistance they have provided.

During the retreat, Tammy did not offer any personal information about her deeper feelings. She had intentionally given no indication that she actually felt concerned, anxious, and angry about being discounted as a junior member of the team—Twos often have difficulty expressing their own feelings and needs, and this can be particularly acute in a group setting.

Analysis of Threes' Team Behavior

Recap

BEFORE Theresa feels perplexed as she considers both the causes of her department's problems and their possible solutions. Outwardly, Theresa appears energetic and cordial. Inwardly, she feels anxious in anticipation of what might be said during the retreat about her leadership style. A week before the retreat, after reviewing the data from Fred's staff interviews, Theresa expresses her anxiety and impatience to him: "What can we do about these issues? What can I do about these staff conflicts? Do you think the agenda for this retreat will really work? Spending our energy on these issues is not a good use of anybody's time!"

DURING Theresa handles herself constructively throughout the retreat. She feels well prepared by Fred, the consultant, who met with her privately before the retreat in order to share the same information the group is now discussing. She starts the afternoon session on Friday by saying, "I know we have some serious issues to discuss, and my goal is to do whatever I can to help resolve them so we can keep adding value to the organization." During the retreat, Theresa decides to share her real feelings about her leadership style with the department members. She tells them, "I want everyone to be successful in this group. I'd feel terrible if anyone were unhappy. I know I've not made time for everyone, and I want to change that. Please be very honest with me when you tell me about my leadership."

With the leadership issues dealt with, Theresa can shift her focus from responding to questions about her leadership to helping guide the group in discussing and resolving the remaining topics. She asks open-ended questions such as these: "Are we making progress?" "Are we meeting our goals for this retreat?" "Do you think it's time to move on, or is there more to discuss?"

AFTER Theresa is appreciative that the retreat went so well, but she feels guilty that she has not been more supportive of Elliot.

Theresa's initial anxiety concerned the feedback she was about to receive from her staff about her leadership style. In addition, she was flustered by the ambiguity of the goals for the retreat. Threes prefer clear, measurable *goals* that link clearly to their own success and to the success of the organization. Theresa's group had strong feelings to deal with, and emotional issues do not lend themselves to clear goals in the same way that task-related problems do. Threes often feel uncomfortable when they have to discuss negative emotions. Theresa's apprehension can be seen in her comments such as, "Do you think

THREES

- **Forming.** Seek group approval early; may assert themselves in order to define goals
- **Storming.** Become disengaged; perceive conflict as a waste of time and too emotional
- **Norming.** Like unification, so refocus group on results and efficient work
- **Performing.** Favorite stage, so encourage others to increase their performance

the agenda for this retreat will really work? Spending our energy on these issues is not a good use of anybody's time! Are we making progress? Are we meeting our goals for this retreat?"

Threes often prefer working on teams with moderate to high *interdependence* rather than working alone, providing that they perceive the other team members as being both competent and willing to learn from one another. Theresa believed she had a highly capable staff, but she did not view them as able to learn from one another. She was, therefore, highly motivated to resolve the team's issues, and she hoped they could begin to share among themselves. She also desired a more affirming, less hostile work environment. Her question to the group, "Do you think it's time to move on, or is there more to discuss?" reflected Theresa's effort to get the group issues dealt with so that the process could evolve into the creation of productive interdependent relationships.

Theresa's primary team roles demonstrate how most Threes behave in groups. Her primary *task role*, defining goals and tracking the task, can be heard in almost every statement she made to the group, with the exception of her comments about her leadership style. For example, she consistently used words such as *goals*, *plans*, and *progress*. Her *relationship role* was one of facilitating the group to move the process forward. Again, her words, "Do you think it's time to move on, or is there more to discuss?" illustrate this role, as does her request for leadership style feedback: "Please be very honest with me when you tell me about my leadership."

During the *Forming* stage, Threes often assert themselves by clarifying the team's goals. Theresa began the retreat by saying, "I know we have some serious issues to discuss, and my goal is to do whatever I can to help resolve them so we can keep adding value to the organization." Threes may also do something at this stage in order to gain approval from the group. This desire for group affirmation can be inferred from Theresa's comment above, in which she implies that she is now ready to take action in the two areas she knows the group feels she has ignored—her leadership style and her unwillingness to mediate conflicts between group members.

During the *Storming* stage, Threes most commonly disengage from the conflict if they can. Theresa's desire to do this is reflected in her behind-the-scenes comment to Fred, "Spending our energy on these issues is not a good use of anybody's time!" She knew, however, that her conflict avoidance was partly responsible for the team's problems and that she now had to face these issues directly.

During the Norming and Performing stages of her team, Theresa lent her approval to every team decision. Threes usually like these later stages; during *Norming*, they can sense the emerging unification that refocuses the team on the work and on achieving results.

Performing is often a Three's favorite stage because he or she can see tangible results. At this time of the retreat, Theresa lent her full support to the team, and she encouraged the others to increase their performance.

The only exception to Theresa's full satisfaction with the team retreat was her remorse about how she had treated Elliot. She had a lingering sense of having failed him, as well as anxiety that this had caused some team members to not respect her. Theresa took her failure with Elliot particularly hard because she took great pride in her skills as a motivator and leader of people.

Analysis of Fours' Team Behavior

Recap

BEFORE After interviewing all of the staff members, Fred, the consultant, has become more concerned about how well the retreat will go. Staff members have told him about a number of sensitive issues, including three major conflicts that, in Fred's opinion, all directly or indirectly involve Theresa. During the interviews, Fred also learned that most of the staff do not want to attend the retreat. They also told

Enneagram Style ④

MOOD

him that they hoped he would be objective and unbiased in listening to them and in facilitating the retreat. Fred is hoping to live up to these expectations. He has other concerns as well: *Will people be forthcoming when they come together? Do I have enough trust and goodwill to draw out some difficult issues? What if this retreat isn't productive? If it isn't, I may never work in this company again!*

DURING Fred feels he is really earning his money conducting this retreat. Although the first morning was relatively easy because the group enjoyed learning about the Enneagram, Fred knew that the hard work lay ahead. For the remainder of the retreat, he has to pay attention to each team member's feelings and reactions, to the group's dynamics, and to moving the agenda forward without spending too much or too little time on any one person or issue. He makes sure that the agenda still meets the group's needs by asking questions such as, "Should we spend more time on this?" "Are we finished with that topic?" "Shall we add another item to the agenda?" He simultaneously pays attention to each person's reaction to the group's dynamics. He watches each person's body language closely and asks questions such as, "Do you have something to say?" "What feelings do you have about that?" "Is there something else on your mind?"

AFTER Fred feels the retreat went as well as it could. The team was feeling relieved and had found their direction. The success of the retreat means that there will probably be more work for Fred in the organization. He is feeling concerned that the conflict between Esther and Theresa was never discussed at the retreat, but he hadn't known how to raise the issues; he only heard about it from Esther, and she had told him she didn't want it brought up.

Fred cared about this project for several reasons. As a Four, Fred felt empathy for the team members most affected by the conflicts—Theresa, Faye, Simon, Esther, and Elliot. He was also concerned about the damaging effects of the group's power dynamics on Tammy, Esther, and Elliot. Fours often do whatever they can to help those whom they perceive to be in pain. The project's *goals*, therefore, met all of Fred's personal requirements. This project was

FOURS

- **Forming.** Focus on own internal feelings in relation to the group more than on the task
- **Storming.** Enjoy realness of explicit, constructive conflict as long as they are not a main participant
- **Norming.** Will suggest and support rules that add clarity but not ones that restrict individuality
- **Performing.** Feel most a part of a group at this stage; work hard toward common goals

personally meaningful; it was challenging; and it was large enough in scope to be worth doing, yet small enough to still be manageable.

Fred felt pleased with the emerging *interdependence* within the team. As a consultant, he could assist the others while not being a real part of the team. This suited Fred very well. Most Fours have an ambivalent reaction to highly interdependent teams. On one hand, Fours enjoy the connection and genuine communication among team members; on the other hand, they like to preserve their uniqueness, avoid rejection, and preserve their autonomy. Consequently, Fours often operate on the margins of teams—never fully outside the team, but never fully inside it, either. Being a consultant allowed Fred an insider view from a peripheral position, which is a very comfortable place for a Four.

Even when Fours are not in the consultant role, they typically act in a facilitative way. The Four's *task role*, similar to Fred's role with this team, often focuses on managing the team's agenda. Fours want to know that what needs to be said is said, and what needs to be covered is covered. Fred's early comments are good examples of this behavior: "Should we spend more time on this?" "Are we finished with that topic?" "Shall we add another item to the agenda?"

The most common *relationship role* for Fours, expressing feelings, refers to both the expression of their own feelings and their drawing out of others' emotions. In his role as the team's consultant, Fred did not share many of his own sentiments with the group, but he did make numerous comments to draw out other people—for example, "Do you have something to say?" "What feelings do you have about that?" "Is there something else on your mind?" Fours on teams often ask these types of questions, whether they are a team member or team leader.

During the *Forming* stage of a team, Fours often focus more on their own internal feelings about the group than they do on the group or the task. This tendency can be observed in some of Fred's initial thoughts—for example, *Do I have enough trust and goodwill to draw out some of the group's difficult issues? What if this retreat isn't productive? I may never work in this company again.* Here, the word *I* appears twice, and Fred's focus is on the group in relation to himself, rather than on the group itself or the individual members.

Fours often feel satisfied during the *Storming* stage, particularly when the conversation is honest and no one is trying intentionally to hurt someone else. They appreciate both the genuine self-expression and the sense of connection that often follow healthy conflict. On the other hand, if they perceive cruelty or disrespect or if they themselves are the objects of someone's hostility, Fours may suggest a change in the process, or they may instead respond with intense anger or back off and withdraw. Fred tried to change the situation when he redirected Simon and asked him to slow down his speech, talk to Faye directly, and give examples.

During *Norming*, Fours may suggest norms that either allow for authentic interaction or reduce the possibility of someone's getting hurt. They may also suggest norms that add clarity to people's roles or future interactions, as long as these rules do not overly restrict individual behavior. Fred watched the Norming phase of the team discussion, but he offered no suggestions because he thought the group was designing norms that were appropriate to their needs.

When a team is *Performing*, Fours often feel most included in the team; the Four's tendency toward "marginal" behavior, such as walking around or leaving, may dissipate. Again, because Fred was the consultant rather than a team member, he was always peripheral to the team. He was, however, very pleased with the results of the retreat.

Fours may have trouble feeling the full pleasure of success; they are sensitive to what is missing or is not as good as it could have been. Fred felt mildly disappointed at the end of the retreat because he knew that Tammy had not fully expressed her deep feelings and that Esther and Theresa had not resolved their differences.

Analysis of Fives' Team Behavior

Recap

BEFORE Faye, a senior human resources specialist, feels frightened and distant as she thinks about the coming retreat. She wants to be in control of what she will say there as well as how and when she will say it. Her preference is to say nothing, although she knows that this is unlikely. She feels agitated as she wonders, *Why does Simon make such nasty remarks about me? I work just as hard as everyone else, maybe harder. Don't clients always come first? Will Simon attack me in this retreat? How should I react if he does?*

DURING Faye says little during the leadership discussion except for supportive statements such as, "I can understand why Theresa has such limited time." She feels nervous about the time when she and Simon will deal with their conflict. She assumes Simon will launch the attack, because she has very little to say to him. In fact, her only problem with him is his negative attitude toward her. When Fred opens the discussion about the conflict between the two,

Simon confronts Faye about her not being a team player. Although Faye initially becomes flustered, she regains her composure and says, "I *am* a team player, as much as anyone else in this group. I attend the staff meetings except in an emergency, and I complete every assignment requested of me. All of us are under tremendous time pressure. Isn't our individual client work our first priority?"

AFTER Faye feels free. She now knows why Simon has been so aggressive with her, and she is relatively confident that he will stop his verbal assaults. She thinks the two of them might even be able to work together.

Fives prefer clear, practical, and tangible *goals* that are manageable in scope. In her work with clients, Faye had goals that met these criteria. Before the retreat, she did not think that team goals existed in the human resources department. Although Faye was not the only team member with this view, she believed she was alone in her perception because the topic of team goals had never been discussed. During the goal-setting part of the retreat agenda, she asked many clarifying questions because she wanted to make sure that the team developed goals they could truly achieve.

Fives enjoy working on teams as long as team members have enough autonomy to accomplish their work. Fives thus usually prefer low to medium *interdependence*, and they often prefer smaller teams to larger ones. Fives typically like responsibility and will take on additional work *if* it comes with a greater degree of control and a higher-level position in the organization. Faye was willing to commit to a higher degree of interdependence than she actually wanted once she understood the rationale for the increased teamwork, and also trusted her teammates. Faye had begun to feel more trusting after she and Simon had resolved their conflict.

FIVES

- **Forming.** Social connections feel frivolous, yet necessary; strong preference for a focus on goals
- **Storming.** Prefer to skip this stage in order to avoid anger and conflict
- **Norming.** Like clear rules and structure as long as these allow sufficient autonomy
- **Performing.** Prefer individual tasks in areas where they feel competent; like being appreciated for their knowledge

At the start of the retreat, Faye was so preoccupied with what Simon might do that she paid limited attention to the team. In a way, she was in her own internal world. However, her *task role* was still apparent: managing group and individual resources. Early in the session, she commented about time as a scarce resource, saying, "I can understand why Theresa has such limited time." She made other references to time—for example, when she lamented, "All of us are under tremendous time pressure." Fives usually guard their time and energy. Because they perceive resources to be a limited commodity, Fives do not typically like to have demands made on them, and they often feel overextended. Faye's *relationship role*, providing perspective, can be seen in her comment, "Isn't our individual client work our first priority?" In this statement, she is defending herself, but she is also trying to influence the group to examine the way they work from a larger perspective. Another way of rephrasing her comment would be the following: "We need to act from our highest priority and I think that it's client work. If not, then what is it?"

Most Fives view spending time on social connections and "chitchat" as frivolous, although necessary at certain times. For this reason, Fives often have limited patience for the "getting to know you" part of the *Forming* stage, preferring to focus directly on the task of the team—goals. Faye's initial goal for the retreat was simply to get Simon to stop attacking her. Once their conflict had been resolved, she was ready to examine the team's goals.

Fives generally do not like the *Storming* stage, because they tend to shy away from conflict. Conflict often demands too much of them emotionally, and dealing with differences forces them into situations in which they are expected to share their feelings. Such situations are difficult for Fives for two reasons. First, Fives typically detach from their emotions and so may not know what they are actually feeling. Second, if Fives are aware of their feelings, they typically prefer not to share them with others. Faye, unfortunately, found herself at the center of a conflict and had no escape route. She handled herself very effectively, but also felt completely drained afterward; Fives often feel depleted after intense emotional interchanges.

Fives often become more energetic at the *Norming* stage because they like clear expectations and want to influence the team's working agreements. In addition, they try to make sure that the new team rules provide for a high degree of individual autonomy. Faye did acquiesce to the norm that each team member should volunteer for one major project. Although she was already very busy, she selected a project in which she would work with one other person, someone whom she knew was highly competent.

When a team starts *Performing*, Fives often become enthusiastic. If they believe they can count on the work of others, Fives will take on tasks within their areas of competence. Faye was able to enjoy the end of the retreat because she had renewed hope in the team, and because she felt acknowledged for her expertise.

On this team, Faye was in a situation that would be challenging and difficult for anyone. However, the situation was particularly frightening for a Five. It was, in fact, a Five's worst nightmare, because it contained the following elements: high emotionality, with the Five at center stage; the demand for expressing feelings spontaneously; the fact that no one could leave the room because it was a retreat setting; the expectation that everyone would take on more work; and the fact that no one knew exactly what would happen. When it began, the two-day retreat contained little that was predictable. It's no wonder that Faye felt freed at the end of the retreat.

Analysis of Sixes' Team Behavior

Recap

BEFORE Simon, also a senior human resources specialist, is ambivalent about this retreat. On the one hand, he wishes he could avoid the whole thing; on the other, he thinks it is finally time to get the issues on the table. As he thinks about his feud with Faye, which began eight months earlier, he

Enneagram Style 6
DOUBT

anguishes, *Faye does not carry her weight in the group. She chooses to do her client work at the expense of our collective human resources projects. She misses departmental meetings and takes credit for the work done by people who report to her. No, she is not a team player! Should I say all this? Will I be forced into sharing my thoughts? What if no one else is willing to be honest? Why does Theresa keep supporting Faye? If I do have to say something, what should I say? Is our consultant capable of handling all of this?*

DURING Simon has not decided in advance whether or how he will confront Faye. When the time comes to discuss their conflict, the room is silent. Finally, Simon sits forward in his chair and begins a series of intense statements: "Faye always puts her work ahead of the group's work. She never volunteers for group projects." Fred, the consultant, asks Simon to make these three changes in his delivery: (1) talk directly to Faye, using words such as *you* rather than *she*; (2) slow down his speech; and (3) give specific examples. Simon continues by saying, "Faye, I don't think you are loyal to the team, only to yourself. I believe this because you choose your client needs over our group's needs, and you sit back when the time comes to volunteer. You may complete the few things assigned, but not always on time."

Once Simon and Faye understood that by their own definitions each was acting in good faith as a team player, their conflict subsided. Faye agreed to volunteer for more tasks and to attend staff meetings regularly, even when she was dealing with an emergency. Simon, for his part, realized that his vision of a team was only one viable way of defining a team; not only did he relax his assault on Faye, but he also apologized to her.

AFTER Simon feels appreciative that Fred managed everyone's negative emotions so well during the retreat, and he is cautiously optimistic that the group will start to act like a team.

Sixes frequently prefer a combination of team and individual *goals* that are substantial and meaningful. Simon was fully aware that everyone had individual goals, but he was dismayed at the lack of team goals and team effort. He felt like Sisyphus pushing the rock uphill when he tried over and over again to get the team aligned behind common goals. In Simon's mind, Faye was the main obstacle to achieving team goals, but he did not perceive her as the only culprit.

As is the case with Fives, Sixes usually like goals that have clearly delineated lines of individual responsibility. In contrast to Fives, however, most Sixes do not like a high degree of individual autonomy. The exception to this desire to be highly connected to teams is the extremely counterphobic Six, who would prefer fewer team-based constraints. Most Sixes, being a mixture of phobic and counterphobic, prefer to work on teams that have a moderate to high degree of *interdependence*, as long as the following criteria are met: each team member can be trusted to do a capable job; team members follow

SIXES

- **Forming.** Prefer watching the group's dynamics, but will clarify issues or ensure that vulnerable members get heard
- **Storming.** May engage in conflict if authority and improper use of power are involved; may also withdraw
- **Norming.** Work actively to secure agreement among group members, with attention to equal participation
- **Performing.** Keep other members focused on deliverables, act as troubleshooter, acknowledge others' contributions

through on tasks; and all team members demonstrate loyalty and commitment to the team. Sixes believe they exhibit these qualities, and they want the others to offer them in return; the reciprocation makes Sixes feel safe. This Six orientation to team interdependence can be heard in Simon's comments to Faye during the retreat—for example, "I don't think you are loyal to the team, only to yourself" and "You may complete the few things assigned, but not always on time."

Simon's *task role* on the team was the one Sixes most often play in team situations: they evaluate the information discussed within the team. Although this role may sound similar to the critiquing behavior of Ones, the evaluation process of Sixes is not that of differentiating between a good idea and bad one, but of anticipating what could go wrong with a particular idea. In anticipation of the retreat, Simon had a number of serious concerns—the agenda, the amount of time to be spent, and the competence of the consultant.

During the retreat, Simon also behaved in the most common Six *relationship role*, that of devil's advocate. After Faye had shared her thoughts in response to Simon's accusations, his reaction was to ask her a series of insightful and incisive questions. He did so to make sure that what Faye was saying was accurate and not merely a defensive reaction.

Simon's behavior during the retreat reflects the ways in which Sixes typically act during the four stages of team development. During the *Forming* stage, Simon was quiet and simply watched the group at work. He was attempting to assess the group's dynamics and to anticipate how the group might evolve. Simon also helped the group to clarify the main issues.

Although Simon was nervous about asserting himself during the retreat, he found the courage to suggest that the group had serious conflicts that needed resolution. While many Sixes may assert themselves to make sure that more vulnerable team members are heard, in this case, Simon did not do this because the most vulnerable team member was Elliot. In this situation, Simon was actually the antagonist, although he did not perceive himself as being in this role.

Most Sixes prefer to remain in the background during the *Storming* stage, because they view team conflict as an unsafe situation. Sixes, like all of us, do not always do what they most prefer, and so they do not always keep a low profile. Because Sixes typically evaluate information or play devil's advocate, team members may perceive them as behaving in a contrarian manner. Sixes' task and relationship roles on teams involve questioning or disagreeing with something that has been said by someone else. This role behavior can actually ignite a conflict. On the human resources team, Simon was a central player in the conflict. He was quite active, particularly in his exchanges with Faye—for example, when he said, "You choose your client needs over our group's needs, and you sit back when the time comes to volunteer." Or when he remarked to Elliot, "Who do you think you are to come into this group, work under me, and assume you know more about how we should do things than I do?"

By the time the team had evolved to the *Norming* stage, Simon felt exhausted, and as a result was rather subdued during this time. Most Sixes, however, become active during Norming and work to secure agreements among the team members. Many of the norms they suggest and support involve assurances that everyone will participate. Simon did not need to become active because everyone was already participating, and he liked all the agreements they were creating.

During the *Performing* stage, Simon became a little more active, particularly when the team designed goals and created action plans. As a senior team member, Simon was able to poke some holes in others' ideas, and he attempted to ensure that the ideas were both practical and concrete. It is at this stage that Sixes typically both play the devil's advocate role and also acknowledge other people's contributions. Simon acknowledged Elliot by commenting on Elliot's enthusiasm and intelligent ideas. He also acknowledged Faye, and immediately after the retreat, went over to speak with her. Although no one could hear their conversation, the other team members could see the emerging rapport between the two of them. They sat close to each other, talked intensely, and had smiles on their faces.

Simon's feeling of apprehension before the retreat is something any of us would have felt had we been in his shoes. However, the high level of his anxiety and the ways in which he showed his fear are more typical of Sixes. For example, the Six's tendency to engage in the creation of worst-case scenarios is apparent in Simon's pre-retreat thoughts: *Should I say all this? Will I be forced into sharing my thoughts? What if no one else is willing to be honest? Why does Theresa keep supporting Faye? If I do have to say something, what should I say? Is our consultant capable of handling all of this?* Simon's worst-case scenario building shows in his "what-if" line of questioning. The self-doubt and anguish of the Six is also apparent in Simon's continual questioning of himself regarding how he should behave at the retreat.

An additional Six tendency can be inferred from Simon's thoughts and behavior—paying close attention to the behavior of authority figures. Before the retreat, Simon had wondered why Theresa, his boss, had supported Faye rather than disciplined her. He also wondered whether the consultant, Fred, was competent to do the job. In the context of this retreat, the consultant was in a temporary leadership role. Sixes often focus on authority figures, looking to these individuals to provide security and protection, yet questioning their ability or willingness to do so.

Analysis of Sevens' Team Behavior

Recap

Enneagram Style
OPTIONS
7

BEFORE Saul, the most experienced senior human resources specialist in the group, wonders if he will have anything to contribute to the retreat. He knows that he has more experience and perspective than the other department members, but he works in a completely separate business unit and rarely sees his coworkers. He thinks, *Why would I want to get involved in their mess? Besides, I could hurt my relationships, especially with Theresa. She and I get along fine. What if something negative happens at the retreat, and I'm somehow involved? I need Theresa's support for my forthcoming promotion. I guess I'll just have to look interested even when I'm not and keep a low profile!*

DURING Saul says very little during any of the three heated discussions: the concerns about Theresa's leadership style, the conflict between Simon and Faye, and the issues related to Elliot. Saul does, however, appear involved, as if tracking the conversations closely. Occasionally, his eyes twinkle as he makes a spontaneous joke, for example, "If our clients could see us now, they might reconsider using our services!" Everyone laughs. During the goal-setting and action-planning discussion, Saul becomes very animated, sharing ideas for strategies and bringing in ideas from his prior experiences: "If we organized ourselves along client and project lines simultaneously, we could continue our individual work and create world-class human resources initiatives. This was very successful in the engineering environment where I last worked. Here's how you do it."

AFTER Saul's plan worked. He stayed active, alienated no one (at least no one of whom he is aware), and made some important contributions.

Saul had disengaged from the team before the retreat even began. This is reflected in his initial thought, *Why would I want to get involved in their mess?* While this sentiment was partly a result of his tendency as a Seven to avoid painful situations, Saul's reaction was also a result of his feelings about the team's *goals*—or, in this case, the lack of them. Sevens commonly become

SEVENS

- **Forming.** Contribute ideas about larger vision, dislike too much structure, can get impatient with lack of progress
- **Storming.** Do not like conflict and perceive many disagreements as trivial or petty; use humor to defuse serious situations
- **Norming.** Will suggest a minimal number of rules that include everyone but react against rules that feel limiting
- **Performing.** Tend to work from their own personal prioritizations and prefer a variety of tasks and roles that include positive social interaction

energized by stimulating, visionary, and action-oriented goals. The human resources department had no such goals.

Sevens usually enjoy working on teams; they enjoy interacting with others, and they are stimulated by new ideas. At the same time, Sevens usually prefer minimal structure to their work, because they believe that too much structure hampers their creativity and freedom. Thus, *interdependence*, whether it is low, medium, or high, is usually acceptable to Sevens as long as certain criteria are met: the roles between and among team members need to be fluid rather than rigid; the team environment must be egalitarian and democratic; and people's interconnections must allow for the full use of their gifts and talents. None of these factors existed in the human resources department.

The *task role* Sevens most often perform on teams is one of generating and elaborating on ideas. Saul demonstrated this near the end of the retreat; for example, he said, "If we organized ourselves along client and project lines simultaneously, we could continue our individual work and create world-class human resources initiatives."

The *relationship role* Sevens commonly exhibit on teams focuses on relieving tension, often through the use of humor. Saul exhibited this behavior when he made a joke so that the team could laugh at itself; he said, with perfect timing, "If our clients could see us now, they might reconsider using our services!"

During the *Forming* stage, Sevens often become impatient with the lack of team progress. Because Sevens typically grasp the big picture, think fast, and like to move to action quickly with a minimal amount of structure, they become frustrated with others who do not work at this accelerated pace. Saul was already annoyed with the group for having created this "mess." Although Saul said very little at the start of the retreat, his impatience showed in his body language, as he tapped his foot and squirmed in his chair.

During the *Storming* stage of the group, Saul also said little. In general, Sevens do not like conflict. They perceive disagreements, particularly those that do not involve them directly, as petty or nonproductive and often use humor as a way of defusing the situation. If the conflict does affect them directly, Sevens will typically reframe the problem in a way that justifies or rationalizes their own behavior. If reframing does not dissipate the tension, Sevens may become agitated and begin to blame others. In this situation, Saul was not directly involved, and he was therefore ready to move on.

During the *Norming* stage, Sevens generally either remain silent or speak up in order to ensure that the new agreements made are not ones that will curtail their individual freedom of action. Saul said nothing during this phase of the retreat, for two reasons: first, the team generated only a few working agreements; second, Saul believed that in any case he would probably not have to live with these rules, as he was anticipating being promoted. The new position would remove him permanently from the team.

In the *Performing* phase, Saul not only made several suggestions, but he also became enthusiastic because he enjoyed the positive team interactions. Saul was not particularly concerned about the team's goals. He knew that if he did not get the promotion and had to stay on this team, he would follow his own counsel. While Sevens do not ignore team objectives, they do tend to work more from their own set of priorities.

Saul's behavior also demonstrates additional ways Sevens tend to act on teams. They often have a general game plan, and Saul entered the retreat with a plan that he then successfully executed: *I'll just have to look interested even when I'm not.* Saul's inner dialogue about his relationship with Theresa and on how she might help or hurt him as he advanced in the organization reveals the Seven's sensitivity to authority: *Besides, I could hurt my relationships, especially with Theresa. She and I get along fine. What if something negative happens at the retreat, and I'm somehow involved? I need her support for my forthcoming promotion.*

Sevens tend to pay a great deal of attention to authority figures and typically perceive leaders as having the decision-making power to increase or curtail their future options. Consequently, Sevens often develop friendships with their bosses. In the Seven's mind, this helps to equalize the power in the relationship and gives the Seven more freedom to do what he or she wants to do. If befriending the boss is not successful, Sevens may ignore the leader, acting as if they have no boss at all. If ignoring the boss is unsuccessful, Sevens may engage in testy interchanges with their superiors, both privately and publicly. The first strategy worked well for Saul. He was Theresa's favorite staff member and her personal confidant.

Analysis of Eights' Team Behavior

Enneagram Style **8**
CHALLENGE

Recap: Esther

BEFORE Esther has the credentials to be a senior human resources specialist, but Theresa refuses to formally raise her level or even to acknowledge Esther's experience and expertise. Esther feels angry as she thinks, *I could be the department head—at least I'm decisive! Is Theresa threatened by me?* Esther's major concern about the retreat, however, is Elliot, the department intern with whom she is very close. She thinks, *He is more capable than most people in this department. Sure, he has a few rough edges, but I thought we were supposed to mentor him. He's a diamond in the rough, and we should be helping him! Theresa should be watching out for him; instead, she just lets Simon attack him.*

DURING Esther has brought some client work with her and sits far away from Theresa. She thinks that perhaps she will do some work in the event that she does not like the conversation. Esther knows that the other group members will not like this, but she doesn't care. During the leadership discussions, she watches closely but says little. She wonders, *Why are we doing this? Is this session going the way it needs to go? Is all this talk, including Theresa's apologetic response, for real?* When the agenda moves to the issues about Elliot, however, Esther initiates the discussion, saying, "We need to take a long, hard look at what we've done here. Elliot is our group intern, and what have we done? Simon is downright rude to Elliot, Theresa has done nothing visible to find him another position, and the rest of us have let Elliot get completely demoralized. Does anyone else care?"

AFTER Esther feels satisfied that there is some closure for Elliot regarding how he was treated in the group. She likes the team better, but she is still not sure that she trusts Theresa.

Recap: Elliot

BEFORE Elliot has been with the group for a year working as a paid intern, but everyone knows that he plans to leave in two weeks. The process of looking for a new job and separating from the human resources department has been exhausting and stressful for him. He tried to excuse himself from having to attend this retreat, but both Esther and the facilitator, Fred, have urged him to attend. Elliot worries, *Why is Simon so hostile to me? Why hasn't Theresa tried to find me a job in this group? I have no idea what I would have done all* *these months without Esther. Sometimes she gives me great advice. Sometimes it's nice just to talk with her and be understood. Could I have done something to upset the others? All I've done is conduct research, make suggestions, and ask the hard questions. Mostly, they've ignored me!*

DURING Elliot feels very vulnerable, but he is also very angry. He wants to stay with the organization and knows that burning bridges is not in his best interests; at the same time, he wants to say something. He wonders, *How much should I say?* After Esther's preamble, the group turns to look at Elliot. Elliot responds by saying, "I will continue working in the company, just in another department. This group means a lot to me, and it was my hope to stay in human resources. Simon not only does not support me, but he is openly hostile. Why? I don't know. Why, Simon? What have I done?"

Simon's answer surprises many group members when he says, "Who do you think you are to come into this group, work under me, and assume you know more about how we should do things than I do? It takes time to learn, but you just assume that you know everything. I don't care if you do have an MBA!"

AFTER Elliot feels exhausted and relieved. He understands more fully what happened to him and why his experience in the department was so painful, but he still thinks the team needs to reinvent the ways it serves clients.

Eights like big-picture, strategic *goals*. Both Esther and Elliot dismissed the team's initial goals because they perceived these as being vague and pedestrian. In addition, Eights often respond well to goals that are aligned with their social values. This team had no explicit values base to either its goals or its actions.

EIGHTS

- **Forming.** Either suggest direction for the group or pull back and watch, deciding whether to be part of the team
- **Storming.** Enjoy the intensity of the interaction as long as people are honest; are often part of the conflict, but if not, they will lead the dialogue
- **Norming.** Will recommend ground rules, particularly ones that allow everyone to be heard
- **Performing.** If they find the productivity exciting, they will stay; if the work is not significant or too predictable, they will move on

Esther and Elliot were, in a sense, team "outlaws," but outlaws with a great deal of personal power. Esther expressed her need for the team to be aligned with her social values when she said, "Simon is downright rude to Elliot, Theresa has done nothing visible to find him another position, and the rest of us have let Elliot get completely demoralized. Does anyone else care?"

Eights like their independence, although they also enjoy *interdependence* if the team members are highly capable. The Eights' desire for independence can be interpreted as needing a sense of their own territory. This is different from the Five's desire for autonomy or space. While *space* means "Leave me alone to do my work, and I'll leave you alone to do yours," *territory* suggests the need to expand one's own areas of competence and responsibility, as in "Give me room to move."

Both Esther and Elliot felt professionally thwarted in the department. Esther thought, *I could be the department head—at least I'm decisive.* She also perceived Elliot as being held back: *He's more capable than most people in this department.* Elliot felt that Simon was very threatened by his competence and knowledge, and this was reinforced when Simon said, "Who do you think you are to come into this group, work under me, and assume you know more about how we should do things than I do? It takes time to learn, but you just assume that you know everything."

Eights also like to create order out of chaos, but often prefer some degree of chaos over too much order. For many Eights, chaos is a challenge; an overly ordered situation does not ignite their enthusiasm about working to get something bigger and more important under control. Eights therefore often prefer a slightly underorganized structure within their interdependent team.

The most common *task role* of Eights is consistent with their preferred team goals; Eights usually try to articulate the team's larger purpose and try to keep the team from focusing only on tactics or goals. Esther thought that the department had no strategic purpose. She also believed that the group could not create a vision until it had dealt with the issue of Theresa's leadership style. Eights are often highly sensitive to power dynamics, and they understand the critical role that leadership plays in a team's effectiveness. The question Esther asked herself, *Is Theresa threatened by me?*, reflects this sensitivity.

From the time Elliot had joined the group, he had attempted to get the others to tackle strategic issues, doing so through his research and benchmarking. However, he had received little support for his endeavors and thought, *All I've done is conduct research, make suggestions, and ask the hard questions. Mostly, they've ignored me!*

The most common Eight *relationship role*, challenging, is clearly demonstrated in the behavior of both Esther and Elliot during the retreat. For example, Esther challenged the team when she said, "We need to take a long, hard look at what we've done here. Elliot is our group intern, and what have we done?" Elliot's plea to Simon was a challenging remark: "Why, Simon? What have I done?"

During the *Forming* stage, Eights tend to do one of two things: suggest a direction for the team to take, or pull back and watch. When they do the latter, they are actually deciding whether or not they want to be part of the team. Esther and Elliot were only partially committed to the group. Esther was considering leaving the company entirely, and Elliot had already located a position in another department. Consequently, they did not assert themselves early in the retreat.

Their behavior became very different during the *Storming* stage. Esther and Elliot both became very active at this point, particularly when the topic of Elliot's treatment by the team was being discussed. During the discussion of the conflict between Faye and Simon, Esther and Elliot watched closely. They wanted the answer to two questions: Was Simon capable of resolving a dispute in a respectful way, and was the team honest enough to deal with feelings truthfully? If the answers to both questions were yes, then Esther and Elliot were willing to discuss their feelings. Eights usually appreciate the intensity of honest, direct conflict and are typically active during the Storming stage. They do not, however, like conflict when they feel blindsided. In this situation, Esther and Elliot were fully aware of what issues were likely to be discussed.

During the *Norming* stage, Eights may suggest a small number of working rules, which are usually agreements that create inclusion for everyone on the team. In this situation, neither Esther nor Elliot did this because they were not highly invested in making the team more effective, believing that they would be leaving the team soon.

When the team began the *Performing* stage, Elliot made a few suggestions about goals and tactics, and Esther volunteered for the tasks that she thought were important. Eights like this stage only when they believe that their own work will be significant and challenging. However, if they think the goals and tactics are either mundane or misguided, they will usually leave the team, and perhaps even the organization.

Eights often behave similarly to the way Esther and Elliot acted during this retreat. When Eights are active on a team, their presence is usually intense and strong. When they are silent, the team still pays attention to them.

Although Elliot felt he was ignored (and he was), it was not Elliot himself but his ideas that were not given full consideration. This was because of his junior status in the human resources department and because his ideas seemed to imply criticisms of the group. However, the others were always aware of Elliot as a person.

An additional aspect of typical Eight behavior is revealed in this case study. Although Eights often appear tough and strong on the outside, on the inside they may actually feel quite vulnerable. Feeling vulnerable is something Eights try to avoid. Elliot felt vulnerable on this team, and especially so at this retreat. Esther rose to his defense, in a sense becoming his protector. She saw herself in Elliot, and his vulnerability made her more painfully aware of her own.

Analysis of Nines' Team Behavior

Enneagram Style
⑨
HARMONY

Recap

BEFORE Nigel, a human resources specialist, has not been looking forward to this retreat. Although he has had a few conversations with his coworkers about the coming event, he has kept his real feelings to himself. His strong preference would be not to attend the retreat. His thoughts are these: *What a pathetic group! The personalities can be so strong and overbearing. There's so much work on my desk—how can I take two days away from the office?*

DURING Nigel wishes all this were not happening. He is caught between wanting to avoid all the group tension and not wanting to be invisible in the group. He knows he will be ignored if he says nothing. During the discussions about conflict in the group, he steels himself and says, "Another factor to consider is Theresa's demanding international travel schedule. Have we thought through the intense pressures on us all to serve so many clients? Maybe Simon and Elliot are both concerned that with the possible restructuring, there may not be jobs for everyone. Maybe we're all worried about this." During the goal setting and action planning, Nigel becomes very relaxed and active. "This can really work. We're finally getting somewhere! We're a team!"

AFTER Nigel thinks the time has been well spent. He looks forward to the team's continued progress.

Nines like to work with clearly defined, concrete *goals* that are developed by team consensus. When Nines find the goals to be personally meaningful, they become even more motivated. Nigel perceived the human resources

NINES

- **Forming.** Have difficulty focusing if progress is slow; may become impatient
- **Storming.** Uncomfortable and looking for a way out
- **Norming.** Ambivalent about developing agreements; like the consensus, but don't like arbitrary rules
- **Performing.** Find getting something accomplished with a harmonious group feels very pleasurable

department's goals to be vague and unfocused. In addition, he disliked the hostility, both subtle and overt, that existed among some of the team members. He would have preferred to be somewhere other than at this retreat, as shown in his pre-retreat thought, *There's so much work on my desk—how can I take two days away?*

Nines often enjoy their *interdependence* with coworkers. They enjoy the warm ambience and the comfort that often come when a harmonious team interacts. However, when a team is highly interdependent for extended periods of time, Nines can become tense because they feel that too many demands and deadlines are being placed on them. In general, as long as team members meet their assignments and there is ample stimulation in a predictable work environment, Nines can be happy with low, medium, or high interdependence.

A Nine's most common *task role* is to give information to the team. When giving this information, Nines tend to present ideas, opinions, and facts that have not been previously discussed. Nines also see multiple points of view, and it is important to them that the other team members take these alternative perspectives into consideration. Nigel was doing this when he said, "Another factor to consider is Theresa's demanding international travel schedule. Have we thought through the intense pressures on us all to serve so many clients? Maybe Simon and Elliot are both concerned that with the possible restructuring, there may not be jobs for everyone. Maybe we're all worried about this." These comments also reflect the common Nine *relationship role*, that of harmonizing group interactions. Not only was Nigel giving additional information to the team, but he was doing so with the intention of mediating the impending conflict. He was trying to get the team members to see one another's points of view. From the Nine's perspective, if everyone considers the other person's feelings and ideas, conflict can be avoided or at least minimized.

Nines often become impatient during the *Forming* stage; Nigel was impatient even before the retreat began. He was frustrated with having to attend the retreat and was thinking about the work on his desk. When Fred reviewed the department data with the group, Nigel thought that this review took too much time. When Nigel heard about the items related to conflict within the group, he became anxious. As a result of these two issues, Nigel did not pay close attention during the Forming stage, but instead let his mind wander to things not related to the retreat.

During the *Storming* stage, Nines often become uncomfortable and may try to make peace within the team. If this does not work, they may try to find a way to extricate themselves from the situation. When the conflict became explicit during the retreat, Nigel tried to mediate. Although he could not leave the retreat because it was an off-site event, he might have tried to do so had it been held at the office.

When the team evolves to the *Norming* stage, Nines often feel relieved because the tension and disharmony are lessening. However, Nines like this stage only if the new working agreements have been developed through team consensus. If the norms come from the leader, with little input from team members, Nines tend to be less satisfied; Nines sense that team agreements developed solely by the leader are often the source of further conflict. Nines may also back away during the Norming stage. While Nines like predictability and consensus, they do not like being told what to do; norms are rules that prescribe and control individual behavior. During this part of the session, Nigel primarily listened, tracked the discussion mentally, and made comments only when he thought the new rules were too restrictive.

Nines usually flourish during the *Performing* stage, and Nigel volunteered enthusiastically for several assignments. The idea of accomplishing goals through the work of a highly productive, harmonious team fit his image of an ideal team situation.

Nigel's behavior at the start of the retreat was dramatically different from his behavior at the end. The reason for this shift was the transformation of the department, which had moved from being simply a group of nine individuals (from which Nigel wished to extract himself) into a real team (which excited him).

Nigel's behavior also demonstrated two other Nine tendencies. When Nines discuss multiple points of view, they often make comments regarding ideas that have not yet been fully articulated by other team members. When this occurs, the team members may not understand exactly what Nines are thinking. Questions such as these may arise in people's minds: *Are they just expressing this perspective, or do they agree with that idea? Since they said some-thing that is the opposite of what I said, do they disagree with me or are they merely raising alternatives?* Considering all points of view can be helpful to teams, but because Nines may not firmly state their own positions, other team members may feel confused and not respond to their comments. At these times, Nines often feel ignored. In addition, because Nines are usually most active at the later stages of team development, they may feel less influential, at least for a period of time, than other team members. This often changes, however, when the team becomes highly productive.

How to Develop and Improve Teams

Now that you understand more about teams and the influence of individual Enneagram styles on the behavior of team members, you are in an excellent position to help your group develop as a team. Taking the following steps will help you to dramatically improve any team's effectiveness.

Step 1: Determine Whether the Group Is a Team

If the members of a group do not share common goals and do not have some degree of interdependence, they will become frustrated if they try to become a team. The members of some groups in organizations actually have little in common—for example, the group may be a staff support unit for whom the only common element is that the individuals work for the same organization. Although these groups can never become real teams, they can still benefit from discussing how they will work together and what they need from the group leader. In addition, the groups can be helped by periodic meetings to provide members with organizational updates and occasional social events to help reduce any sense of individual isolation.

The first step with any group is to discuss whether the group has the potential to meet the two essential criteria for becoming a team: (1) members share common goals, and (2) members have some degree of interdependence. If either or both of these criteria are not present, please skip to Step 2. The activity in Step 2 can still help individuals who are part of groups—but not part of a real team—learn to strengthen and expand the roles they play in group meetings.

If, on the other hand, both team criteria are met, continue with the activities for Step 1. These two activities will help the team to develop common goals and articulate the ways in which members need to depend on one another's work to accomplish their goals.

CLARIFY COMMON GOALS The most direct way to determine a team's common goals is to simply ask this question: *What are our current and/or potential common goals?* Team members may have different opinions, in part because of differences in Enneagram styles. Knowledge of the Enneagram helps team members to understand that their own preferences reflect their perspectives. With this insight, team members often become more flexible, and reaching consensus becomes far easier.

There is a second way that the Enneagram can be useful in developing team goals. While it is nearly impossible to create goals that completely satisfy individuals of all Enneagram styles, the Enneagram can highlight a way to accommodate and, therefore, enlist all nine styles. This can be accomplished by finding the team's common ground—that is, goals that appeal to everyone. The accompanying chart of ideal team goals by Enneagram style reveals a number of explicit as well as implicit similarities across Enneagram styles (Figure 5.4). Four basic principles underlie the common ground for creating ideal team goals, regardless of the Enneagram styles of the team members.

Team Goals: Common Ground for All Enneagram Styles

1. All nine styles like team goals because these focus the work of all team members and provide a way for all members to be allied with the larger team efforts.

FIGURE 5.4 Ideal Team Goals for Each Enneagram Style

1 Clear, realistic, and purposeful

2 Common and meaningful, utilizing the talents of others

3 Specific, measurable goals linked to individual and organizational success

4 Significant and challenging, broad in scope, with specific benchmarks

5 Precise, concrete, useful, and manageable

6 Substantial and meaningful for both the team and individuals

7 Stimulating, energizing, visionary, and action oriented

8 Reflect the big picture and move the organization

9 Concrete and meaningful, developed by consensus

2. All nine styles become energized by team goals that are linked to an important organizational or social purpose.
3. All nine styles work best from clear, actionable goals.
4. All nine styles feel motivated when they see results from their work.

Developing goals based on the above principles will put your team on the path to success. When these four principles are followed, team members of all nine Enneagram styles will experience very little discrepancy between their ideal goals and those of the team, thus increasing everyone's level of satisfaction with the team.

DELINEATE INTERDEPENDENCIES Once common goals have been determined, the next step is to identify interdependencies among team members. This may sound like a complex task, but it can be made simple through the following group exercise:

Bring the team together to define the ways in which each person's work depends on someone else's work (see, for example, Figure 5.5). Ask the team to answer the following question: *What are the specific ways in which each of us depends on someone else's work in order to get our work done?* As team members do this activity, create a chart similar to Figure 5.5 to reflect their comments. Continue this activity until all of the interdependencies within the group have been articulated.

FIGURE 5.5 Interdependence Chart

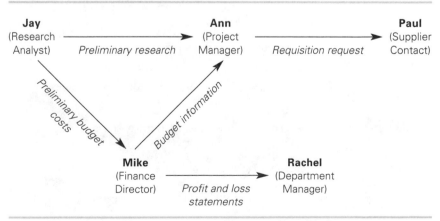

After this activity has been completed, have a team discussion to help members become more aware of the team's need for interdependence. The following discussion questions can be very helpful:

- How would you describe the current level of interdependence within this team?
- Which dependencies are inefficient and should be eliminated?
- What additional dependencies that do not currently exist could help our team achieve our goals more effectively?
- Given our team's level of interdependence, what are the implications for how we need to work together?

There are wide variations in Enneagram style preferences regarding team interdependence, as summarized in Figure 5.6.

Anchoring the ends of these variations are Fives, who typically prefer interdependencies with a great deal of individual freedom, and most Sixes, who often like a high degree of team interdependence. While this wide spectrum may seem impossible to bridge, in real life almost everyone will accept what-

---

FIGURE 5.6 **Ideal Interdependence for Each Enneagram Style**

1 Unambiguous interdependence with competent and responsible team members

2 Moderate to high interdependence in a warm, supportive environment

3 Clear lines of interdependence, appropriate to the task, with focused, capable team members

4 Interdependence that allows independence, in a self-expressive and creative environment

5 Low interdependence, high degree of autonomy, with capable and efficient team members

6 Moderate to high interdependence in a like-minded, capable, and loyal team

7 Fluid roles in a democratic, stimulating, and productive environment

8 Interconnections that allow for one's own territory, with effective, enjoyable team members

9 Interdependence with specific tasks in a stable, harmonizing environment

ever level of interdependence is best for the team *as long as they fully understand why that level of interdependence is important.*

More often than not, team members will bypass their personal preferences for the greater good of the team. The critical element is to provide a common understanding of the rationale for the degree of optimal interdependence. The preceding exercise provides a useful way to achieve this important individual and team alignment.

Step 2: Encourage Team Members to Experiment with Different Team Roles

While individuals of all nine Enneagram styles play varied roles in teams, there are certain roles that people of each style tend to exhibit consistently. The following activity helps individuals try out new behaviors in team settings. Since this activity can help change the behavior of individual members of a team, it is also a provocative and highly effective way to alter a team's interpersonal dynamics. When one person changes, this change will affect the way everyone on the team behaves. When several people shift their behavior, the resulting changes in team dynamics are even more profound.

During a team meeting, have each team member try a new *task role* and a new *relationship role*. These roles will be very different from each person's customary roles.

Figure 5.7 summarizes the most common task and relationship roles for individuals of each Enneagram style and suggests alternative roles for each style. The alternative roles are the opposite of each style's most common team roles: when people try behaviors opposite to those that are customary for them, changes in both individual behavior and team dynamics are more dramatic.

This activity is usually challenging, educational, and fun to do. The challenge arises because each person is asked to behave "out of character." That is also what makes this activity so educational. Often we don't realize that we are playing consistent roles until we try a different role. At first, many people will feel awkward, but with a little practice they will begin to expand their behavioral repertoire. The team will benefit (and everyone may have a good laugh!).

Trying an unfamiliar behavior can be extremely challenging, but behaviors that challenge us also help us to grow. Following are brief synopses of opposite task and relationship roles for each Enneagram style.

Opposite Task Roles
- **Ones** can learn the skill of soliciting information from others rather than giving their own opinions.
- **Twos** can practice giving their own opinions instead of soliciting information from others.

FIGURE 5.7 **Team Roles for Each Enneagram Style**

Style	Common Task Role	*Opposite Task Role*	Common Relationship Role	*Opposite Relationship Role*
1	Structuring tasks and giving opinions	*Soliciting information*	Suggesting norms (working agreements)	*Facilitating the positive resolution of conflict*
2	Soliciting information	*Giving opinions*	Facilitating the process to encourage participation	*Facilitating to move process ahead*
3	Defining goals and tracking task	*Managing the agenda*	Facilitating to move process ahead	*Facilitating the process to encourage participation*
4	Managing the agenda	*Defining goals and tracking task*	Expressing feelings	*Providing perspective*
5	Managing resources	*Defining larger purpose*	Providing perspective	*Expressing feelings*
6	Evaluating information	*Generating and elaborating on ideas*	Playing devil's advocate	*Relieving tension*
7	Generating and elaborating on ideas	*Structuring tasks (but not giving opinions)*	Relieving tension	*Playing devil's advocate*
8	Defining larger purpose	*Managing resources*	Challenging	*Harmonizing group interactions*
9	Giving information	*Evaluating information*	Harmonizing group interactions and facilitating the positive resolution of conflict	*Challenging*

- **Threes** can experiment with managing the agenda to make sure it is meeting the team's needs, rather than defining goals early on and then making sure that everyone stays on task.
- **Fours** can benefit from defining the team's goals and tracking the task, rather than managing the agenda so that the agenda meets everyone's needs.

- **Fives** can stretch themselves to help the team define its larger purpose (including vision and strategy), rather than focusing on managing resources to make sure there are sufficient resources to get the job done.
- **Sixes** can practice generating and elaborating on ideas instead of reacting to the ideas of others by evaluating information.
- **Sevens** can learn from structuring tasks, a role that delineates and clarifies the work, rather than generating and elaborating on ideas, a role that expands and creates more work. They should be careful, however, not to adopt the role of giving opinions, as this is very similar to their usual task role.
- **Eights** can try managing resources to ascertain whether there is enough to go around, versus defining the larger purpose, which often requires more resources than originally anticipated.
- **Nines** can challenge themselves by evaluating information, a role that can produce conflict, instead of giving information.

Opposite Relationship Roles

- **Ones** can learn from facilitating the positive resolution of conflict instead of suggesting norms or working agreements because this new behavior stretches Ones to spend the time and have the patience to draw out the concerns of others.
- **Twos** can challenge themselves by facilitating to move the process ahead rather than encouraging participation—behavior that can keep the team focused on where it is rather than where it is going.
- **Threes** can grow by facilitating the process to encourage participation instead of facilitating to move the (task) process ahead; this shift forces Threes to focus more on involvement and less on results.
- **Fours** can learn by providing perspective instead of expressing feelings, because the new behavior causes Fours to be more objective and less affected by feelings and emotional tone.
- **Fives** can challenge themselves by expressing feelings, both their own and other people's, moving away from the more cerebral role of providing perspective.
- **Sixes** can add joy and humor to the team if they try the role of relieving tensions rather than that of playing devil's advocate.
- **Sevens** can switch roles to playing devil's advocate by asking tough questions, although not in a critical way, rather than relieving tensions through humor and the infusion of upbeat energy.
- **Eights** can challenge themselves by harmonizing group interactions, a behavior that requires them to bring out the truths of multiple perspec-

tives, rather than engaging in their more usual role of challenging people and ideas.

- **Nines** can expand their behavioral repertoire by challenging others, rather than working to harmonize group interactions and mediate the resolution of conflict.

You may have noticed that in many cases, the opposite for individuals of one Enneagram style is the common behavior for individuals of the Enneagram style right next to it. For example, the new task role for Ones (soliciting information) is the common task role for Twos, and vice versa. In the relationship role column, the new relationship role for Nines (challenging) is the common relationship role for Eights, and vice versa. This is not a chance happening. The styles on either side of an Enneagram style are the "wings" of that style, as discussed in Chapter 1, "Discovering Your Enneagram Style." Our wings can be very helpful to us in our growth and development. When we integrate some of the characteristics of our wings into our daily behaviors, we are claiming some of our underdeveloped potential.

The exceptions to the pattern of exchanging roles with the wing styles can be seen in the task role column for styles Five, Seven, Eight, and Nine. For these Enneagram styles, the opposite task role comes from either the stress point or the security point (see Chapter 1, "Discovering Your Enneagram Style"). The opposite task role for Fives is the common task role for Eights, and vice versa; Eight is the security point for Fives, and Five is the stress point for Eights. For Sevens, the opposite task role is structuring tasks, which is the common task role for Ones, their stress point. Nines also draw their opposite task role from their stress point, Six.

Step 3: Educate Team Members About the Stages of Team Development

Most teams go through the four stages of team development without being aware they are doing so. In addition, most team members experience some degree of anxiety and frustration during the Forming, Storming, and even the Norming stages. Consequently, teams often try to jump over these first three stages and move directly to the Performing stage.

Catapulting over these early stages rarely creates a high-functioning team. For example, a group that has not completely formed as a team will have a difficult time dealing with conflict, because sufficient trust has not yet been developed among the members; dealing with conflict requires a belief in a positive outcome that grows from trust and goodwill. In addition, at this point in a team's life cycle, there is usually only preliminary commitment to the team. After a team has formed, however, conflict can usually be resolved more easily. Team members will have a sufficient sense of direction and enough investment in the team that they will be willing to invest the time and energy needed for resolving differences.

When team members learn about the stages of team development and understand the dynamics that occur at each stage, as well as their related Enneagram style behaviors, they often act less impatiently and more effectively throughout the entire process of team development. The four stages of team development model is not only extremely helpful, but it is also simple to use.

The first two activities here provide guidelines for working with the four stages of team development model *before* showing the team members how to integrate the insights of the Enneagram with it. The third activity shows how to use the insights of the Enneagram to expand each team member's behavioral repertoire at each of the four stages.

TEAM ACTIVITY 1 Explain the four stages of team development model and discuss how these ideas apply to the team. Following are key questions for discussion:

- What stage is our team in right now, and why do you think this is so?
- *If the team is past the Forming stage:* What were our team's particular dilemmas or issues at the prior stage(s), and how did we resolve these issues?
- Are there any unresolved issues left over from any prior stages? If so, how can we effectively deal with these issues?
- What do we need to do to address the issues of our current stage?

If the team is a start-up team, this model can still be used with great success, as it can prevent team-development obstacles before they arise. The following additional topics and questions are particularly useful for new teams, who will always be in the Forming stage:

- Think about other highly productive teams of which you have been a member. How have they functioned at each stage of development, and how did this contribute to their success?
- Think about unproductive teams of which you have been a member. How have they functioned at each stage of development, and how did this team behavior contribute to their difficulties?
- What can we (as a new team) learn from our cumulative past experiences?
- What agreements do we want to make now about how we will function at each of the four stages?

TEAM ACTIVITY 2 Have each team member assess his or her own behavior at each stage of team development, with individuals making a commitment to change behaviors that currently impede the team's development and progress or could do so in the future.

Once all of the team members have learned the importance of constructively meeting the challenges of each stage of team development and understand the central issues of each stage, the individual members are ready to learn what they can do to help the team's progress at each stage. Each person should ask himself or herself the following questions; while these questions can be answered individually without any team discussion, it will have a stronger impact if team members discuss their assessment results with the entire team.

• How do I act during each stage that helps or hinders the team's progress?
• How can I ensure that I maintain the behaviors that help the team?
• How can I stop doing those things that hinder the team?
• What can I do more of or add to my behavioral repertoire that will assist the team in its growth and development?

TEAM ACTIVITY 3 Have each team member compare his or her answers to the four questions above with the related Enneagram style behavior described in Figure 5.8, "Enneagram-Related Behavior at Each Stage of Team Development." After this individual analysis, conduct a team discussion, with team members highlighting what they have learned from using this Enneagram-based information in conjunction with the four stages of team development model. Based on this new information, ask each team member to adjust his or her commitments to make changes in behavior and to verbalize these new commitments to the entire team.

It is particularly useful to assess and change team members' behavior during the Forming and Storming stages, as it is during these stages that teams tend to have the most problems. If teams experience difficulties later, in the Norming or Performing phases, the issues that arise can often be traced to individual team member behavior and unresolved issues from the first two stages.

As you review the common behaviors for all nine Enneagram styles during the Forming stage of team development, you will find that something intriguing emerges. You may have noticed that Twos are the only Enneagram style whose common team behavior is to help team members orient to the team and get to know one another. Individuals of other Enneagram styles either tend to become impatient with the formation process and want to move quickly to doing the task, or they focus on the task rather than the people. As a result, many teams are left with a deficit in the relationship area. At the Forming stage, the core issue for all Enneagram styles except Twos is to shift individual behav-

FIGURE 5.8 **Enneagram-Related Behavior at Each Stage of Team Development**

Style	Forming *orientation to people and work*	Storming *conflict*	Norming *developing working agreements*	Performing *high performance and team synergy*
1	Task-focused, with minimal need for social connection; may suggest ways to structure work	Frame conflict as a problem to be solved, exert leadership to do this and grow impatient if the conflict endures	Suggest rules for working better together	Embrace high production of excellent quality
2	Encourage people's contributions; facilitate organizing group around a central purpose	Assist others to express feelings toward a quick resolution; may give advice or distract through humor	Push group for clear, shared agreements	Like performing, particularly in support of star performers
3	Seek group approval early; may assert themselves in order to define goals	Become disengaged; perceive conflict as a waste of time and too emotional	Like unification, so refocus group on results and efficient work	Favorite stage, so encourage others to increase their performance
4	Focus on own internal feelings in relation to the group more than on the task	Enjoy realness of explicit, constructive conflict as long as they are not a main participant	Will suggest and support rules that add clarity but not ones that restrict individuality	Feel most a part of a group at this stage; work hard toward common goals
5	Social connections feel frivolous, yet necessary; strong preference for a focus on goals	Prefer to skip this stage in order to avoid anger and conflict	Like clear rules and structure as long as these allow sufficient autonomy	Prefer individual tasks in areas where they feel competent; like being appreciated for their knowledge

continued

FIGURE 5.8 Enneagram-Related Behavior at Each Stage of Team Development

Style	Forming *orientation to people and work*	Storming *conflict*	Norming *developing working agreements*	Performing *high performance and team synergy*
6	Prefer watching the group's dynamics, but will clarify issues or ensure vulnerable members get heard	May engage in conflict if authority and improper use of power are involved; may also withdraw	Work actively to secure agreement among group members, with attention to equal participation	Keep other members focused on deliverables, act as troubleshooter, acknowledge others' contributions
7	Contribute ideas about larger vision, dislike too much structure, can get impatient with lack of progress	Do not like conflict and perceive many disagreements as trivial or petty; use humor to defuse serious situations	Will suggest a minimal number of rules that include everyone but react against rules that feel limiting	Tend to work from their own personal prioritizations and prefer a variety of tasks and roles that include positive social interaction
8	Either suggest direction for the group or pull back and watch, deciding whether to be a part of the team	Enjoy the intensity of the interaction as long as people are honest; are often part of the conflict, but if not, they will lead the dialogue	Will recommend ground rules, particularly ones that allow everyone to be heard	If they find the productivity exciting, they will stay; if the work is not significant or too predictable, they will move on
9	Have difficulty focusing if progress is slow; may become impatient	Uncomfortable and looking for a way out	Ambivalent about developing agreements; like the consensus, but don't like arbitrary rules	Find getting something accomplished with a harmonious group feels very pleasurable

ior to include addressing the need for people to get to know each other as people and to discover the hidden talents of all participants. Of course, a team leader who understands the importance of relationship building in team formation can structure an activity that helps team members to become acquainted with one another, but it also helps when several team members are actively supportive of team members spending the time to know one another.

Ninety percent of the time, the Storming stage will go far more smoothly if the challenges of the Forming stage have been met. The conflicts that do emerge will often be less severe because of the team's common purpose and trust; in addition, the team will typically have the courage to address issues as they emerge. Team problems that are not addressed do not usually go away on their own; they tend to go underground, either emerging later with greater intensity or never surfacing but continuing to impede the team's ability to become high-performing.

Some teams may never experience what they would define as conflict. This situation, however, is usually the result of effective team formation. When differences of opinion do arise on these well-developed teams, this conflict does not lead to overt or covert hostility because it is treated as a problem to be solved and is handled expeditiously.

As can be seen in Figure 5.8, individuals of all Enneagram styles except Fours, Eights, and, sometimes, Sixes typically prefer either not to face conflict or not to deal with it for very long. It can be extraordinarily helpful to teams when individuals who prefer to avoid conflict learn to be more direct about it and to stay with issues until they are resolved. Those team members with Enneagram styles Four, Six, and Eight can help their teams by continuing to support dealing with conflict, although lowering the intensity of their approach will be more likely to encourage others to join the discussion.

Additional Suggestions for Improving Teams

Teams are an integral part of organizational life, and almost any team can become more effective. The following suggestions can help both team members and team leaders to make these improvements.

Suggestions for Team Members

1. Work to change your own individual behavior, using the ideas and suggestions in this chapter for your Enneagram style.
2. Make suggestions either to the team leader or to the whole team regarding the importance of team goals and interdependence. In order to help the team articulate its goals, you can say, for example, "It would

be helpful to me if we spent some time discussing our team goals in order to make sure we're all on the same page." If the team does not have a common understanding of the team's interdependence, you can suggest the following: "Can we spend some time examining the ways in which we depend on each other's work, so that we can make sure we're giving each other the necessary information or work products?"

3. Suggest to the team leader that he or she recommend to the team that they experiment with new task and relationship roles.

4. Make the following suggestions to help the team progress through the first three stages of team development:

- **Forming.** Suggest that the team members get to know one another: "It might be helpful for us to spend some time getting to know each other's backgrounds, so that we can better understand how to use one another as resources." If the team has an unclear direction, you could say, "Can we examine what our team's purpose or charter is supposed to be so that we'll be sure to move in a common direction?"

- **Storming.** Encourage the team members to share their honest feelings and opinions by suggesting, "I think it would be a good idea to discuss this issue in more detail, because it isn't clear whether everyone agrees with our recent decision."

- **Norming.** Make suggestions about the ways in which the team can work even better together. An example of this is the following: "If we were to meet twice a month instead of once a month, we could stay more up-to-date on the latest organizational changes. What do the rest of you think?"

Suggestions for Team Leaders

In addition to taking all of the actions suggested above for individual team members, as a team leader you can leverage your leadership role in the following ways:

1. Make certain that your team has clear goals and that team members have a realistic understanding of their interdependence. Use the activities for developing team goals and identifying interdependence that are described earlier in this chapter.

2. Design your team and your team meetings so that the team forms, storms, and norms effectively.

- **Forming.** Ask team members to take three to five minutes each to discuss their backgrounds and experiences in relation to the team's goals and central tasks.

- **Storming.** Elicit the team members' feelings and thoughts about topics on which differences exist.
- **Norming.** Ask team members for their ideas regarding working agreements, or make some suggestions of your own and then solicit reactions.

3. Educate the team members about teams, using the information in this chapter, so that all members are prepared to behave constructively on the team.

   - Have team members examine their common team roles, and suggest that they experiment with new roles for at least one team meeting; use the activities, charts, and explanations from Step 2 of this chapter as an aid.
   - Teach the members about the stages of team development and related Enneagram style behaviors; use the four stages of team development model from this chapter to analyze the connection between individual behavior and team performance.

Whether you serve as a team member or team leader, taking the actions described in this chapter will enable you to help your team to become high performing. You will also be helping all team members, yourself included, increase their emotional intelligence. The members of the team will also be able to apply their new knowledge and skills in their roles on other teams, thus building greater overall capability not only for your team, but for the whole organization.

Chapter 6

Leveraging Your Leadership

Research from the Center for Creative Leadership in Greensboro, North Carolina, found that a primary cause of executive derailment is a deficit in emotional competence. The intense emotional challenges of leadership are complex, demanding, unpredictable, exciting, and rewarding, and they require the ability to manage oneself and to interact effectively with hundreds of others in both stressful and exhilarating circumstances. For these reasons, leaders must spend time in honest self-reflection. Individuals who become extraordinary leaders grow in both evolutionary and revolutionary ways, as they push themselves to meet the challenges even they cannot predict in advance.

Excellent leadership comes in many forms, and no Enneagram style has a monopoly on greatness. However, your Enneagram style shows you both your strengths as a leader and the areas that would most likely cause you to derail. This chapter presents insights about each Enneagram style: the paradigm of leadership—a worldview based on assumptions and beliefs, often unconscious, that influence how we behave and what we tend to overlook; leadership strengths and derailers—weaknesses that often impede a leader's success; a description of how each leader's greatest strengths, when used to excess, can become his or her greatest weaknesses; an analysis of the common leadership behaviors of the Enneagram style under discussion; and three ways to dramatically improve your leadership style.

Ones' View of Leadership

Enneagram Style
① DILIGENCE

"My job is to set clear goals and inspire others to achieve the highest quality."

Strengths	Derailers
Leads by example	Reactive
Strives for quality	Overly critical
Pursues perfection	Defends when criticized
Organized	Unaware of own anger
Consistent	Detail focused
Perceptive	Controlling
Honest	Opinionated

Their greatest strength becomes their greatest weakness when . . . In their diligent striving for the highest quality and perfection, One leaders can exhaust themselves to the point of illness and cause others to feel inadequate, criticized, or micromanaged.

One leaders commonly set the standard for exemplary work and behavior in their organizations; others seek to emulate them, with varying degrees of success. With an inner instinct for quality, One leaders work with diligence to make sure the work is organized, standards are met, and the right people are in the right jobs. For them, good is not good enough; they do not settle for anything less than 100 percent excellence.

Even if One leaders make every effort to control their critical predispositions, others often sense that they are being judged by the One. They sense this through the leader's nonverbal behavior and also through what is both said and not said. For example, criticism may be inferred through the leader's behavior in offering elaborate praise for one person's excellent work but silence for another's less-than-stellar performance.

One leaders work hard to interact graciously and to keep their own behavior above reproach. For instance, while their perceptiveness allows them to understand the assets and frailties of other human beings, One leaders are loath to make negative remarks about someone to a third party. First and foremost, they believe that belittling a person to someone else is disrespectful and also sets a bad example. Second, One leaders know that even when they have strong opinions about someone else, their conclusions could be wrong;

thus, they would not knowingly take the risk of hurting someone else without solid grounds for making a comment.

Although it may not always be apparent, One leaders are more demanding of themselves than they are of others. Because of their tendency to be self-critical, they often take negative feedback from others personally, whether the feedback is implied or direct. Such perceived criticism can fuel their predilection for self-deprecation. When Ones receive critical feedback, their first reaction may be to try to prove the other person wrong. Later, however, they will consider the feedback, and they may even apologize. To most One leaders, self-improvement is a lifelong task, and honesty—particularly as it pertains to taking an unbiased look at themselves—is a core value.

On the other hand, if One leaders disagree with a critique of them, they may not say anything to the person who has given the feedback. Inside, however, feelings of resentment may begin to simmer. These unexpressed feelings begin to build up over time, and the anger will erupt, often unpredictably. When such an explosion occurs, the One leader's feelings and thoughts tumble out, with the One bringing up events that may have taken place far in the past or behaviors that they think the other person has displayed. They may elaborate on their feelings, but only if they trust the other person.

When One leaders feel resentful, angry, or very frustrated over a period of time, they can become deeply discouraged (as they move under stress to Enneagram Four). When One leaders are relaxed, most often in situations away from their work and responsibilities, they can become lighthearted and playful (as they move when secure to Enneagram Seven).

Three Ways to Improve Your Leadership

- **Replace being right with being effective.** Every time you feel deeply critical of someone else, have a strongly held opinion, or believe in the rightness of a specific course of action, challenge yourself with this question: *Would I rather be right or effective?*
- **Delegate more.** Delegate work to other people and remember the following: delegate the whole task, rather than only part of a project; initiate a discussion of the goals, time frames, deliverables, and process; check in periodically; and give plenty of positive reinforcement.
- **Have more fun at work.** Make work less serious and more fun. Have your favorite picture on your desk. Bring in your preferred tea for everyone at work to try. Show your humor at work so others can enjoy your lighter side. Pass around an amusing article.

Twos' View of Leadership

Enneagram Style
GIVING

"My job is to assess the strengths and weaknesses of team members and to then motivate and facilitate people toward the achievement of our organizational goals."

Strengths	Derailers
Develops excellent relationships	Accommodates
Empathic	Indirect
Supportive and generous	Difficulty saying no
Optimistic	Angry when unappreciated
Likeable	Unaware of own needs
Responsible, hardworking	Overemphasizes relationships
Insight into others' needs	Enraged when others are mistreated
Motivates others	Unaware of "giving to get"

Their greatest strength becomes their greatest weakness when . . . In their dedicated efforts to give to everyone else, Two leaders often lose touch with their own needs to the point of self-neglect, may create dependency in others, and may end up leaving the ones they most want to help.

The Two leader often has several people in his or her office at the same time, with others waiting outside. Two leaders like to listen to people, support them, and then send them on their way feeling a little better and trying a little harder. If the person does not seem up to the task, Two leaders will lend a hand, intervening on behalf of an employee in whom they have faith.

This focus on others' well-being leaves Two leaders very little time for taking care of their own needs. On one hand, resentment can build as the Two thinks, *What about me?* On the other hand, Two leaders may not actually know what they need; focusing on others has the effect of keeping Twos from having to focus on themselves. When asked what they need, many Twos will respond with a puzzled look or will say, "I need to be needed."

The Two leader often ends up with many organizational friends, a situation that potentially causes some inner conflict. The Two leader may then wrestle with concerns such as these: *How do I take care of everyone in the organization? When I have special relationships with so many different people, what should I do if they are all in the same room at the same time? What should I do when there is conflict between two or more people, and I want to protect everyone?* However, there is one situation in which Two leaders feel absolutely no internal pressure to support both sides, and that is when they perceive abusive behavior: the Two leader will take the side of a person who has been the victim of abusive behavior, whether the abuse came from a manager or another employee.

The most difficult idea for Two leaders to internalize is that they give to get. Two leaders see themselves as being extremely giving, and they often are. Nonetheless, underneath this apparent selflessness is an intense desire for something in return. While thank-yous and notes of appreciation feel good to Two leaders, what they truly want is to be liked, to be considered indispensable, and to be treated as worthy human beings by the recipients of their generosity. When they are treated in this manner, Twos feel deeply satisfied. When they are not clearly appreciated, Two leaders can become dejected, deeply resentful, or both.

If Two leaders believe an injustice has been done or will be inflicted on someone else, they will fight this to the end (as they move under stress to Enneagram Eight). Sometimes Two leaders will, finally, take time for themselves, perhaps following a prolonged struggle or an exhausting work schedule, or in a moment of self-reflection in which they ask themselves, *What do I need?* Twos can then be found appreciating the pleasures of life by pampering themselves, engaging in artistic endeavors, or pondering life's philosophical issues (as they move when secure to Enneagram Four).

Three Ways to Improve Your Leadership

- **Learn to say no!** Say no to work activities before you become overextended, get sick, sacrifice your family time, or become resentful.
- **Help the organization become less dependent on you.** Empower others to do their jobs, make their own decisions, and think through difficult issues without coming to you.
- **Bring more objectivity and less emotional reactivity into your leadership.** When you respond favorably to people who make you feel important and negatively to those who challenge you or your ideas, this may not always lead to your making the best decisions. Focus more on strategy and less on people.

Threes' View of Leadership

Enneagram Style
PERFORM

"My job is to create an environment that achieves results because people understand the organization's goals and structure."

Strengths	Derailers
Success oriented	Overly competitive
High energy	Not always forthcoming
Reads an audience well	Abrupt
Overcomes problems	Hides deep-level feelings
Optimistic	Becomes overextended
Entrepreneurial	Limited time for personal
Confident	relationships
Accomplishes results	Impatient with others' feelings
	Believes that his or her image is the true self

Their greatest strength becomes their greatest weakness when . . . In the relentless pursuit of accomplishment and success, Three leaders can focus on a task at the expense of deeper human issues, including both their own feelings and those of people around them.

Three leaders are usually very successful; they have learned over time how to read a situation to know what it takes to be successful in it, and they adjust their personas and behaviors to meet that challenge. Energetic and goal-oriented, they focus on results and seek recognition for their accomplishments. With the Three leader's focus on *doing*, there is often little room for simply *being*—that is, enjoying the moment, taking time for friends outside the work environment, and spending time on one's internal life.

Because the Three Enneagram style is part of the Heart (Emotional) Center, people sometimes wonder why Three leaders do not seem to deal readily with feelings, whether their own or those of other people. Threes are keenly interested in emotions, but when they focus on the feelings of others, it is usually for the purpose of gaining the respect of those individuals. While many Three leaders are aware of their own feelings, they often prefer not to spend much time either thinking about or sharing them. They will deal with a feeling if they must, then move quickly back to the work in front of them. Other

Three leaders may experience generalized feeling sensations but are unable to differentiate one emotion from another. The reasons for this difficulty in differentiating the subtleties of emotion are both lack of interest and limited practice, with the Three often preferring to *do* rather than feel something.

Three leaders do like affirmative feelings—as long as they aren't too intense—because positive emotions support their forward-moving, "can-do" orientation. In the feeling world, however, positive and negative emotions coexist; negative emotions, theirs or other people's, interfere with the optimistic outlook of Three leaders. Feelings such as anger, sadness, and fear are associated with the Three's greatest avoidance—the possibility of failure.

If you were to ask a Three leader whether she or he has ever failed, the most common responses would be either great puzzlement over what this question means or a question in return: "What do you mean by failure?" If Three leaders acknowledge having experienced a failure, they will call it by a different name—most commonly, a "learning experience." This language reframes a painful and potentially embarrassing event. It is also a true statement, as Three leaders do learn from their mistakes and try not to make the same error twice.

When they are feeling overly pressured or worried, Three leaders will suspend their forward momentum and engage in activities that will help them temporarily forget their concerns (as they move under stress to Enneagram Nine). When they are not driving themselves so hard, Three leaders take the time to think and reflect, tapping their insights about events, people, and ideas (as they move when secure to Enneagram Six).

Three Ways to Improve Your Leadership
- **Pay more attention to the impact on people.** Your dual focus on goal achievement and efficiency can have the effect of minimizing the human side of work. Conduct a human impact analysis each time you make a decision and take the results very seriously.
- **Curtail your competitiveness.** Remember that not everything is a competition, something you must either win or, at least, not lose. Make sure that your conversations are not debates, but become collaborations through your openness and receptivity.
- **Consciously tell the whole truth about yourself.** When you feel yourself start trying to impress someone else, consciously stop doing this. Become more familiar with the whole truth behind your facade of impressing others.

Fours' View of Leadership

"My job is to create organizations that give people meaning and purpose so that they are inspired to do excellent work."

Strengths	Derailers
Seeks meaning through interpersonal connection	Intense
	Self-conscious
	Moody
Inspiring	Easily bored
Creative	Guilt-ridden
Introspective	Difficulty accepting criticism
Expressive	
Intuitive	Becomes disillusioned and then deeply critical of others
Compassionate	
Searches for excellence	

Their greatest strength becomes their greatest weakness when . . . In the unending quest for meaning and connection, Four leaders can become encumbered by interior mood swings, leaving those around them to focus primarily on the leader instead of the work.

Four leaders are usually warm, creative, visionary, and engaging. They tend to be reflective, empathic, and deeply sensitive to suffering; they can also be moody and take things personally.

A Four leader often spends hours on his or her internal life, replaying past scenarios involving both positive and negative emotions. The opposite can also be true of Four leaders, with a great amount of time spent in dreaming of the future and conjuring up creative ways to get things done.

The attention of the Four goes automatically to what is missing or falls short of the mark. With a feeling-based intuition, Four leaders often know immediately what is wrong with a situation, as they are quick to see the gap between the real and the ideal. They then feel compelled to try to close the chasm, and they often can. If a remedy is not possible, the Four leader usually becomes distressed, resulting in the moodiness that others perceive and then may try to avoid.

Four leaders like to understand, and they may ask penetrating questions of people around them in order to fully comprehend a situation. They also want to be understood, or, more accurately, to not be misunderstood. When they feel that they have been misunderstood, Four leaders generally become agitated, although they may not show this outwardly. They will discuss the issue repeatedly until they feel they have been heard in the way they intended. If that does not happen, the Four leader often becomes angry; beneath this anger lies hurt.

This feeling of hurt, which is like a generalized sorrow, is what makes the Four leader so empathic. It is also this sensitivity that becomes activated when something negative happens to them. Four leaders often have trouble internalizing positive feedback even if they receive it regularly; they do hear the message, but it does not stay with them very long. Negative messages, however, whether perceived or real, penetrate to the Four leader's inner core. Four leaders thus tend to take things personally; any perceived slight or accusation, or any misinterpretation of their words or actions, feels personal to them because it taps into their primary fear, that of being rejected.

When they feel rebuffed, Four leaders feel disheartened. They begin to wonder whether they did something wrong, whether what happened was the other person's responsibility, or whether the situation was caused by a multitude of other people and things. What this shows is that Four leaders can have difficulty in differentiating the boundary between what is their responsibility and what properly belongs to someone else. This confusion causes Four leaders to engage in a flurry of thoughts, feelings, and activity as they try to understand.

In order to reduce their distress, Fours may spend a great deal of effort to reestablish the perceived broken relationship (as they move under stress to Enneagram Two). On the other hand, Four leaders can be upbeat and enthusiastic, dreaming up ideas, making things happen, and achieving excellence themselves while inspiring it in others (as they move when secure to Enneagram One).

Three Ways to Improve Your Leadership
- **Focus on others more than yourself.** Use personal stories and the words *I*, *me*, *my*, or *mine* only 10 percent as much as you currently do. Think about how others feel, not how you would respond if you were in their position.
- **Turn down your intensity.** In both what you say and how you say it, cut your intensity level in half. Let conversations end before you want them to, don't feel a need to constantly hold the other person's attention, and learn to express yourself in less dramatic ways.
- **Learn to forgive and let go.** Learn to think, feel, experience, and then move on, rather than dwelling on difficulties or holding something against another person for a long period of time. Followers need this sort of emotional balance in their leaders.

Fives' View of Leadership

"My job is to create an effective organization through research, deliberation, and planning, so that all systems fit together and people are working on a common mission."

Strengths	Derailers
Analytic	Detached
Insightful	Aloof
Objective	Overly independent
Systematic	Unassertive
Thorough planning	Underemphasizes
Excellent in crises	relationships
Persistent	Doesn't share information
Expert	Stubborn
	Critical of others

Their greatest strength becomes their greatest weakness when . . . In their predisposition to be self-contained and their unending thirst for intellectual understanding, Five leaders run the risk of not being appreciated for all of their talents, as well as of not fully integrating an emotional component into their organizations.

Five leaders prefer to understand their organizations completely before they take strategic action. Once they have grasped the complexity of the organization's component parts—for example, strategy, structure, skills, and rewards—and have placed these pieces in the context of environmental trends, Five leaders are ready to garner the organization's resources. Then, they take action. The preliminary rigorous analysis undertaken by the Five leader takes time, but the results are usually always on target.

The Five leader may also neglect both his or her own emotional life and that of the organization. Accustomed to detaching from their feelings at the time these occur, Five leaders will actually feel these feelings later—sometimes deeply, and sometimes much less so. "Later" might mean minutes or hours, or it might even mean months. Because Five leaders may not fully factor emotions, whether their own or other people's, into the organizational equation, some decisions may end up incomplete. In addition, employees may feel unacknowledged or less motivated when their feelings are not considered.

The preceding description doesn't mean that Five leaders never respond to their own personal needs or the needs of others. In times of great emotional turbulence, whether it be personal or organizational, Five leaders remain steadfast. They can focus their full attention on both the issues and the persons affected and stay fully present in the situation. This, coupled with their objectivity, makes Five leaders excellent crisis managers: they remain levelheaded about the issues, and at the same time they are compassionate toward the individuals involved.

Five leaders do not like sharing personal information in either work or nonwork situations. To their thinking, this sort of information (for example, where they live, whether they are married, or what they did over the weekend) is irrelevant at work; a discussion of it also feels like an invasion of privacy—something very important to a Five. Five leaders value autonomy and self-reliance, and they develop only as much interdependence with others as they feel is necessary. They do not like surprises, expectations they have not agreed to, or demands. A demand, for example, can be time they didn't expect to give or information they didn't plan to share. While Five leaders usually like people and take great pleasure in human interaction, they usually prefer to go it alone. They often carve out a private space for themselves and make it very clear to others in the organization when they want to interact and when they do not.

Five leaders are keen observers of life and often have astute insights about others. Their quest for knowledge leads them to accumulate a great deal of information from written material or other sources. Despite all of their talents and knowledge stores, not to mention their sense of humor, Five leaders don't always let their attributes show. They are reluctant to toot their own horns, they do not want everyone looking at them or talking about them, and they sincerely don't want to impose or intrude on anyone else. Marketing in general, and especially marketing of themselves, can be a real challenge for Five leaders.

Sometimes, however, the Five leader is bold, funny, and highly interactive. This shift typically occurs when the Five leader is either very comfortable with someone or is expected to perform, as in giving a speech. In a pressured situation such as the latter, particularly because it involves presenting oneself in public, Five leaders often become more extroverted and polished (as they move under stress to Enneagram Seven). When they are extremely comfortable, Five leaders can become commanding and authoritative, stepping into new situations with vigor and certainty (as they move when secure to Enneagram Eight).

Three Ways to Improve Your Leadership

- **Focus on team interdependence.** Pay attention to helping your team optimize their handoffs to one another and increase their coordination, rather than focusing on how to optimize the competence and autonomy of each individual.
- **Pay more attention to politics.** Know the political players and learn how to influence them in productive ways, rather than dismissing, ignoring, or not paying enough attention to these social relationships.
- **Stop strategizing and start acting.** Thinking is not the same as doing and strategizing is not the same as taking action. Err on the side of action, and if you're not sure what to do, seek the counsel of others whom you respect, but move to action quickly.

Sixes' View of Leadership

"My job is to solve organizational problems by developing a creative problem-solving environment in which each person feels that he or she is part of the solution."

Enneagram Style
6 DOUBT

Strengths	Derailers
Loyal to company and employees	Wary
	Worrying
Responsible	Overly compliant or
Practical	overly defiant
Collaborative	Dislikes ambiguity
Strategic	"Analysis paralysis"
Sharp intellect	Projects own thoughts
Persevering	onto others
Anticipates problems	Defensive
	Martyring

Their greatest strength becomes their greatest weakness when . . . With their tendency to doubt—intertwined with their sharp insight about themselves, others, and their environment—Six leaders can create a work climate of great loyalty, of distrust, or of both in a back-and-forth pattern.

Six leaders can be stimulating and sometimes perplexing to those who work with them. They are sometimes bold and confident and sometimes worried or fearful, causing people to wonder what is behind this alternating pattern of confidence and fear. Both types of behavior are part of the Six leader's character traits.

Adept at sensing potential problems, Six leaders can be bold and assertive for two different reasons. When concerned or afraid, Six leaders may bypass their apprehension and go full force into a problem, as though they feel no fear at all. This frontal response is the Six's *counterphobic* response—that is, going directly against a fear or phobia. This bravery may also appear when the Six leader feels very confident in his or her chosen solution to a particular problem.

The opposite behavior, called the *fearful* or *phobic* response, occurs when Six leaders continue to doubt themselves, others, and the situation. This fear response, coupled with a subsequent "analysis paralysis," can immobilize the Six, causing the Six leader to procrastinate. It is not, as some may believe, that they are forgetting to do something, but rather that they are not sure what to do.

Sixes often focus their attention on authority even if they themselves are the leaders. A leader's job, in the Six view, is to use power fairly—that is, to not abuse anyone. Consequently, Sixes often have an ambivalent relationship with people in authority. Sometimes they befriend their bosses and maintain a stance of extreme loyalty. At other times, they react strongly against authority, particularly when they feel unsafe or perceive a misuse of power. Many Sixes engage in both behaviors.

Six leaders have relationships with their superiors that are very positive, very negative, or mixed, depending on whether they trust, agree with the decisions of, and feel supported by the particular boss. With their own staff, Six leaders usually have extremely close relationships—providing that the employees are loyal to both the Six leader and the organization. For Six bosses, loyalty is a key issue. They are loyal to their organizations and to those who work for them, protecting employees in every way possible. In return, they expect unerring support and dedication to the job.

With their peers, Six leaders most frequently develop strategic alliances. These business friendships with like-minded individuals serve several purposes. If Sixes express controversial opinions during a meeting, they do so with the belief that there are others in the room who will support them. These special relationships also give Six leaders someone with whom to talk things over before and after the meeting. Before the meeting, there may be a strategic conversation in which the Six reviews his or her opinions and develops a plan for delivering them. After the meeting, if Six leaders feel any discomfort or anxiety about what they have said and the responses they have received, they can review the events and share perspectives with trusted others.

Six leaders can be prone to either inaction (if they are feeling fearful or phobic) or to highly bold action (when going against the fear, in a counterphobic reaction). However, with a small to moderate amount of pressure, they can also focus on results, and their behavior can become clear and decisive (as they move under stress to Enneagram Three). When their worry abates, Six leaders often engage in satisfying, rhythmic activities, such as walking, cooking, writing, or other pastimes they find relaxing (as they move when secure to Enneagram Nine).

Three Ways to Improve Your Leadership
- **Deal with your authority issues.** Take a serious look at your history with bosses and authority figures, particularly in those cases where your reactivity to authority may have either hurt your career or those with whom you work. Try to learn from your past experience.
- **Learn to manage your anxiety.** Manage your anxiety by learning its early warning signs and then de-escalating it (by walking, talking, or whatever works well for you) rather than fueling it with worst-case scenario development. Remember that fretting is not problem solving.
- **Cultivate worthy adversaries.** With the same fervor that you seek loyalty from those with whom you work, also cultivate worthy adversaries from the ranks of your peers and subordinates. These individuals are most likely to push your growth and development as a leader.

Sevens' View of Leadership

Enneagram Style
OPTIONS

"My job is to get people excited and to create innovative ventures so that the organization can take advantage of new and important business opportunities."

Strengths	Derailers
Imaginative and creative	Impulsive
Enthusiastic	Unfocused
Curious	Rebellious
Engaging	Avoids painful situations
Multitasking	Inconsistent empathy for others
Upbeat	Reactive to negative feedback
Quick thinker	Rationalizes
Connects disparate data	Dislikes routine

Their greatest strength becomes their greatest weakness when . . . With tendencies to be highly creative and to pursue multiple options, Seven leaders can move fast in so many directions that their followers may become exhausted, unfocused, and frustrated.

Seven leaders can lead their organizations to great heights through new ideas, projects, and ventures. Their minds work like automatic synthesizers, bringing in ideas from a variety of disciplines, past experiences, and new inventions. Seven leaders have a contagious enthusiasm, and they are thus able to get people excited about a project and then to enlist them in the effort.

Seven leaders can also create a hectic work environment for their employees. While many Enneagram styles multitask, handling numerous ideas and activities simultaneously, Sevens do this continuously, and others may have to scramble in order to keep up. When Seven leaders get wholeheartedly enthused about something, as often happens, their excitement builds and builds. Seven leaders are capable of maintaining an extraordinarily high level of energy for a long period of time, and those around them can become exhausted.

Seven leaders are quick studies; when they are given information to read, they are capable of quickly absorbing large quantities of data. What Sevens often do not realize is that in this rapid consumption of data, they may miss some important information; even if they do not, others may not believe that the Seven leader has given the material its proper attention. When Seven leaders feel they are being perceived as unprepared or only partially informed, they usually feel unfairly and inaccurately judged and become confused and angry.

Seven leaders are usually engaging and enjoyable to be around, but they also have a serious side. They are highly sensitive; when they allow themselves to feel things, they can be deeply moved. When face-to-face with someone who is suffering, they will usually listen, console, and offer creative and helpful solutions.

Sevens prefer affirmation and are highly sensitive to criticism, particularly unsolicited negative critiques. When they feel criticized, Seven leaders tend to rationalize their behavior by reframing the issue positively. For example, they may have been very late for a meeting but will reframe this in a positive way, noting that it was good because it gave those already present a chance to talk with one another. If reframing doesn't work, the Seven leader will often blame something or someone else for the problem. The reframing or blaming behavior occurs rapidly, as the Seven leader's mind jumps from one thought to the next. This reactive response occurs because the Seven's major area of avoidance has been activated—pain and discomfort.

The Seven leader's challenge can be stated in one word: *focus*. When faced with deadlines or other forms of pressure, Seven leaders focus on deliverables and details (as they move under stress to Enneagram One). When they focus on themselves, they become highly introspective, taking time alone to read and reflect (as they move when secure to Enneagram Five).

Three Ways to Improve Your Leadership

- **Slow your pace.** Slow your speed to 50 percent of your natural rate. Speak half as fast about half as many items. Breathe twice as deeply for twice as long.
- **Find the truth in a criticism.** Instead of defending against a criticism by rationalizing, blaming, or critiquing the critique, ask instead, *What really is true about the criticism and what can I learn from it?*
- **Complete your tasks.** Follow through on every task you start, and don't start a task that you do not complete.

Eights' View of Leadership

Enneagram Style 8 CHALLENGE

"My job is to move the organization forward by leading decisively, getting capable and reliable people into the right jobs, and empowering competent people to take action."

Strengths	Derailers
Direct	Controlling
Self-confident and authoritative	Demanding
Highly strategic	High expectations of self and others
Overcomes obstacles	Impatient
Energetic	Agitated with a slow pace
Protective of others	Feels used when others do not perform to expectations
Moves projects forward	Disdains weakness
Supports others' success	Overextends to the point of exhaustion

Their greatest strength becomes their greatest weakness when . . . With their strategic ability, authoritative leadership, and ability to both sense and support greatness in others, Eight leaders can either create exemplary organizations or deplete themselves and create intimidating, underperforming work environments in the process.

Eight leaders like to make important things happen and to create order from chaos. They usually take a very large view and are able to integrate the many components of an organization into strategic action. They grasp the complexities of the marketplace and anticipate the moves of competitors. They are willing to restructure the company and retrain all employees if necessary, and they reward people for excellent performance. When the organization has been made effective and stable, Eight leaders might choose to create new challenges, to remain with the company but disengage from its core workings, or to move on.

Commanding and demanding, Eights commonly lead by example and expect others to follow suit. With an ability to sense potential in people, Eight leaders offer others both support and opportunity, most often behind the scenes. Insightful, Eights often spend time alone attempting to analyze both themselves and the people who work for them. Eight leaders try to be understanding and supportive, yet they still hold people accountable.

In situations in which their ability to get things under control does not work or in which people who work for them do not take initiative and perform to expectations, Eight leaders take the disappointment personally and become frustrated. When Eight leaders reach their frustration level, which is usually sooner than is the case for many other Enneagram styles, their feelings and sensations begin to rise internally. The frustration leads to anger, which the Eight leader usually tries to contain. However, it is very difficult for Eight leaders to hold back strong feelings; they are very likely to say what is on their minds, whether it is during a meeting or a one-on-one conversation. The Eight's honesty, insight, directness, and intensity combined with their frustration and anger invariably leads to combustion. Those on the other end can feel intimidated, furious, blindsided, or all three. This is not usually the intention of the Eight leader, who afterward may feel a sense of guilt. At the same time, the Eight leader may not feel regret; after all, he or she was just being honest!

Eight leaders do not appreciate being blindsided themselves. They strongly prefer advance warning of difficult issues so that they can strategize and prepare. They will surround themselves with people whom they perceive as able to provide wise counsel, and they seek input before making big decisions. Ultimately, however, the decision is theirs, and Eight leaders stand behind their choices. Eight leaders actually appreciate people who face them directly, without backing down. Eights like having their energy met, and they respect strength in others.

Eight leaders will also stand up for what they believe is just and fair in the organization, even if this has negative consequences for them. Eight leaders will shield those who need their help; at the same time, they dislike weakness in others. This may sound like a contradiction, but it is not: the difference lies in whether the Eight leader perceives the other person as someone truly in need of help or as a weakling, since Eights are disdainful of weakness in those who can defend themselves. This issue touches on what lies hidden behind the Eight leader's bold exterior—a soft and vulnerable interior that is often only seen by those closest to the Eight.

When Eight leaders choose to take time for themselves instead of sacrificing themselves for the organization, they can become very quiet and reflective (as they move under stress to Enneagram Five). When they allow themselves to relax, Eight leaders show a deeply warm and generous side (as they move when secure to Enneagram Two).

Three Ways to Improve Your Leadership

- **Never yell at work!** As frustrated as you may feel and even if you are not directing a raised voice toward a particular person, the price paid for yelling (fear, disrespect) is never worth it.
- **Be careful about blaming others.** When something for which you are responsible does not succeed as planned, be careful that your tone of voice, line of questioning, and general approach do not make others feel blamed. The perception of being blamed shuts down candid conversation and effective problem solving.
- **Consider opposing points of view.** Ask yourself every day, *Who and what am I not listening to?*

Nines' View of Leadership

Enneagram Style
HARMONY ⑨

"My job is to help achieve the collective mission by creating a clearly structured and harmonious work environment."

Strengths	Derailers
Diplomatic	Avoids conflict
Assimilates big picture through attention to operational details	Unassertive
	Forgets priorities
	Procrastinates
Easygoing	Passive-aggressive when pushed
Consistent	
Inclusive and collaborative	Indecisive
	Uncertain
Develops lasting relationships	Low energy
Patient	
Supportive of others	

Their greatest strength becomes their greatest weakness when . . . In the effort to foster collaboration, provide clear structure, and stay on top of operational details, Nine leaders can create organizations that avoid conflict, do not respond quickly enough, and have insufficient work delegation.

Nine leaders usually create inclusive, collaborative, and harmonious work environments in which people enjoy working together to get the job done. Nines enjoy the complexity of running an organization, with its variety of challenges and tasks. Employees typically find Nine leaders approachable and supportive. In general, Nine leaders tend to be nonjudgmental and sincerely interested in other people. Employees find that being on the receiving end of a Nine leader's accepting behavior is encouraging and satisfying.

Through gathering organizational details and drawing on their strong operational instincts, Nine leaders are usually able to assimilate the organizational big picture and can lead with a strategic vision. They like to know what is going on, and they often involve themselves in the daily details of running the organization. While this hands-on orientation can be useful, it can also create bottlenecks, particularly on the desk of the Nine leader, who often has stacks of materials to review. This tendency to examine all information, combined with the Nine leader's tendency to procrastinate, can lead to organizational inaction or, at the least, to frustration among employees who require the leader's stamp of approval to move forward on a project.

Although Nine leaders are hard workers, they tend to put off tasks because they have difficulty setting priorities. With many tasks to do, Nine leaders tend to move from one thing to another rather than completing the most pressing task first. They may start one thing, move to another, perhaps forget that the first item needed their immediate attention, and then go on to a third piece of work. Tired of it all, the Nine leader may simply go for a walk or a jog.

This difficulty with setting and following priorities is related to the Nine leader's avoidance of conflict. While Nine leaders are usually astute at mediating differences and creating accord, they also tend to avoid making decisions or doing anything that might create disharmony in the work environment or cause someone to become angry at them. Making a decision means that someone might not agree with them; doing work for one person may mean that someone else will be unhappy because another task must be left undone for the time being. Conflict typically makes Nines very uncomfortable, and they have a particular aversion to having anger directed at them. Nine leaders try to do all they can to prevent others from becoming upset. Eventually, everything does get accomplished, though not always on time.

Asserting themselves is not easy for Nine leaders, who dislike having to make demands on others. Their often humble, low-key style can be endearing and wins them many friends. However, Nine leaders can also feel that they are being overlooked, with their opinions taken less seriously than those of other people. Because Nines often state their positions in an easygoing manner, others may not be aware when an opinion expressed by a Nine leader is a strongly held one.

Nine leaders also tend to approach serious issues from multiple viewpoints, explaining how several different alternatives might work. When discussing a conflict or decision that does not involve them directly, Nine leaders may present both sides of the argument or explain only the side that has not been expressed by anyone else. Because they believe all of the different possible ways of viewing a conflict should be considered, the Nine's own position may be difficult for others to discern.

This nonassertive verbal style is evident even when they deal with issues that are very important to them. For example, Nine leaders almost always want to follow their own timetables and make their own decisions. If they feel that someone else is pushing them to do something, they often feel resentful but have trouble saying no directly. The Nine leader may say nothing and do nothing. If pressured, the Nine leader might say yes, but then not do what was asked. This passive-aggressive behavior means that a Nine leader will not usually confront someone else directly and will thus avoid the conflict. Others, however, can be left perplexed about the leader's actual decisions and plans.

Nine leaders do not like demands, and as a result they often become agitated, incisive, and skeptical when they feel pressured. They may begin to doubt others' motives or to make sharp negative comments to others (as they move under stress to Enneagram Six). When Nine leaders feel comfortable and relaxed, they become high performing and results oriented (as they move when secure to Enneagram Three).

Three Ways to Improve Your Leadership

- **Assert yourself more.** Instead of first finding out what others are thinking, express your own thoughts and feelings and let others react to you.
- **Emphasize what is most important.** Instead of talking in paragraphs and using abundant detail, practice communicating with others by highlighting the key points you want to make, as if you are making a PowerPoint presentation.
- **Move things off your desk.** Make sure you are not an organizational bottleneck by delegating more, moving administrative items quickly from your desk, and spending a specified amount of dedicated time each day for paperwork.

Conclusion

The nine Enneagram styles of leadership are very different from one another and are all highly effective. The leaders profiled in this chapter have paradigms of leadership that are subtly, yet significantly, different. How a leader defines leadership often determines how that leader chooses to behave; the converse may also be true. We all have certain strengths and weaknesses based on our place on the Enneagram. Our behaviors are reinforced by success or failure, and we develop our leadership paradigms in our own images and based on our own experiences.

Leaders from each of the nine Enneagram styles illuminate one important aspect of leadership. We can all benefit from each of the nine different Enneagram perspectives on leadership. (See Figure 6.1.)

Each leadership gift can be useful in specific situations. For example, an organization with concerns about quality would benefit from a One leader's pursuit of excellence. Problems with low morale can be helped by Two leaders, who can serve the organization by concentrating on employee motivation. If an organization is having productivity problems, a Three leader's focus on results can help. Many organizations go through a crisis of meaning and purpose; Four leaders can help in the pursuit of passion.

During times of organizational crisis, Five leaders can use their objectivity to keep a clear organizational course. Organizations with a philosophy of acting first and asking questions later can use the insight and planning gifts of Six leaders. Seven leaders can inspire stagnating and complacent organizations

FIGURE 6.1 **The Gifts of the Nine Styles**

to new heights through their innovation and flexibility. Organizations experiencing a crisis of direction can use the services of Eight leaders, who can "move mountains" and make important things happen. Finally, Nine leaders' gifts in gaining consensus are invaluable in creating a climate of inclusion and consensual decision making in organizations.

Imagine what would happen if all leaders were to serve their organizations using all nine Enneagram perspectives. The leaders' paradigms of leadership and subsequent behaviors would be dramatically enlarged and enriched; every organization would be more successful, with highly motivated and thus more productive employees.

Suggestions for Working on Change

Because your leadership style is directly connected to your Enneagram style, the Enneagram will be an invaluable tool as you move forward and increase your leadership capability. The following suggestions will help you get started.

- **Appreciate and use your special leadership gifts.** Learning to appreciate what comes naturally to you can be a challenge. Every leader must have followers, and these gifts are what attract people to you. Know who you are and appreciate what you bring to leadership.
- **Expand your leadership paradigm.** Your leadership paradigm or worldview determines what you think is important, which in turn influences how you behave. Paradigms are not necessarily good or bad; they are useful, yet they also limit behavior. Expand your leadership paradigm, and you will expand your leadership repertoire.
- **Leverage your leadership strengths, but do so in moderation.** Strengths, used to excess, invariably become weaknesses. Know your strengths and use them, but not to an extreme. Using your strengths in moderation will also encourage you to expand your skills into new areas and to rely on the strengths of others in new and productive ways.
- **Take your leadership derailers seriously.** Derailers can take even the best leaders off track. It is best to know what these areas are and to work on them as a preventive measure *before they cause any serious difficulties.*
- **Solicit feedback.** Discuss the strengths and derailers associated with your Enneagram style with people who know you well at work, and ask them for honest feedback on how these compare with your leadership behavior.
- **Work with a coach.** You might find it useful to work with an experienced executive coach, preferably someone familiar with the Enneagram. As you work toward the goals mutually agreed upon by you and your coach, you

can use the Enneagram to help you better understand your leadership style, and you can further your explorations to include the deeper issues related to your Enneagram style.

- **Dare to do something different.** Read Chapter 7, "Transforming Yourself." Pick some activities that you know you can and will do, and also choose some that may seem unusual to you or are out of character for you. The latter choices may end up being the best because they are more likely to stretch you beyond your comfortable behavior patterns.

Transforming Yourself

his chapter describes developmental activities specific to each style. Feel free to select the particular activities for your style that you think will be most beneficial to your growth. Whichever activities you select, it is very important that you continue doing them long enough to experience the difference they can really make—for example, three to six months or longer. Sometimes you will see immediate results, while at other times results will be cumulative and more long-term.

This chapter is organized into sections by Enneagram style. Each section includes five activities, the first three of which are specific exercises intended to be done on a daily basis. The fourth activity involves your mental processes and is intended to help you change your thinking patterns or habits. In the final activity, you will work on emotional patterns and habits. These last two activities are not for daily use, but are designed instead to help you in the exact moments when you are in the throes of a style-based reaction that you really want to change. When you read these final exercises for changing your thinking and emotional patterns, you will realize that they overlap with the daily activities for your style. This overlap is intentional, as all of the activities focus on the core issues of your particular Enneagram style.

You may choose to go directly to the section for your Enneagram style. If you do so, consider then going back and reviewing the activities for the other eight styles. Doing this gives you a way to compare and contrast the activities for your style with those of others, and it may help clarify for you why certain activities work best for each Enneagram style. You may find that exercises for styles other than your own also appeal to you. If this occurs, feel free to use these activities as well, with these points in mind: (1) it is best to first pursue the activities for your own Enneagram style, and (2) as a supplement to the exercises for your own style, the exercises for your wing styles and stress and security points may be of particular value to you.

As you embark on the activities for change, it will help you to be aware that your attitude will make an enormous difference in both your enjoyment of the exercises and your ultimate success with them. The most productive orientation to take is that of an anthropologist—someone who is engaged in exploration, discovery, and a search for the truth. When you treat yourself with curiosity, respect, objectivity, and understanding, the self-development process becomes as rewarding and beneficial as the end goals themselves.

Please be gentle with yourself in this process of change; do not pressure yourself to change too quickly. If you become discouraged when you reach a self-insight that makes you feel uncomfortable, try to appreciate the courage you have shown in being honest with yourself. Any discouragement will pass, and new thoughts, feelings, and behaviors will ultimately emerge. The whole process of self-awareness and change can be an extraordinary journey.

Daily Activities for Ones

Enneagram Style
1 DILIGENCE

Pay Attention to Your Patterns of Right/Wrong Thinking

Keep a daily journal and note the times you engage in judgments, opinions, criticisms, or any other behavior that reflects right/wrong thinking on your part. At the end of each week, review your journal and note the patterns related to this thinking—for example, the frequency of the behavior per day and per week; what you actually thought or said, along with the accompanying feelings, physical sensations, and body language; and the external or internal events that triggered your reaction. After four weeks of keeping and reviewing this journal, note the overall patterns you discover. For example, is your behavior consistent throughout the day and week, or are you more prone to right/wrong thinking late in the day or at other times when you are fatigued? Do you tend to exhibit this behavior toward those you know best or least well? Do you tighten all your muscles or primarily those muscles in your face and jaw? Do you tend to react more strongly when you feel criticized, when someone else is responding too slowly, or under some other condition?

Once you become aware of your patterns related to right/wrong thinking, locate a point early in the process where you could actually intercept your typical reaction—for instance, an early physical sensation (such as a jerking back of your head) or a particular line of thought (such as the thought that another person is too slow or that an idea won't work). This interception point can be thought of as a choice point. Once you are aware of your choice point, you can begin to choose to react in a different way. At that moment, you can say to yourself, *I'm about to go into my typical reactive pattern. Do I want to do that?* If your answer is no, then substitute another behavior, such as deep breathing combined with a refocusing of your thoughts to something else, particularly something positive. The new thoughts can be something positive about the other person, the event at hand, or about something you like—for example, your favorite hobby or food. Every time your choice point arises, substitute these alternative behaviors. You may need to experiment with alternative behaviors until you find those that work best for you.

Use Your Feelings of Resentment as a Clue to Deeper-Seated Anger

Ones are usually more familiar with resentment—a mild form of anger—than they are with deeper forms of anger, such as fury and rage. However, a deeper, suppressed anger often underlies the One's feelings of resentment. These angry feelings lie below the surface, where they accumulate and simmer. When something occurs that upsets or distresses Ones, their resentment can become fueled by these unexpressed or unresolved latent feelings. If Ones want to use their feelings of resentment as a clue to more deeply felt anger, they must first recognize their feelings of resentment as these occur.

To do this, keep a pad of paper with you and write down each time you feel resentful or experience such less intense variations of resentment as displeasure, irritation, or distress. Pay special attention to your body's cues, your thought processes, and your emotional reactions, and make notes of these responses.

After two weeks, review your notes and identify the patterns of your responses. This will help you to recognize that you are actually feeling resentful at times when you otherwise might not have even noticed your reaction. It is not uncommon for us to not recognize feelings and reactions that we feel regularly, because we become so accustomed to them. After doing this exercise, however, you will be more likely to notice when you feel resentful. Now that you are able to identify this feeling, each time it occurs, ask yourself, *Am I only upset about what just happened, or is there more behind this?* Write down all the things that may be bothering you that are related to or contributing to your feelings of resentment.

Make this list as long as possible by going as far back and as deeply as you can. For example, someone at work may have annoyed you by taking full credit for work in which you made a significant contribution. Write down everything else that this person has done that is irritating to you and why. Write down other examples when others have either taken credit for your work or when you have failed to receive the acknowledgment you deserved. Write down the values you hold dear that have been violated. Write down earlier examples of times when these values have been violated. Continue the above process until the underlying causes of your deeper anger become apparent to you; because these feelings may be deeply buried, do not be discouraged if the process takes several months.

Learn to Appreciate What Is Positive in Everything—Events, Inanimate Objects, and the Behaviors of Other People

On the first day of this activity, go on an hourly treasure hunt for all that is *right* in the world; do this activity for two or three minutes *every hour*. You may still notice things that contain errors or behavior that does not reflect your standards, but try to focus instead on the elegance, beauty, or positive aspects of what you observe. For example, when you read an e-mail or letter and notice a typographical error on it, pay more attention to and acknowledge the quality of the ideas and/or the excellence in the choice of words. Similarly, when you attend a meeting that may not be running efficiently, notice and appreciate something positive about the meeting—for example, the effort that the meeting chair puts into gaining everyone's participation.

Continue practicing this exercise every day—for the next three weeks or longer, particularly at times when you find yourself overfocusing on the negative—until focusing on the positive becomes a more natural part of your thought process. When you feel you are ready, continue doing the exercise for five minutes every day before you go to work. You can also use this exercise if you notice yourself suddenly reverting to a pattern of faultfinding only, rather than appreciating the positive as well. At these times, five minutes of a positive treasure hunt will help you to regain your balance.

Activities for Transforming Mental and Emotional Patterns of Ones

MENTAL ACTIVITY When you become aware that you are continually thinking about flaws and errors, think about one or more times when you were able to accept the perfection of all things as they are in their natural state, imperfections and all. Remember those moments, and relive what was occurring within you at those times. Sustain your memory of these times until you feel completely calm and accepting. Thus, you will transform the mental pattern of *resentment* (paying attention to flaws so that nothing ever seems good enough) into the higher belief of *perfection* (the insight that everything is as it should be and that even imperfection is perfect).

EMOTIONAL ACTIVITY When you become angry about how someone is acting or something that's taking place, remember one or more times in your life when you initially felt angry but were able to find peace and tranquility by accepting the situation as it was, not as you wanted it to be. If you can't recall such a situation, then imagine how you might feel if you could simply feel serene about life's events without trying to change them. Hold this feeling as long as possible, or until you feel relaxed and appreciative. In this way, you will transform the emotional habit of *anger* (the feeling of chronic dissatisfaction with how things are) into the higher awareness of *serenity* (an openhearted acceptance of all that occurs).

Daily Activities for Twos

Spend Time Alone

As you spend time alone, you will most likely begin to understand the degree of dependency you have on others. This can be especially enlightening for Twos, who often believe that other people are dependent on *them*. However, it goes both ways. When Twos give continuously, this giving often creates a dependency in the other person. At the same time, the Two then becomes dependent on the need to be needed, the ability to influence others behind the scenes, and the need for personal affirmation.

Enneagram Style
GIVING

Spending time alone allows Twos to understand who they really are, without the influences of other people's reactions and perceptions. This new sense of independence can be liberating for Twos.

As you practice spending time by yourself, keep in mind that for the purposes here, being alone means no phone calls, no e-mails, no letter writing, and no extended conversations with anyone. Spend one full hour each day alone, without any interaction with others. On the weekend, carve out two to three hours solely for yourself to do exactly what you want to do, but make sure your choice of activity focuses only on you. For example, if you choose to engage in physical activity, choose an individual activity such as jogging, walking, or gardening by yourself. If you want to go to a museum, do so, but go alone and do not engage in conversation with others while there. During this time, make sure you turn off your cell phone.

Ask Yourself: What Do I Really Need?

Twos usually have their emotional antennae extended to pick up cues about other people's needs; however, a continual focus on the needs of others usually results in Twos having less awareness of their *own* real needs. Eventually, most Twos feel shortchanged in relationships. They expend so much effort on behalf of other people that they end up feeling, *But what about me?*

Twos do have needs, but because these are often unconscious or unexpressed, it becomes difficult for most Twos to get their needs met directly. Consequently, Twos often use indirect methods, and their indirect behavior can have the effect of unconsciously controlling or manipulating other people. As Twos become more fully aware of their own needs, they usually become more direct in expressing them and get more of them satisfied. For example, they may take better care of themselves by not working every night until nine o'clock or may ask someone to help them on a large project.

When you have returned home from work each day, do the following activity. Take a sheet of paper and divide the paper into four columns, with these headings:

1. Today's needs
2. Needs met? (yes/no/partially)
3. If yes, how I let my needs be known
4. If no or partially met, other options

Then, write down the answers to the following questions under the appropriate headings: *What needs did I have today?* (Put your answers in column 1.) *Did I get each of these needs met?* For each *yes* answer, detail exactly what you did to get this need met. For each *no* answer, write down one explicit way in which you could get this need met.

After you have completed your lists, analyze what you have written. Did you have very few needs (three or less) or many needs (more than fifteen)? Are there themes that arise as you review the types of needs listed—for example, a need for more time for yourself or for more support from others? Are most of your needs being met? Are most of your needs ones that you yourself can meet, or are they dependent on other people? Are you being mostly direct or mostly indirect in expressing your needs to others?

Do the above activity for two weeks, dating each day's work. At the end of that time, review your lists in sequence. You will probably notice some interesting patterns to your needs, which will help you to develop greater self-insight. Did your needs (both quantity and type) change over time? For instance, did you become better at getting your needs met? Did you become more direct about getting your needs met? Congratulate yourself on your accomplishments, and make a commitment to work on any areas you find troublesome, such as needing to be more direct or becoming better at meeting your needs yourself. Continue the entire activity for two more weeks, and you will begin to see marked improvement.

Examine the Ways That You Give in Order to Get Something in Return

Twos usually give a great deal to others, but beneath their generosity is a tacit expectation that they will receive something in return. The most common expectation or hope is that the Two will be needed by others, become important to others' lives, and be perceived as a worthy human being.

Although the giving behavior of Twos may be greatly appreciated, it can also create problems. For example, Twos may give or offer things that other people don't truly want. In these cases, the other person can become angry, and/or the Two may feel unappreciated and distressed. At other times, the other person may appreciate something that the Two has done, but may not have known that there was an expectation for anything in return; the other person can feel hurt or angry, believing that the giving was done with no strings attached. And on yet other occasions, the other person may end up involuntarily dependent on the Two. This can be an unhealthy situation, fraught with potential conflict on both sides.

The following questions constitute an exercise that can be very helpful to the Two in changing the behavior of giving with the expectation of getting something back. Each time you offer, or even think about offering, to do something for someone else, ask yourself, *What am I really wanting in return from doing this? Am I doing this so that others will need me?* (the creation of dependency); *Am I doing this so that I will later feel proud that I can take care of things better than others?* (the passion of pride); *Am I doing this so that I will feel like a worthy person?* (the need for personal affirmation). At the end of each day, make a list of every single thing you either did do or thought of doing for someone else and what inside you really motivated you to want to help this person. After you have honestly answered this question, reconsider whether in each case your giving behavior was really in the other person's best interests, *and* whether it was in your best interests. If you do this activity daily for two weeks, you will be in for some startling discoveries.

Activities for Transforming Mental and Emotional Patterns of Twos

MENTAL ACTIVITY When you realize you are complimenting someone frequently and/or giving him or her more continual attention and focus than you truly want to give, think about one or more times when you were truly in tune with and able to acknowledge your own needs both to yourself and others. Recall those times and relive what was occurring within you. Pay particular attention to what you needed and how you expressed those needs, and also to any feelings of independence and liberation you experienced. This allows you to transform the mental pattern of *flattery* (the gaining of acceptance through giving compliments or other forms of attention to others) into the higher belief of *free will* (the insight that acknowledging oneself and one's own needs leads to autonomy and freedom).

EMOTIONAL ACTIVITY When you become aware of feeling prideful—feeling either elated about what you have done for others and how important you have become to a cause or a group, or feeling deflated because you were not appreciated enough or all of your efforts did not come to fruition—remember one or more times in your life where you experienced true humility. Humility is not the same as self-effacement or self-deprecation; it is more akin to having a modest and realistic appreciation and valuation of yourself without inflating your self-image because of your "good works," and without basing your self-worth on the opinions and reactions of others. Maintain your feeling of true humility, and carry it with you as you think about and interact with others. Thus, you can transform the emotional habit of *pride* (the inflated self-esteem and self-importance derived from doing for and being needed by others) into the higher awareness of *humility* (the feeling of self-acceptance and appreciation without either self-inflation or deference to the opinions of others).

Daily Activities for Threes

③ Enneagram Style
PERFORM

Spend the Time to Get to Know Yourself

It is important for Threes to regularly spend time with absolutely nothing on their agendas. There are several ways to do this—for example, spend fifteen minutes a day or one hour a week with nothing on your schedule except being by yourself with no work, no interruptions (such as telephones or pagers), and no distractions (such as television). This time by yourself should be time to think about who you are, what you like and dislike, and what you most value.

Alternatively, you can use meditative techniques to help you stay focused on the present moment, instead of thinking about what you have to do. Meditation calms the mind and body and settles the emotions. These practical guidelines can get you started: find a quiet, private location and sit upright in a chair, on a couch, or on the floor for fifteen minutes or more. With your eyes closed, focus on one item from the following list: your breath going in, down, up, and then out; numbers, starting from one and moving upward; or a simple image in your mind such as a lighted candle, the sun, a white light, or some similar object.

You will find that it is almost impossible during this fifteen-minute period to stay focused on only what you have chosen. The goal, however, is just to notice when your attention shifts away to other thoughts, feelings, bodily sensations, or noises in the environment, and then to simply shift your attention back to your intended focus.

If you need something more active to do, instead of or in addition to the above activities, take a ten-minute walk each day during which you focus only on your physical experience. For example, take inventory of your body as you walk. Begin with your head, noting, for example, the level of clarity or congestion, the wind on your face, the degree of tension or relaxation in your face, and other physical sensations. Move down through the neck to your shoulders. Threes often hold a great deal of tension in their shoulders, so it can be very helpful to consciously drop and relax your shoulders. Continue down your body and eventually focus on your feet, including the sensation of your feet touching the ground as you walk.

All of the above activities are helpful for Threes to do *every single day*.

Learn to Avoid Overidentifying with Your Work

Most Threes believe the following statement: "I am what I do and accomplish," and this belief causes them to overidentify with their work. When individuals overidentify with anything, whether work or another of life's roles, they tend to believe that that is who they really are. Overidentifying with only one aspect of ourselves limits us as human beings. In reality, people possess multiple facets, such as roles, attributes, behaviors, interests, talents, thoughts, feelings, physical characteristics, skills, and values, as well as their accomplishments.

The following activity can help Threes understand and overcome their overidentification with work. Make a precise list of at least twenty ways in which you identify with work—for example, how many hours a week you work, how much work you bring home nightly, and how you schedule yourself in general. Then, write down as many answers as you can think of to this question: *If I am not my work, then who am I?* Finally, ponder the next two questions for ten minutes every day: *Who am I, really? If I were valued for something other than my work accomplishments, what would that be?*

Acknowledge Your Weaknesses

All of us have weaknesses, and Threes are no exceptions. Threes, however, are often more reluctant to reveal their flaws or Achilles' heels, even to themselves. The crux of the issue for Threes lies in the belief that they are valued only when they are seen as competent and successful. Because of this, they have learned to mask or otherwise hide their shortcomings. The following activity can help with this issue. Make two long lists, heading them "Things I am good at" and "Things I am not good at." Discuss one item from the second list with at least one other person (and do so within the week). At first you may feel uncomfortable, but it gets easier with practice. You are also likely to have the opposite experience from what you might expect: rather than finding that people value you less because you're discussing your flaws, they will probably value you *more* because they will perceive you as more human and sincere. You may also find that your relationships with others become closer; interpersonal relationships usually grow when one or both parties reveal personal information to one another.

Feel free to add to these lists as you proceed. For the next three weeks, continue to share items from the second list with a new person each week and ask for reactions. Once you have done this, make a commitment to share one thing each day with someone else that suggests a flaw, weakness, or shortcoming you may have—for example, a statement such as "That's not my greatest strength" or "I wish I could be better at that."

Activities for Transforming Mental and Emotional Patterns for Threes

MENTAL ACTIVITY When you become aware that you are trying to impress others with how successful or desirable you are, stop for a moment and ask yourself, *What if I were not focusing on creating a positive image and thought of myself as valuable for who I truly am, not what I do?* Then try to remember one or more times when you believed in yourself, completely separate from any accomplishments. Stay in that thought, reliving what was occurring within you at that moment. Stay with this feeling of well-being about who you are, not what you do, for at least two minutes. This will help you to transform the mental pattern of *vanity* (the strategic thinking about how to create an idealized image based on being or appearing to be successful) into the higher belief of *hope* (the faith that you can be valued and appreciated for who you are rather than what you do and accomplish).

EMOTIONAL ACTIVITY When you realize you are not telling the complete truth to yourself or someone else, ask yourself, *What is the truth here? What am I really feeling and thinking, and how am I shading or changing my reporting of events so that I look good?* Then remember one or more times in your life when you told the whole truth and were completely accepting of yourself. Remember how you felt and what you experienced during those times. Keep replaying those truthful moments until you feel reconnected with the deeper part of yourself. This will lead you to transform the emotional habit of *deceit* (the feeling that you must do everything possible to appear successful, hiding parts of yourself that do not conform to that image, and believing that your image is the real you) into the higher awareness of *truthfulness* (finding true self-acceptance through acknowledging both your successes and your failures, and realizing that your image is not your essence or true self).

Daily Activities for Fours

Appreciate the Ordinary

Because Fours tend to gravitate toward the unique and avoid the commonplace, they can grow enormously from focusing on and learning to appreciate the ordinary things in life. When the following activities are done every day, the results will be profound. First, make a long list of tasks you consider to be ordinary or boring—for example, doing paperwork, filing expense reports, or washing dishes. Each day, select one of these items, and do it until you find the pleasure in it.

Enneagram Style 4
MOOD

Second, take a fifteen-minute walk every day and notice commonplace things in your environment. Reflect on each item and what there is about it that you can deeply appreciate.

Third, when you are given a task that you perceive as being boring or insignificant, do it with relish, finding the joy and pleasure in it. You can do this by focusing on the actual activity rather than thinking about what you'd rather be doing instead or how boring the task is. Almost anything can be meaningful and interesting if your focus is in the present rather than the past or the future.

Take Pleasure in Other People's Positive Qualities and Accomplishments

Fours consciously and unconsciously compare themselves to others. These comparisons can be about small things, such as an item of clothing that someone else is wearing, or large, such as the promotion of a friend or peer. This phenomenon of invidious comparison, or envy, results in Fours comparing themselves to someone and then feeling superior or inferior to that person.

When you notice you are comparing yourself to others (and this will become more apparent the more you pay attention to it), instead of feeling either superior or deficient, look at the person or situation again. If you initially felt inferior, continue looking at the person until you genuinely feel some pleasure for him or her. If you felt superior to the other person, continue looking and search for positive qualities in him or her that you truly admire.

Doing the above activity requires a commitment on your part. It means paying attention to yourself every day. Don't be surprised to find that you have to use this activity fifteen times a day or more. The frequency of use demonstrates to you that you are becoming more and more aware. When you use this process over several months, you will find that you compare yourself less often, that you spend less time thinking about it when you do compare yourself to someone else, and that you can more easily change your feelings of envy and inferiority or superiority into feelings of true appreciation.

Minimize Your Self-Referencing Behavior

The self-referencing behavior of Fours comes in many forms, including e-mail, conversation, and even thoughts and feelings. In order to eliminate self-referencing behavior, one must first recognize it—for example, the frequent use of the words *I*, *me*, *my*, and *mine*; the frequent sharing of personal stories and/or emotions; the redirection of a conversation back to oneself; the continual thinking about one's own thoughts, feelings, and experiences; and, most importantly, a worldview that sees most events as emanating from or reverberating back to oneself, as if one is the hub in the center of a wheel and outside events are spokes to that hub.

Once Fours begin to recognize the extent to which they engage in self-referencing behavior, they can begin to minimize this behavior, one step at a time. E-mail is an easy first step, as we often write e-mail messages multiple times per day, and we are able to review them before sending them. Once your e-mail language becomes less self-referencing, your everyday conversations are likely to change as well.

A more difficult area to change is the redirection of conversations back to yourself. Not only is this behavior often unconscious, but many Fours do not even think of it as redirection. They think of it as showing empathy and personal warmth. If you want a greater understanding of your frequent telling of personal stories, refrain from telling personal stories to anyone for one day. As you do this, notice the number of times you have an impulse to say something personal about yourself and the amount of energy it takes for you to restrain yourself. Do this again for the second day and notice whether restraining yourself is becoming easier. Continue this activity for two more days or until not sharing personal stories feels easier. For the following two weeks, allow yourself to share only two or fewer stories per day. This activity will greatly reduce this aspect of your self-referencing behavior.

The most important thing to remember is that what occurs in life is not all about you or about any single person. Each person has his or her own universe of experience, and events do not occur in reference to only one person. This is particularly important to remember when you feel criticized or slighted by someone else; the other person's behavior may have nothing or very little to do with you. Saying the following words to yourself when you feel hurt, angry, or have in some way personalized someone's response to you can be very helpful: *This isn't all about me! What might be occurring in relation to this other person's experience?*

Activities for Transforming Mental and Emotional Patterns for Fours

MENTAL ACTIVITY When you become aware that you are noticing what is missing or lacking in a situation and underplaying or ignoring what is positive, try to remember one or more times when you perceived both the positive and the negative in a situation and truly appreciated what you had as well as your deep connection with everything and everyone. Try to remember both ordinary moments and big events. Allow those times to come back into your mind, and relive what was occurring within you at those times for a minimum of three minutes. Thus, you will transform the mental pattern of *melancholy* (thinking continually about what is missing, with accompanying thoughts of being disconnected or separated from others) into the higher belief of *original source* (the insight that nothing is missing and everything and everybody is ultimately deeply connected, because we all emanate from the same source).

EMOTIONAL ACTIVITY When you find that you're comparing yourself to others, remember one or more times in your life when you didn't compare yourself or anything in your situation to anyone or anything else. Remember how you felt during those times—it's likely that things seemed to be going well without any effort whatsoever, and that your thoughts, feelings, and actions were balanced, clear, and working in harmony. Keep replaying those moments in your mind and heart until you feel fully reconnected with the experiences. In this way you can transform the emotional habit of *envy* (consciously or unconsciously comparing yourself repeatedly to others in large and small ways, with accompanying feelings of deficiency or superiority) into the higher awareness of *balance* (experiencing emotions in such a clear and centered way that thought, feeling, and action emanate from your inner self).

Daily Activities for Fives

Enneagram Style
KNOWLEDGE

Allow Yourself to Need Others

Because Fives value their autonomy and have come to believe that they really don't need other people very much, it can be enlightening to realize that you either do, or could, need others far more than you currently believe. Take a piece of paper and fold it in half. On the left side, write down at least ten ways in which you currently do or could need others, if you allowed yourself to do so—for example, a need for attention or a need for intellectual rapport. On the right side, write down ten ways in which you hold yourself back from getting your needs met by others—for example, not knowing how to start a conversation. Some of the ways in which you hold yourself back may be related to specific needs listed on the left-hand side. When this is the case, draw a line between these related items from the two lists—for example, not knowing how to start a conversation would be a probable barrier to engaging in an intellectual conversation.

The next day, select one of these needs from the first list and make a commitment to take action to get this need met. A very logical and helpful first step would be to remove the relevant barriers from the second list. Continue working on this one need for a full week. The second week, select another need from your list and follow the same process. Each week, proceed to take action on a new item from your needs list until you have completed the entire list. You may find that new needs or barriers come to your attention, so feel free to add these to your lists.

Connect with and Express Your Feelings

In their thirst for knowing everything that can be known, Fives also tend to take a more cerebral view of the world of feelings. Fives have learned how to disconnect from their feelings the moment these occur so they can bring them up for examination later, at a time of their choosing. This way of dealing with feelings makes Fives believe that they are able to understand their feelings, and it also makes them feel less vulnerable and more in control. Fives do this disconnecting from feelings in various ways. Some Fives, for example, simply start thinking intensely about something else when their feelings arise; others may hold their breath until the feelings subside; and still other Fives may pull their attention into their heads and begin to observe themselves as if they were objects to study. For all Fives, however, the process of emotional disconnection is so automatic and habitual that they are usually unaware of doing it. Consequently, the very first step in the development process for Fives is to pay close attention to exactly how and when they disconnect from their feelings.

For one week, simply observe the ways in which you disconnect from your feelings. Write down these observations in very precise terms, but don't attempt to change your behavior yet. There will be numerous times each day that you do this; consequently, one week will give you ample information. The following week, practice *not* doing the behaviors you noted doing when you disconnect from your feelings. As you do this, make sure you breathe deeply; this will help your feelings to surface. Continue to practice allowing yourself to connect with your feelings until it becomes easy for you to do so. At this point, you can choose either to be connected to your feelings or to disconnect from them at will.

Once you have learned how to experience your emotions at the time these actually occur, you will also become more aware of the variety of feelings you actually have. The next step is to share these feelings with others. It is easiest to begin by discussing some feelings you have had recently with those you trust. For one week, select three different people to talk with. An effective conversation opener is, "Do you have a minute? I wanted to get your reactions to some feelings I had recently." Feel free to talk about anything you like as long as you are sharing emotions—for example, *I've been wondering if I should take a vacation abroad* is a thought, whereas *I want to take a vacation abroad, but I'm terribly worried about leaving my sick mother* is a feeling. Do the above activity for two more weeks, selecting different individuals each week. Once you feel comfortable discussing recent feelings, then practice discussing feelings in the present. Choose three people per week—you can choose the same people if you wish—and share spontaneous feelings, such as *That project was so much fun* or *I really didn't like the way the meeting we attended was run*. Continue this phase of the activity for two more weeks, selecting different individuals each week.

Finally, you are ready to practice communicating your feelings with people whom you know less well. Select two people each week with whom you will practice. Choose to communicate either recent or spontaneous feelings with each of them. There is no reason to bare your heart to this person. Simply make sure that you take the risk and get practice in revealing information about your feelings to him or her. A good conversation starter might be, "Do you have a few minutes to talk about the project? I'm feeling more and more nervous that we may not make our deadline," or "Wasn't that a great meeting? I felt so pleased when they honored our team for its accomplishments."

Increase Your Capacity to Engage Rather Than to Withdraw

Everyone has cycles of engagement and withdrawal, but Fives tend to withdraw from others far more than they are likely to engage with them. In fact, Fives tend to disengage as a matter of habit. Some Fives literally or figuratively sit outside of groups they belong to. Other Fives say very little in social encounters or leave events early. Still others give monosyllabic answers to questions, thereby giving the impression that they prefer not to converse.

The first step in learning to engage is to *want* to engage with others. The second step involves specific actions that foster engagement. To begin with, Fives need to consider why they would want to engage with others and to find some compelling reasons to do so. Otherwise, there will be no motivation to change behavior. Once you feel that you do want to learn how to engage more frequently with others, make three lists, side by side. In the first column, write down how you will benefit if you do engage with others more frequently. In the second column, write down what you believe you may be missing because of your pattern of withdrawal. In the third column, write down the specific things you do that allow you to disengage from interaction—for example, bringing work with you to meetings, not communicating with others unless they ask you a question, or standing literally outside of groups.

Over the next two weeks, observe other people with respect to their actions of being engaged with others. When you observe individuals who seem very effective at interacting with others, notice their behavior in detail—where they stand or sit, what they say and how they say it, their timing, their body language, and so on. Next, experiment with trying some of these behaviors yourself, and notice the effects of your new behaviors both on you and on your interactions with others.

After you have done this for two weeks, pick someone you know well who appears to be able to engage effectively, and ask this individual for some tips on how to engage others. Open up with a simple statement to him or her such as, "I've noticed you're quite skilled at networking, and this is something I'm exploring how to do more effectively. Can you give me a few tips on what you've learned about doing this?" Then try each of these suggested behaviors yourself.

The following testimonial illustrates the effectiveness of these techniques: "I would say that using the Enneagram has been a big success for me as a Five, and I have achieved some of the goals I set ten months ago. Since then I have completed the Los Angeles, San Francisco, Chicago, and New York Marathons and became a board of directors member and a mentor for my running club, and a pace leader for Nike's Club Run. I have successfully moved from an observer to a participator."

Activities for Transforming Mental and Emotional Patterns for Fives

MENTAL ACTIVITY When you become aware that you are thirsting for and withholding information, distancing yourself from direct experience, or engaging in extended strategizing about how to control your environment, remember one or more times when you understood that true wisdom can be achieved only through complete engagement with your direct experience. Allow those times to come back into your thinking, and relive what was occurring within you at those moments. Then you can transform the mental pattern of *stinginess* (a scarcity paradigm that leads to an insatiable thirst for knowing, a reluctance to share—knowledge, time, space, and personal information—and to strategizing about how to control one's environment) into the higher belief of *omniscience* (the insight that only through direct personal experience and complete engagement can one know all things).

EMOTIONAL ACTIVITY When you become aware that you are withholding anything from others—for example, your knowledge, time, physical space, and feelings—remember one or more times in your life when you were fully sharing and present to others. Remember the circumstances and how you felt, and what you experienced during those times. Keep replaying those completely engaged moments until you feel fully reconnected with the experiences and can transform the emotional habit of *avarice* (the intense desire to guard everything related to oneself—information, physical and emotional privacy, energy, and resources—combined with automatic detachment from feelings) into the higher awareness of *nonattachment* (the firsthand experience that detachment—from feelings, people, and experience—is not nonattachment, and that one must fully engage and become attached to something before one can learn to be truly nonattached, appreciating something without coveting or trying to possess it).

Daily Activities for Sixes

Shift Your Focus from Half Empty to Half Full

Enneagram Style (6)
DOUBT

Because Sixes tend to focus on what could go wrong, it can be said that they usually view the glass as being half empty. To change your focus from observing something and worrying about the negative, you have to consciously shift your focus and view the glass as being half full. To do this, you have to purposely think of all the things that are right, effective, and in place. For example, if you are planning a business trip, instead of being worried that the cab may forget to pick you up, that you may miss the airplane, or that a presentation you'll be giving may not go well, think instead about how well organized the cab company usually is, how important it is for your safety that airports have expanded their security procedures, and how useful others will find the information that you will be covering in your presentation.

The following activity can also help you to focus more on positive scenarios. For two weeks, spend ten minutes at the end of each day making a list of all the things that went right that day. Then, for the next two weeks, make a list each morning of at least five things that will occur that day that are likely to go well.

The following month, take ten minutes each evening and make a list of everything that went well during the day. Next to each item, write down exactly what you did that contributed to the success. At the end of the month, you should see your focus shift to include positive as well as negative scenarios, and your self-confidence will increase because you better understand your role in creating a positive outcome.

Trust Your Own Authority

It is not unusual for Sixes to seek the counsel of other people, and often several people, before making a decision. With their self-doubt high, Sixes may actually trust an outside authority's judgment over their own, even in the face of facts that would indicate that the Six's own assessment is superior. Sixes thus sometimes give their power to someone else when they really need to trust themselves.

Ironically, Sixes often give others excellent advice, then turn around and ask someone else for advice on the exact same matter. The following technique works well with Sixes because it tricks the mind into releasing its own wise inner authority. When you think you need to solicit the counsel of someone else on a particular topic, stop yourself and ask, *What do I think about this?* If your answer is *I don't know,* ask yourself, *Well, if I did know what to do about this issue, what would it be?* Usually, the self-advice that is elicited is worth following. Another variation on this technique is to ask yourself, *If someone else were coming to me with a similar request for advice, what advice would I give?*

Differentiate Between an Insight and a Pure Projection

One of the most difficult tasks for Sixes is to learn to differentiate between an insight and a projection. Insights are astute perceptions that are accurate and therefore actionable. Projections are also perceptions, but they reflect the psyche of the perceiver more than the truth about the person or thing being observed. What can make differentiating between the two even more difficult is that sometimes ideas are projections but are also accurate, and so they are insights. Thus, Sixes actually need to discern among pure projections, pure insights, and ideas that are *both* projections and insights.

Two activities can help Sixes with this discernment. The first is to recognize that pure insights are really keenly intuitive perceptions and almost always have very little emotion attached to them by the perceiver. Consequently, the more emotion you feel with a perception, the more likely it is to be a projection; the less the emotion, the more likely it is to be an insight, something you can trust to be real. When you discover a perception that you sense is a projection or at least partly a projection, the best way to test this is to ask yourself, *Is what I have just thought true in any way about me?* For example, if you imagine someone is not being truthful with you, ask yourself, *How am I not being truthful with that person?* Once you have discovered how you are not being honest with the other person, ask yourself, *Now that I understand how I am not being honest, are there any other reasons to suggest that this person is not being honest with me?*

The second way to test a projection is to ask others for feedback about the thought you have had. If you check with several people who have no particular reason for bias, you can confirm or disconfirm the veracity of the thought. Over time, this will help you to understand the pattern of your projections and the nature of your insights.

Activities for Transforming Mental and Emotional Patterns for Sixes

MENTAL ACTIVITY When you become aware that you are plagued with self-doubt and worry, and are creating worst-case scenarios, remember one or more times when a situation or outcome was uncertain, yet you had complete trust in yourself and others to rise to the challenges in a constructive and meaningful way. Allow those times to come back into your thinking, and relive what was occurring within you at those moments. This will enable you to transform the mental pattern of *cowardice* (the thoughts of doubt and worry that cause you to continually create worst-case scenarios) into the higher belief of *faith* (the belief that both you and others can capably meet life's challenges, and that there is some certainty and meaning in the world).

EMOTIONAL ACTIVITY When you become aware that you are feeling fear, anxiety, and deep concern or panic, remember one or more times in your life when you were courageous and were able to overcome your fears in a fully conscious and calm way. Remember the circumstances and your feeling of being capable of taking action, and recall what you experienced during those times. Keep replaying those completely engaged moments until you feel fully reconnected with the experiences. This will allow you to transform the emotional habit of *fear* (feelings of anxiety, deep concern, and panic that the worst will occur, that others cannot be trusted, and that you are not up to the challenges that present themselves) into the higher awareness of *courage* (the feeling of being able to overcome fear through fully conscious action, rather than turning to either inaction or to action designed to prove that you have no fear).

Daily Activities for Sevens

Enneagram Style
OPTIONS

Listen Fully to Others

Sevens usually listen more with their heads than their hearts; listening fully, however, means listening with both your head and heart. When you are listening to others, ask yourself, *What are they saying about what they think **and** how they feel?* In addition, Sevens often believe that they know what the other person is saying before the person has completed his or her thoughts, so they often stop listening and/or interrupt the other person. To help yourself listen more fully, allow at least three or more seconds between the time the other person finishes speaking and the time you begin to speak.

It can also be helpful to paraphrase both the content and the feeling of what you have just heard. A paraphrase is a restatement of what a person has said and includes both the thoughts and feelings. For example, when a colleague says, "This place is so disorganized," you can paraphrase what he or she said as follows: "You sound very frustrated. Something must have happened." When you do paraphrase, be sure to listen to the other person's affirmation or disconfirmation of your paraphrasing. This feedback can be of great help to you in increasing the accuracy of your listening skills. For example, the colleague in the above scenario might respond, "No, I'm beyond frustrated—I'm furious! They told me I'd be receiving a raise, but no one can find my paperwork." It is not uncommon, as in this example, for a paraphrased statement to lead to a deeper level of communication between two individuals.

Stay Focused

Staying focused on one thing at a time can be one of the most difficult tasks for Sevens, because the Seven's mind and attention tend to move quickly from one area of interest to another. The following exercise is very helpful and can be applied to every area of your life. In everything you do—for example, considering an idea, eating a meal, experiencing a feeling, having a conversation, or engaging in any activity—try to notice when your attention becomes diverted from that activity, thought, or feeling. Then bring your attention back to it, and stay focused on it for at least one more minute. As you become proficient at refocusing your attention, expand the areas of your life in which you do this, and also prolong the amount of time in which you give consciously concentrated time and attention to the experiences.

One structured way to practice this skill is to spend eight minutes every morning simply focusing. First, sit or stand with minimal body movement, and focus on an object you see, hear, or smell in your environment. Concentrate only on that object for two full minutes; if your attention becomes diverted to anything else, just notice this shift and bring your attention back to the original object. For the next two minutes, focus on something inside yourself, such as a feeling, a bodily sensation, or your breathing. Follow the same process as in the first part: try to stay focused for two minutes, and simply observe attention shifts and return to your intended focus. Next, follow the same two-minute procedure with an external object as your point of focus. For the final two minutes, focus on something inside yourself. Focusing may be difficult at first, but with practice you will find that it will become easier and more enjoyable. This should become a daily practice.

Note: A kitchen timer or a watch with an alarm may be useful to keep track of the two-minute intervals.

Develop Your Emotional Repertoire

Expanding one's emotional repertoire and developing a deeper empathy for others can be a major challenge for many Sevens. While Sevens can be very emotionally engaging and tend to express positive feelings easily, they often restrict their access to the emotions of fear, anger, and particularly sadness by thinking interesting thoughts or pursuing stimulating activities. Unfamiliarity with their own feelings can hinder Sevens from being able to deeply empathize with the emotions of other people. Several approaches can be helpful to the Seven in changing this pattern. It is important to be patient with yourself, keeping in mind that the development of a deeper emotional repertoire is a long-term process.

First, the activity above—staying focused—can be very easily applied to emotions. Second, the Emotional Index in Chapter 1, "Discovering Your Enneagram Style," can be useful for identifying your current repertoire in the four basic emotional groups—Mad, Sad, Glad, and Afraid. Once you have identified your emotional repertoire, you can work to increase the range of your emotions by allowing yourself to feel more emotions in the feeling categories in which you had a low number of marks, and/or by allowing yourself to feel your emotions more fully, thus increasing your intensity levels in all four emotional groupings.

Third, you can increase your emotional repertoire by talking about your feelings in depth, as well as by listening to other people talk about their own feelings. Fourth, you can go to movies or plays that evoke emotions, then discuss the experiences with a confidant afterward.

Note that sadness is the emotion that Sevens often have the most difficulty allowing themselves to feel. Part of the foundation of the Seven personality is the seeking of pleasure and the avoidance of pain—and sadness is emotional pain. Here are some ideas that can help you to stop avoiding pain, which is a natural part of the human experience. First, make a list of all the things that make you feel sad. You may find that it is not very long at first, but keep this list and add to it every day. Once you begin to pay attention to your own feelings, you may be surprised to find that a number of feelings related to pain are lurking below the surface. Second, whenever you feel even the slightest twinge of sadness, make sure that you keep breathing normally and deeply. Shallow breathing typically cuts people off from their feelings, while deeper breathing tends to allow feelings to become strong enough so that we can recognize them.

Activities for Transforming Mental and Emotional Patterns for Sevens

MENTAL ACTIVITY When your mind starts moving in rapid succession from one thing, person, or idea to another, remember one or more times when you were able to sustain your mental focus and change the focus of your thoughts at will. Allow those times to come back into your thinking, and relive what was occurring within you at those moments. Sustain your focus as you remember these incidents for several minutes, thus transforming the mental pattern of *planning* (the mental process by which the mind goes into "hyper gear," moving in rapid succession from one thing to another) into the higher belief of *work* (the ability to direct and control the focus of one's mental attention to the work at hand, and to sustain that focus).

EMOTIONAL ACTIVITY When you become aware of constantly needing new stimulation, remember one or more times in your life when you felt integrated and complete as a person because you were able to absorb the difficult as well as the pleasurable aspects of an important event. Remember the circumstances, how you felt, and what you experienced during those times. Keep replaying each of those moments until you feel fully reconnected with the experience and can transform the emotional habit of *gluttony* (the insatiable, unrelenting thirst for new stimulation of all kinds—people, things, ideas, and experiences) into the higher awareness of *sobriety* (the feeling of being a full and complete person, which comes from pursuing and integrating painful and uncomfortable experiences as well as pleasurable and stimulating ones).

Daily Activities for Eights

Take Care of Yourself Physically

Enneagram Style
CHALLENGE (8)

More often than not, Eights take action continuously and often run themselves down, becoming like a car running out of gas or oil. We all do this to some degree, but Eights tend to do it regularly and excessively. When they get run down, they often come to a complete stop; it can take weeks or even months for them to recharge their batteries. Worse, Eights may not even realize they are becoming run down until they have become very ill. Physical awareness and exhaustion prevention are crucial issues for most Eights, as they have a tendency to go into denial related to their physical limitations until it is too late.

First, make sure to get a full night's rest every night and to eat healthfully every day. Second, take time daily to ask yourself, *Am I running myself down?* If the answer is *Yes*, then take time that same day to do something that will replenish your reserves. If your answer is *Not yet*, do not take this to mean you can and should keep pushing yourself. Instead, *stop and relax* for at least an hour or more. Don't wait until you are forced to stop by the limitations of your own body. When you take care of yourself regularly, you will be calmer and more patient, and you will get agitated less easily. This will give you more genuine self-control so that when something occurs that you don't like, you will be able to respond to it in a less intense and more constructive way.

Exercise can also be very helpful. However, when Eights exercise, they tend do so excessively—for example, not exercising for a month, then going to the gym for two-hour workouts for a full week, and then getting no exercise at all for another month. Please exercise regularly *and* in moderation. Not only will you feel better physically, but you'll also discharge some of the physical energy that accumulates in your body.

Slow Down Your Impulse to Take Action

In almost every situation, Eights take direct and rapid action. This tendency, combined with the Eight's authoritative stance, often leads others to think of Eights as controlling or dominating. The easiest way to alter this behavior is to be alert to each time you are about to suggest a course of action—whether it is a strategic action to take, a way of organizing a committee, or a choice of restaurant—and stop yourself. The most difficult response at these times, and probably the most useful for your growth, would be to say nothing at all for several minutes and simply see what happens. At first, others may look to you for direction, but if you say nothing, they will eventually begin to voice their opinions. If you feel compelled to say something, then ask the other individuals involved, "What do you think is best?" Make sure that your response or reaction to someone else's suggestion involves either asking for more information about the thinking behind the suggestion, or making a suggestion that builds on the other person's idea.

If you want to practice this new behavior every day, you can do the following exercise: when you arrive at work, write down one item you will need to act on that day. Ask at least two people for their advice, and consider these suggestions before you act. Each day, select a new item for which you will solicit the opinions of others. While you may think that asking other people for their opinions will make you appear indecisive, it is far more likely to make you look like a person who both respects people and makes important decisions by thoughtfully weighing alternatives.

Share Your Feelings of Vulnerability

The notion of being vulnerable or sharing vulnerabilities can be very anxiety-producing for many Eights. While feelings related to anger or joy may come readily, feelings of sadness or fear can be more difficult to acknowledge, as these feelings are often more indicative of uncertainty and vulnerability.

The first step for Eights is to acknowledge to themselves that they are feeling vulnerable. One way to do this is to examine the deeper issues that may lurk behind the feelings of anger. When you begin to experience a surge of anger, ask yourself, *What vulnerability could my anger be protecting or covering?*

Eights can also use their drive to action as a possible clue to their softer feelings, such as weakness, anxiety, or hurt. When you find yourself ready to act quickly on something, ask yourself, *Before I move to action, what am I trying to prevent from occurring? What does this indicate about feelings I would prefer not to expose?*

Once Eights become more aware of their own feelings, the next step is for them to share these feelings with other people. Begin by sharing your feelings with those people whom you trust most, then move on to others with whom you feel comfortable. Make a commitment to share your vulnerable feelings at least once a day for one week. During the second week, communicate two areas of vulnerability, and so on, until you become more at ease acknowledging and sharing this side of yourself. Some examples of items to share include the following: uncertainty about what course of action to take; confusion about what occurred at a meeting; and some information that someone or something is important to you.

Activities for Transforming Mental and Emotional Patterns for Eights

MENTAL ACTIVITY When you find yourself thinking about wrongs that have been done and the injustice of situations, and begin blaming others or considering ways to stand up to or intimidate other people, remember one or more times when you were able to solicit and integrate points of view that were contrary to your own. Allow those times to come back into your thinking and relive what was occurring within you at those moments. Keep your attention on those times when your understanding of the truth was highly expanded. This will help you transform the mental pattern of *vengeance* (the process of rebalancing wrongs through thoughts related to anger, blame, and intimidation) into the higher belief of *truth* (the ability to seek and integrate multiple points of view in search of a higher or bigger truth).

EMOTIONAL ACTIVITY When you become aware that you are pursuing an activity in a relentless or excessive way, remember one or more times in your life when you felt the pure, innocent openness of a child without needing to control the situation or protect either yourself or others. Remember the circumstances, how you felt, and what you experienced during those times. Keep replaying those innocent moments until you feel fully reconnected with the experiences. Thus you can transform the emotional habit of *lust* (excessiveness in a variety of forms—for example, work, food, or pleasure—as a way of avoiding and denying one's feelings and vulnerabilities) into the higher awareness of *innocence* (the childlike feeling of vulnerability and openness, such that the need to control situations or to protect oneself or others is no longer present).

Daily Activities for Nines

Express Your Needs Directly

Nines, of course, have needs like everyone else, and they often know what these needs are. At the same time, they can be reluctant to express their needs directly—for example, by stating, "I would like to do this" or "I need some time to think about this"—because they tend to believe that their

Enneagram Style ⑨
HARMONY

needs don't matter, or that expressing their needs will create conflict and disrupt the harmony they feel with other people. Learning to express your needs directly often starts with affirming that your own needs are as important as anyone else's. Ask yourself this question: *Do my needs really matter?* If your answer is no, then ask yourself, *Why do I feel that other people's needs matter, but not my own?* Write down your answer on a piece of paper and read it several times. Then, add any additional thoughts you may have regarding why you believe that your needs don't matter.

Next, divide the paper into two columns and write the answers to this question: *If I were to express my needs directly, what would I gain?* (column 1) and *What would I lose?* (column 2). Analyze your responses. Is there sufficient benefit to you for expressing your needs directly compared to what you might lose? If your answer is no, it will be difficult for you to put the effort forth and take the risk to state your needs directly. In this case, you will need to follow the above activity once a week until the balance of gains versus losses tips in the positive direction.

Once you have affirmed to yourself that your needs do indeed matter and that you would benefit from expressing them directly, practice expressing them daily. Express one need per day for the first week, two needs per day the second week, and so forth. You can select individuals you know and trust, or strangers—for example, you might say to a store cashier, "Please put that item in a bag with handles for carrying." Practice this daily activity until it feels completely comfortable and natural.

Set Priorities, and Keep Them

Nines often have difficulty setting priorities and sticking with them. This leads to procrastination as one thing gets started, then another, and then both tasks get put aside for an activity such as cleaning the desk or organizing the files. First, you have to be really honest about your tendency to shift priorities and put things off. You need to notice how and when you do this, and then assess the consequences of this behavior. Your self-assessment should answer the following two questions: *How do I really benefit from not setting or sticking with my priorities?* Be aware that an answer of *I don't benefit in any way* is not helpful, because there must be some benefit or the behavior would not be recurring. After you have answered the last question honestly, ask yourself, *What do I lose by not setting or sticking with my priorities?* If the costs of not setting and keeping priorities outweigh the benefits of doing so, then you are ready to change. Each day, make a priority list of key items to accomplish and rank order each item, with the most important item first and the least important last. Begin your tasks in order of their priority. Keep this list in front of you, and check it hourly. If you stray from this list or reorder the priorities, get yourself back on track.

Take a Position

Can you dare to be provocative? Nines usually prefer to not take a stand or a strong position on issues for fear of creating conflict and disrupting positive relationships. Think about the issues that really matter to you, particularly those you generally keep to yourself. The issue can be something as significant as *I do not want to buy that new house* or as simple as *I don't like that music on the radio*. Make a list of these issues, and add to them daily. Once a day, take the risk of actually saying something about one of these issues to someone else. After you become comfortable doing this, try communicating a position twice a day. Once this seems to work well, increase the number of times you do this to five times per day. You are likely to find that rather than disrupting relationships, letting people know where you stand actually builds relationships.

Activities for Transforming Mental and Emotional Patterns for Nines

MENTAL ACTIVITY When your focus becomes diffused, you begin forgetting your priorities, or you engage in any other behavior that helps you to avoid conflict, remember one or more times when you were able to sustain your attention and also recognize that there was an underlying harmony between people based on their deep regard and/or affection for each other. Allow those times to come back into your thinking and relive what was occurring within you at those moments. Sustain your focus, remembering these incidents for several minutes until you can transform the mental pattern of *indolence* (the process of mentally diffusing your attention so that you forget what is important to you and also refrain from stating your opinions and positions, thereby minimizing your conflict with other people) into the higher belief of *love* (the belief that there is an underlying universal harmony in the world based on unconditional regard and appreciation for one another).

EMOTIONAL ACTIVITY When you become aware that you are not paying attention to yourself and your deeper feelings and needs, remember one or more times in your life when you felt totally present and aware of both yourself and others and thus knew instinctively what you must do. Remember the circumstances, how you felt, and what you experienced during those times. Keep replaying those fully aware moments until you feel fully reconnected with the experiences. Then you will be able to transform the emotional habit of *laziness* (lethargy in paying attention to your own feelings and needs, thus disabling you from taking the action you most desire) into the higher aware-ness of *right action* (the state of feeling fully present to yourself and others so that you know exactly what action you must take).

Some Concluding Thoughts

At this point, the following questions may be on your mind: *What am I really changing? My behavior? My feelings? My thoughts?* The answer is yes to all three. Sometimes this answer makes people both anxious and excited, because it raises another question: *If I change all these things, then who will I be?* Many of our thoughts, feelings, and behaviors have been with us since childhood. Con-sequently, the thought of changing them—even those that are counterpro-ductive or that cause us anguish—can be quite alarming. To address this concern, some additional insights may be helpful. First, it is unrealistic to think that you will change *all* of your thoughts, feelings, and behaviors. Instead, you will simply become more aware of what they are and have a more realistic and accepting attitude toward yourself. And when you do change—and you will—the choice of what to change will be yours.

Second, it can be very helpful to think of the personality as an implicit mental model about how the world works and how the individual should func-tion in it, a paradigm that comes with an unconscious set of thoughts, feel-ings, and behavioral patterns. Paradigms, of course, do change as we learn new ideas, have different experiences, and gain information—as people changed, for example, when the paradigm changed from *the world is flat* to *the world is round*. The world itself remained the same world, but our understanding of it and our capabilities for navigating it advanced.

So it is with the individual personality. You are still yourself when you change, albeit a deeper and expanded self. One might say that gaining a true understanding of your personality frees you from being constricted by certain aspects of it, allowing you to use all facets of yourself to become more of who you really are.

Resources

For information on training materials to accompany each of the chapters in this book as well as in-house training, consulting, and coaching services, go to www.TheEnneagramInBusiness.com, or contact Ginger Lapid-Bogda at (310) 829-3309 or ginger@bogda.com.

Behavioral Sciences

General

Block, Peter. *Flawless Consulting*. Austin, TX: Learning Concepts, 1981.

Massarik, Fred, and Marissa Pei-Carpenter. *Organization Development and Consulting: Perspectives and Foundations*. New York: John Wiley & Sons, 2002.

Pfeiffer, J. William, ed. *Theories and Models in Applied Behavioral Sciences*. 4 vols. San Diego: Pfeiffer & Company, 1991.

Conflict

Walton, Richard E. *Managing Conflict: Interpersonal Dialogue and Third-Party Roles*. Reading, MA: Addison-Wesley, 1987.

Leadership

Bradford, David L., and Allan R. Cohen. *Power Up*. New York: John Wiley & Sons, 1998.

Kouzes, James M., and Barry Z. Posner. *Credibility*. San Francisco: Jossey-Bass, 1993.

Teams

Katzenbach, Jon R., and Douglas K. Smith. *The Wisdom of Teams: Creating the High-Performance Organization*. New York: HarperCollins, 2003.

Reddy, W. Brandon, and Kaleel Jamison, eds. *Team Building: Blueprints for Productivity and Satisfaction*. Alexandria, VA: NTL Institute for Applied Behavioral Science, 1988.

Smith, Kenwyn K., and David N. Berg. *Paradoxes of Group Life*. San Francisco: Jossey-Bass, 1987.

The Enneagram

Business

Goldberg, Michael J. *The 9 Ways of Working*. New York: Marlowe & Company, 1999.

Nathans, Hannah. *The Enneagram at Work: Towards Personal Mastery and Social Intelligence*. The Netherlands: Scriptum Management, 2003.

Enneagram Styles

Daniels, David N., and Virginia A. Price. *The Essential Enneagram*. San Francisco: Harper San Francisco, 2000.

Hurley, Kathleen V., and Theodore E. Dobson. *What's My Type?* San Francisco: Harper San Francisco, 1991.

Palmer, Helen. *The Enneagram in Love and Work*. New York: HarperCollins, 1995.

Riso, Don Richard, and Russ Hudson. *The Wisdom of the Enneagram*. New York: Bantam Books, 1999.

Wagner, Jerome P. *The Enneagram Spectrum of Personality Styles: An Introductory Guide*. Portland, OR: Metamorphous Press, 1996.

Webb, Karen. *The Enneagram*. London: Thorsons, 1996.

Psychology

Naranjo, Claudio. *Character and Neurosis: An Integrative View*. Nevada City, CA: Gateways/IDHHB, 1997.

Bartlett, Carolyn. *Enneagram Field Guide: Notes on Using the Enneagram for Counselors, Therapists, and Personal Growth*. Portland, OR: Enneagram Consortium, 2003. Forthcoming.

Spirituality

Addison, Rabbi Howard A. *The Enneagram and Kabbalah*. Woodstock, VT: Jewish Lights, 1998.

Almaas, A. H. *Facets of Unity: The Enneagram of Holy Ideas*. Berkeley, CA: Diamond Books, 1998.

Empereur, James. *The Enneagram and Spiritual Direction: Nine Paths to Spiritual Guidance*. New York: Continuum Publishing Company, 1997.

Maitri, Sandra. *The Spiritual Dimension of the Enneagram: Nine Faces of the Soul*. Los Angeles: J. P. Tarcher, 2001.

Rohr, Richard, and Andreas Ebert. *Discovering the Enneagram: An Ancient Tool for a New Spiritual Journey*. New York: Crossroads, 1990.

Specialty Books

Condon, Thomas. *The Enneagram Movie and Video Guide.* Portland, OR: Metamorphous Press, 1999.

Levine, Janet. *Knowing Your Parenting Personality.* Hoboken, NJ: John Wiley & Sons, 2003.

Searle, Judith. *The Literary Enneagram: Characters from the Inside Out.* Portland, OR: Metamorphous Press, 2001.

Websites

* Find additional Enneagram books through the Enneagram Consortium website at www.sa-inc.net/ec/ec.html.

* The Emotional Intelligence Consortium website at www.eiconsortium.org contains more information on EQ research.

* The International Enneagram Association (IEA) website, www.internationalenneagram.org, provides an extensive list of books and periodicals with information on the Enneagram, as well as a listing of Enneagram-related research efforts.

* *Enneagram Monthly*, a monthly Enneagram journal, can be found at www.ideodynamic.com/enneagram-monthly.

* To find an Enneagram-trained coach or therapist in your area, go to www.internationalenneagram.org.

Index

About the Author

Ginger Lapid-Bogda, Ph.D., is a senior organization development consultant with over thirty years of consulting experience, working with companies such as Apple Computer, Kaiser Permanente, Whirlpool, Disney, First Union Bank, the Clorox Company, Hewlett Packard, TRW, Sun Microsystems, Time Warner, Raytheon Electronic Systems, and numerous law firms. Dr. Lapid-Bogda is also an internationally recognized Enneagram consultant and currently serves as president of the International Enneagram Association (IEA). An expert trainer and facilitator, Dr. Lapid-Bogda is a member of the Organization Development Network (ODN) and National Training Labs (NTL).

Her consulting firm, Bogda & Associates (Santa Monica, California), provides an integrated organization development–Enneagram approach that guides organizations in their ongoing quest for improvement and excellence. The firm's areas of expertise include the development of organizational vision and strategy; organizational problem solving and learning; organization design;

executive team development; in-depth executive coaching; leadership development; communications; conflict management; team development; diversity; and organizational power and politics.

Dr. Lapid-Bogda teaches leadership, organizational change, consulting skills, and the Enneagram at colleges and universities, and her writing has appeared in numerous publications. She has been the recipient of speaking awards from the American Management Association, and of writing awards from the *National Business Employment Weekly*.

For further information, go to www.TheEnneagramInBusiness.com. You may also contact Dr. Lapid-Bogda directly with questions or comments by calling (310) 829-3309, or by sending an e-mail to ginger@bogda.com.